August 2015

For Jeb,

Robert

THE ESSENTIAL
AUROBINDO
Writings of Sri Aurobindo

I hope you will be able to visit the Sri Aurobindo Ashram and Aeroville, for which see pp. 238-52.

D1550852

SRI AUROBINDO, 1920, AGE 42

THE ESSENTIAL
AUROBINDO
Writings of Sri Aurobindo

Edited with an Introduction and an Afterword by

Robert A. McDermott

Lindisfarne Books

©1987, 2001 Lindisfarne Books
Selections from the works of Sri Aurobindo are
reprinted by permission of the Sri Aurobindo Ashram.

Afterword Copyright ©1987, 2001 Robert A. McDermott

Published by Lindisfarne Books

www.lindisfarne.org

Library of Congress Cataloging-in-Publication Data

Ghose, Aurobindo, 1872-1950
    [Selections. 2001]
    The essential Aurobindo / edited with an introduction and new after-
word by Robert A. McDermott.
    p. cm.
    Includes bibliographical references.
    ISBN 0-9701097-2-5
    1. Philosophy. I. McDermott, Robert A.
B5134.G42 A2 2001
181'.4—dc 21   2001029226

For Sri Aurobindo

स महात्मा सुदुर्लभः

sa mahātmā sudurlabhah

Such a great soul is very difficult to find.

—Bhagavadgita, VII. 19

A Greater Evolution is the Real Goal of Humanity

The coming of a spiritual age must be preceded by the appearance of an increasing number of individuals who are no longer satisfied with the normal intellectual, vital, and physical existence of man, but perceive that a greater evolution is the real goal of humanity and attempt to effect it in themselves, to lead others to it, and to make it the recognized goal of the race. In proportion as they succeed and to the degree to which they carry this evolution, the yet unrealized potentiality which they represent will become an actual possibility of the future.

—Sri Aurobindo, *The Human Cycle*

CONTENTS

PART ONE

MAN IN EVOLUTION

PART TWO

INTEGRAL YOGA

PART THREE

TOWARD A SPIRITUAL AGE

PART FOUR

EPILOGUE

BIBLIOGRAPHIES AND GLOSSARY

ACKNOWLEDGMENTS

SELECTIONS FROM Sri Aurobindo's and the Mother's writings are reprinted with the kind permission of the Mother of the Sri Aurobindo Ashram. Arrangement for copyright permissions and related matters was greatly facilitated by André Morisset and Udar Pinto.

Throughout the progression of my work on Sri Aurobindo, I have been aided by the small community of disciples at Matagiri, Mount Tremper, New York, especially by the encouragement of Muriel Spanier and the expertise of Eric Hughes.

I am grateful to Joseph E. Cunneen and William Birmingham, editors of *Cross Currents,* for having published a special issue on Sri Aurobindo (Winter 1972), and for having encouraged me to expand that edition to book length. I am also grateful for the generous help of Dr. Oscar Shaftel, Professor of Humanities at Pratt Institute and editor at Schocken Books.

During the summer of 1972 I had the privilege of helping to establish an Auroville-inspired experimental community in upstate New York with Bob Lawlor and Deborah Lee, both of whom had pioneered at Auroville for five years; by example and insight, they profoundly influenced my appreciation of Integral Yoga as an individual and communal discipline. Similarly, Mrs. Marjorie Spalding has enabled me to see more clearly the transforming effect on those committed to Sri Aurobindo's and the Mother's discipline and vision.

The choice of selections and introductions are hopefully more appropriate than they might have been were it not for the helpful responses of students to whom I have introduced Sri Aurobindo in philosophy courses at Manhattanville College and Baruch College, the City University of New York. I

9

have of course benefitted from discussions with colleagues who share my interest in Indian philosophy and religion; a partial list of those to whom I am indebted would include Thomas Berry, Harry M. Buck, Haridas Chaudhuri, Eliot Deutsch, Thomas Hopkins, V. S. Naravane, H. Daniel Smith, and Frederick J. Streng.

As ever, my wife, Ellen Dineen, generously sacrificed her own work so that I could conduct research on Sri Aurobindo—at home, in libraries, in a summer community, and during two trips to India.

PREFACE

THE POSITIVE reception accorded Sri Aurobindo's *The Mind of Light* (New York: E. P. Dutton, 1971) and articles in scholarly journals and news magazines, published in observance of the Sri Aurobindo Centenary in 1972, has demonstrated the need for an American edition of Sri Aurobindo's essential writings. The recent wave of enthusiasm for Indian spirituality has helped to prepare this receptivity—positively by showing the need for a new spiritual discipline in the West, and negatively by failing to discriminate the genuine representatives of the Indian tradition from the peddlers of arrant nonsense.

Scholars and seekers alike will find in Sri Aurobindo an original philosopher committed to natural and human evolution, a yogi second to none in spiritual power, a visionary with a profound sense of the historical process, and the generator of a worldwide movement whose legacy, under the direction of the Mother of the Sri Aurobindo Ashram, includes the UNESCO-sponsored city of Auroville. The four components of Sri Aurobindo's legacy essentially correspond to the four sections of this edition: Sri Aurobindo's systematic philosophy, principally his theory of man in evolution and concept of rebirth; his spiritual discipline, based on the Bhagavadgita and fully developed in his system of Integral Yoga; his vision of the historical and spiritual evolution of man; and, finally, the implementation of this vision by the Mother, his spiritual collaborator, who continues to direct the spiritual lives of the several thousand Sri Aurobindo disciples at the Ashram, at Auroville, and in other parts of the world, including America.

In response to the variety of levels and perspectives from which readers will approach this work, the introductions and selections have been arranged so as to render Sri Aurobindo's teachings intelligible to the beginning student as well as to those familiar with Indian philosophy, religion, and culture. In addition to the general introduction, which attempts to place Sri Aurobindo and the Mother in a context meaningful to the Western reader, brief explanatory essays precede each of the four sections. The glossary identifies the important names and terms, and the bibliographies will direct the reader to books and periodicals on related topics.

INTRODUCTION
by Robert A. McDermott
Vision of a Transformed World

Politics and Yoga

WHAT ERIK ERIKSON CALLS "the strange reversal of the traditional roles of East and West," by which Gandhi has become
"a model of activism in our culture,"[1] may be less strange
than most Westerners are prepared to admit. Not only Gandhi,
but equally the other three giants of modern Indian
thought—Tagore, Radhakrishnan, and Sri Aurobindo—were
all effective activists with a profound sense of social and historical realities. What is distinctive, and distinctively Indian, about
these personalities is their practiced conviction that action must
be disciplined. This practical sense of their own national needs,
quickened by the press of British political and cultural
influence, is at the same time rooted in one or more Indian
spiritual disciplines. But the common characterization of Indian
spirituality as world-negating misses the significance of these
four dominant figures of modern India. Each of these thinkers
has developed and exemplified his own thoroughly humanistic
synthesis of national and cultural values.

Although informed Westerners have long been familiar
with the vision and influence of Tagore, Gandhi, and Radhakrishnan, the less-known work of Sri Aurobindo predates and
will almost certainly outlast the influence of his Indian contem-
poraries.[2] More than any figure of modern India, Sri Aurobindo
dramatically exemplifies the ideal blending of social-political
activism and spiritual discipline. In addition to rivaling the
aesthetic creativity of the poet Tagore,[3] the social and moral
achievement of Gandhi,[4] and the philosophical accomplish-
ment of Radhakrishnan,[5] Sri Aurobindo stands out as the single
most accomplished yogi of modern India. Unlike traditional
Indian yogis, and most modern yogis as well, Sri Aurobindo's
yoga is influenced by and enhances his vision for a transformed
world.

Although Sri Aurobindo more than once cautioned the biographer that his life "has not been on the surface for men to see,"[6] some understanding of his development is essential for a grasp of his intellectual and spiritual force. The relationship between Sri Aurobindo's observable life and his inner life exemplifies his insistence that a transformation in consciousness precedes and molds personal and historical forms. Thus, in his life, as in all human experience, the inner precedes the outer realization; his work for Indian independence, the formation of a yoga based on action and historical evolution, and the emergence of a spiritual community devoted to the creation of a spiritual age—all took shape in Sri Aurobindo's consciousness before receiving historical and institutional expression.[7]

During his years as a political activist, especially his years of revolutionary leadership in Calcutta (1905–10), Aurobindo Ghose sought to prove that so long as India remained politically oppressed it could not express its distinctive spiritual and cultural genius. Like Gandhi, who assumed leadership of the nationalist movement several years after Aurobindo's withdrawal from politics, he was more deeply committed to the liberation of Indian consciousness than to political independence. Similarly, his seemingly precipitate withdrawal from active political life into spiritual retreat in 1910 can retrospectively be explained as a coherent expression of his developing spiritual awareness. What appears to have been a conflict between political and spiritual activity is better understood as a dramatic instance of Sri Aurobindo's conviction that the historical form will adapt to the prior spiritual realization.

Thus, his work in the nationalist movement, both as a political revolutionary (until 1910) and subsequently as an indirect influence, conforms to his belief that historical evolution expresses the demands of spiritual consciousness. While a revolutionary in Calcutta, and during his years as a yogi in Pondicherry, Sri Aurobindo argued that the appropriate form of protest would be found, and would be successful, once his countrymen realized the need and possibility of political independence. By 1910, four years prior to Gandhi's return from South Africa, Aurobindo concluded that the necessity of political independence was so clearly growing in Indian consciousness that its attainment was virtually inevitable. According to his vision of historical and spiritual evolution, first conceived with the passion of a political revolutionary and later articulated in scholarly detail, historical progress is determined by the growth and refinement of consciousness. Whether plotting the strategy for the Indian independence movement or charting the course of civilizations, Sri Aurobindo read the historical process in terms of possibilities and necessities first realized in man's inner life. Since the more profound and ultimately successful realization can only be grasped by the receptive or disciplined personality, the spiritual discipline of yoga and the practical concerns of history function as equally necessary ingredients in the evolutionary process. History without yoga is blind; yoga without history is empty. Sri Aurobindo's life, thought, and influence have so creatively related the spiritual and historical that they jointly serve as a model for spiritual evolution.

Early Life

Although biographical and historical events[8] are merely "on the surface" in relation to the depths and significance of Sri Aurobindo's consciousness, they provide the raw materials which the inner life absorbs and transforms. Just as any account that treats Sri Aurobindo solely in terms of history or philosophy would miss the uniqueness of his spiritual force, so any account dealing exclusively with his yoga would miss the changes effected by his yoga. As the clash of British and Indian interests set the stage for Sri Aurobindo's political and spiritual achievements, these achievements have in turn affected a wide range of political and spiritual developments.

The most fortuitous influence on the young Aurobindo

Ghose was the positive blending of Western and Indian values. Although he eventually transcended—and has urged both India and the West to transcend—the limitations of any one culture, he was able to move beyond Indian and Western ideas precisely because he had so thoroughly assimilated the creative elements of both traditions. Just as the impact of his vision may eventually be felt most keenly in the West, the first ingredients in his intellectual formation were Western, specifically the classical British education he received in London and Cambridge from 1879 to 1893. Since the young Aurobindo Ghose was educated by Irish nuns in Darjeeling from the age of five to seven, and in England from seven to twenty-one by ministers and dons of the Church of England, the formative influences on his attitudes and thought were entirely Western. When he returned to India after completing a degree with honors at King's College, Cambridge, he spoke English and French, read Greek, Latin, and Italian, but of Indian languages he knew only a little Bengali, which he had begun to learn at Cambridge.

Aurobindo's natural affinity for his homeland was kept alive by secondary sources such as *The Bengalee*, a newspaper that frequently included stories recounting the maltreatment of Indians at the hands of Englishmen, and of Indian students such as those who organized Indian Majlis, a student society dedicated to Indian independence. These influences enabled Aurobindo to sustain a sense of identity with the nation to which he subsequently devoted his developing talents and energies. Even though he did not achieve a deep and informed commitment to Indian culture and nationalism until after living in India, his anticipation of India was so compelling that upon reaching the Bombay Gate in 1893 he enjoyed a profound spiritual experience. During his years as a professor of English at Baroda College (1893–1905), he achieved proficiency in Sanskrit, Marathi, Gujarati, and Bengali, wrote numerous poems (later published at Pondicherry), and developed a deep identification with Indian culture. The literary works, translations, and political writings he completed during these years reveal his determination and ability to raise the level of Indian self-consciousness. But the Western emphasis on the implementation of ideas he undoubtedly observed during his years in England led him to act on his beliefs in the social and political as well as in the scholarly communities. At the same time that he was experiencing a series of remarkable—and seemingly accidental—spiritual events, he joined forces with political radicals in Bombay. Thus, the interpenetration of spiritual and political activity dates to his years in Baroda, but the creative synthesis of these two activities developed during the political years in Calcutta, most particularly during his year in the Alipore jail (1908–9).

Politics, Prison, and Karmayoga

Aurobindo's year in the Alipore jail (including several months in solitary confinement), while waiting trial for conspiracy against the British Government in India, dramatically reveals the range and intensity of his commitment to India's regeneration. Although the combination of inner and outer life, or spiritual and historical concerns, runs throughout his lengthy career, it was during his year in prison, at the conclusion of three years of intense revolutionary activity, that Aurobindo meditated on the Gita, felt the presence of Krishna and the inspiration of Vivekananda, and resolved to work for the renewed spiritualization of Indian culture. The roots of this synthesis ran deep in the Indian and Western traditions from which he was drawing. Although clearly exhibiting the influence of the Western historical sense, this new vision of historical and spiritual evolution, with India at the center, was obviously based on the spiritual discipline of the Bhagavadgita.

In a passage remarkably close to Augustine's description of his own conversion,[9] Sri Aurobindo explains that while in prison God placed the Gita in his hands:

His strength entered into me and I was able to do the *sādhanā* of the Gita, I was not only to understand intellectually but to realize what Sri Krishna demanded of Arjuna and what He demands of those who aspire to do His work, to be free from repulsion and desire, to do work for Him without the demand for fruit, to renounce self-will and become a passive and faithful instrument in His hands, to have an equal heart for high and low, friend and opponent, success and failure, yet not to do His work negligently.[10]

In his "Prison and Freedom," written while in prison, Aurobindo reveals the basis on which he would subsequently expound the theory of spiritualized activity:

The central ethical injunction in the Gita—"Fixed in yoga do thy actions" (II. 48)—this freedom is that yoga of the Gita. When the interior joys and sorrows, instead of depending on external good and evil, well-being and danger, become self-generated, self-propelled, self-bound, then the normal human condition is reversed, and the outer life can be modelled on the inner, the bondage of action slackens.[11]

Sri Aurobindo's concerted effort to reverse the normal condition for India climaxed during his year of meditation on the Gita, and took a decisively new direction when he withdrew from active politics in order to practice yoga at Pondicherry, in southern India. The full impact of his yoga experience just prior to his year in prison, and obviously during that year, is evidenced by a comparison of his writings before and after 1908. The editorials he wrote for *Bande Mataram,* the weekly newspaper he edited from 1907 to 1908, emphasized political considerations; but in *Karmayogin,* which he edited from 1909 to 1910, the emphasis was on the spiritual discipline of *karmayoga,* or selfless action. In "The Ideal of the Karmayogin," written in 1909, Sri Aurobindo explicitly recasts the ideal of *karmayoga* in terms of a newly defined national *dharma* (or duty):

There is a mightly law of life, a great principle of human evolution, a body of spiritual knowledge and experience of which India has always been destined to be guardian, exemplar and missionary. This is the *sanātana dharma,* the eternal religion. Under the stress of alien impacts she has largely lost hold not of the structure of that *dharma*, but of its living reality. For the religion of India is nothing if it is not lived. It has to be applied not only to life, but to the whole of life; its spirit has to enter into and mould our society, our politics, our literature, our science, our individual character, affections and aspirations. To understand the heart of this *dharma*, to experience it as a truth, to feel the high emotions to which it rises and to express and execute it in life is what we understand by *karmayoga*. We believe that it is to make the yoga the ideal of human life that India rises today; by the yoga she will get the strength to realise her freedom, unity and greatness, by the yoga she will keep the strength to preserve it. It is a spiritual revolution we foresee and the material is only its shadow and reflex.[12]

As this passage suggests, India for Sri Aurobindo was a kind of Kurukshetra[13]: as a warrior in the struggle for India's liberation, an Indian's highest duty must be to fight the just battle because it is just—and in so doing bring the historical situation into proper relation with the divine will. Like Gandhi after him, Sri Aurobindo was less concerned with political independence than with what India would do with independence; a political solution would be temporary at best if it were not based on a heightened consciousness and the discipline of selfless action.

Soon after his year in prison, and four decades before India achieved independence, Sri Aurobindo had expanded his political and spiritual concerns to include the entire sweep of human history. Equipped with front-line experience in revolutionary politics and advanced yoga techniques, he settled in Pondicherry in order to concentrate on the elevation of Indian consciousness through spiritual and psychic forces. Although he continued to be concerned with his own and his disciples' spiritual discipline, and was consistently if indirectly involved in India's struggle, his Integral Yoga system and his program for historical transformation gained a universal expression essential for contemporary religious thought. In the following discussion of India and world history, for example, it will be seen that his commitment to India presup-

poses a more fundamental commitment to historical evolution
on a transnational or global basis.

India and World History

Sri Aurobindo's address on Indian Independence Day,
August 15, 1947, was as much a retrospective on his own
political life and mystical vision as on India's political independence. As early as 1905, the young Aurobindo Ghose wrote
to his ill-fated, nineteen-year-old wife, Mrinalini,[14] that he
was afflicted with three madnesses: the first was his realization
that his talents and resources had to be used exclusively for
God's work; second, that he "must get a direct realisation
of the Lord"; third, that for him India was the Mother, the
embodiment of the divine *shakti* (or the divine creativity).[15]
Although in later years he greatly widened his commitment,
he never abandoned it. The larger vision described in the
1947 independence address is not limited to, but certainly
includes, his commitment to Mother India, proclaimed in his
letter to Mrinalini more than four decades earlier:

> The third folly is this: whereas others regard the country as
> an inert object, and know it as the plains, the fields, the forests,
> the mountains and rivers, I look upon my country as the mother,
> I worship her and adore her as the mother. What would a
> son do when a demon sitting on the breast of his mother
> is drinking her blood? Would he sit down content to take
> his meals, and go on enjoying himself in the company of
> his wife and children, or would he, rather, run to the rescue
> of his mother? I know I have the strength to uplift this fallen
> race; it is not physical strength, I am not going to fight with
> the sword or with a gun, but with the power of knowledge.
> The power of the warrior is not the only kind of force, there
> is also the power of the Brahman which is founded on knowl-
> edge. This is not a new feeling within me, it is not of recent
> origin, I was born with it, it is in my very marrow. God
> sent me to the earth to accomplish this great mission. At
> the age of fourteen the seed of it had begun to sprout and
> at eighteen it had been firmly rooted and become unshakable.[16]

At the age of seventy-five, Sri Aurobindo was able to take a retrospective view, in his address on independence, not only of the accomplishments of "this great mission," but of the progress toward several larger missions—specifically, the emergence of Asia, spiritual evolution, and the eventual unification of man.

> To me personally it must naturally be gratifying that this date which was notable only for me because it was my own birthday celebrated annually by those who have accepted my gospel of life, should have acquired this vast significance. As a mystic, I take this identification, not as a coincidence or fortuitous accident, but as a sanction and seal of the Divine Power which guides my steps on the work with which I began life. Indeed almost all the world movements which I hoped to see fulfilled in my lifetime, though at that time they looked like impossible dreams, I can observe on this day either approaching fruition or initiated and on the way to their achievement. . . .
>
> For I have always held and said that India was arising, not to serve her own material interests only, to achieve expansion, greatness, power and prosperity—though these too she must not neglect—and certainly not like others to acquire domination of other peoples, but to live also for God and the world as a helper and leader of the whole human race. Those aims and ideals were in their natural order these: a revolution which would achieve India's freedom and her unity; the resurgence and liberation of Asia and her return to the great role which she had played in the progress of human civilisation; the rise of a new, a greater, brighter and nobler life for mankind which for its entire realisation would rest outwardly on an international unification of the separate existence of the peoples, preserving and securing their national life but drawing them together into an overriding and consummating oneness; the gift by India of her spiritual knowledge and her means for the spiritualisation of life to the whole race; finally, a new step in the evolution which, by uplifting the consciousness to a higher level, would begin the solution of the many problems of existence which have perplexed and vexed humanity, since men began to think and to dream of individual perfection and a perfect society.[17]

As this text indicates, Sri Aurobindo gradually came to see both his own life and Indian spirituality as agents of historical evolution. Like many contemporary Indian thinkers, Sri

Aurobindo increasingly emphasized the need for a cosmic or universal view of history and claimed a unique role for India in the future evolution of man. He advanced both of these goals by theoretical and practical means; indeed the strength of Sri Aurobindo's vision is precisely that it is grounded in and addressed to the most pressing of social and historical problems. His *Human Cycle,* for example, is as penetrating an analysis of the world situation as it was when written in 1918, and it has served as a basis for the Sri Aurobindo Ashram, Auroville, and many other potentially significant projects generated by Sri Aurobindo's disciples.

Thus, Sri Aurobindo's importance is not limited to his early revolutionary activity or to his spiritual teachings, but embraces a wide range of concerns which successfully demanded his attention. In addition to his political activities and mature political thought, Sri Aurobindo's legacy includes his systematic philosophy, literary works, yoga system, and the spiritual force attributed to him by his disciples. Like his political thought, these other areas of his teaching issue from his intensely personal experience but have implications far beyond the confines of his life and time.

The Experiential Basis

Although Radhakrishnan claims that "philosophy in India is essentially spiritual,"[18] Sri Aurobindo's is perhaps the only comprehensive philosophical system that issues from spiritual experience. While many of the great modern Indian spiritual personalities—such as Ramakrishna, Ramana Maharshi, Śivananda, and J. Krishnamurti—have expressed their experience in philosophical terms, none has developed an original and critical philosophical system, including theories of knowledge, existence, the self, natural order, and the aim of life. On the other hand, a few Indian philosophers—such as Radhakrishnan, K. C. Bhattacharya, and Datta—have attempted to develop a comprehensive system, but none surpasses Sri

Aurobindo's range of topics, precision of argument, or richness of detail. More significantly, however, Sri Aurobindo's philosophical system is unique in its autobiographical authenticity. In its philosophic comprehensiveness, Sri Aurobindo's philosophy finds its contemporary Western analogue among the systematic thinkers—Royce, Bergson, Whitehead, and Heidegger; in its spiritual and autobiographic quality, it more closely resembles Kierkegaard and Buber, and perhaps Heidegger and Wittgenstein. But in the end it must be said that the primacy of the yogic discipline and achievement in Sri Aurobindo's experience renders his philosophical system almost unique.

As he explained in 1935 to his disciple Dilip Kumar Roy:

> Let me tell you in confidence that I never, never, never was a philosopher, although I have written philosophy, which is another story altogether. I knew precious little about philosophy before I did the yoga and came to Pondicherry—I was a poet and a politician, not a philosopher! How I managed to do it and why? First, because Richard proposed to me to cooperate in a philosophical review—and as my theory was that a yogi ought to be able to turn his hand to anything, I could not very well refuse: and then he had to go to the war and left me in the lurch with sixty-four pages a month of philosophy, all to be written by my lonely self! Secondly, because I had only to write down in the terms of the intellect all that I had observed and come to know in practising yoga daily, the philosophy was there automatically.[19]

The philosophy that Sri Aurobindo found to be "there automatically" was serialized in *Arya*, the philosophical monthly created for Sri Aurobindo by Paul Richard (whose wife, Mira Richard, later became the Mother of the Sri Aurobindo Ashram). During the years 1914–21 Sri Aurobindo published, by monthly installments, all of his major works except *Savitri*—i.e., *The Life Divine, The Synthesis of Yoga, Essays on the Gita, The Human Cycle, The Ideal of Human Unity,* and *The Secret of the Veda.* Along with *Savitri: A Legend and a Symbol,* the twenty-three-thousand–line epic poem which he continued to revise until immediately before his death, Sri Aurobindo also revised *The Life Divine* and *The Synthesis of Yoga* in order to express the more advanced spiritual experiences of his later years. The revisions of these three major works and his voluminous correspondence during his *sādhanā* reveal Sri Aurobindo's spiritual ascent from the mental to the edge of the supramental level of consciousness. The gulf between these levels can be bridged by what Sri Aurobindo calls the Triple Transformation:

> There must first be the psychic change, the conversion of our whole present nature into a soul-instrumentation; on that or along with that there must be the spiritual change, the descent of a higher Light, Knowledge, Power, Force, Bliss into the whole being, even into the lowest recesses of the life and body, even into the darkness of our subconscience; last, there must supervene the supramental transmutation—there must take place as the crowning movement the ascent into the supermind and transforming descent of the supramental Consciousness into our entire being and nature.[20]

Sri Aurobindo achieved the first transformation during, if not before, his year in the Alipore jail; by that time his self-awareness had demonstrably given way to a divine force. The second transformation corresponds to the descent of the Overmind. Sri Aurobindo explains that this descent was first accomplished on his "Day of Siddhi" (day of spiritual victory), November 24, 1926. Immediately after this event, Sri Aurobindo explained that the third, or supramental, transformation was assured by the overmental descent; and shortly before his death in 1950 he announced that the Supermind would be manifest on the mental and physical plane through the Mother. In 1956, the Mother announced that the Supermind had indeed descended through her. This claim can best be rendered intelligible in terms of the Mother's place in Sri Aurobindo's spiritual discipline and force. Just as the credibility of Sri Aurobindo's spiritual claims for himself must depend to some extent on the quality of his political and philosophical bequest, so the credibility of the Mother would seem to depend on the deference paid to her by Sri Aurobindo and the disciples, and by the quality of her historical legacy. Since this is a time in our society when claimants to privileged spiritual status and multitudes of uncritical disciples continue to proliferate, when self-proclaimed avatars and genuine gurus are being divinized by zealous disciples, it is the more essential that this introduction to Sri Aurobindo and the Mother include a clear presentation of their own self-conception.

Sri Aurobindo on Himself and the Mother

Sri Aurobindo defines a spiritual master as one who has risen to, and is regarded as, the manifestation of a higher consciousness. The master or guru assists the *sadhak*, or disciple, by his teaching and his "power to communicate his own experience."[21] His own and the Mother's status as a manifestation of a higher consciousness is described at length in his writings on himself and the Mother. The experience of both Sri Aurobindo and the Mother varies according to the receptivity of the observer—whether disciple or curious outsider—but there seems to be far more receptivity to the claims made for Sri Aurobindo than for the Mother. Both because of this resistance, especially in the West, and, more importantly, because it is her function to lead people to Sri Aurobindo rather than to herself, the Mother has not emphasized her own significance in Sri Aurobindo's legacy; rather, it has been Sri Aurobindo and the disciples who have insisted on the spiritual eminence of the Mother.

Although the concept of the Mother—or *shakti* (Divine Energy)—is well established in the Indian spiritual tradition, it remains a stumbling block for most Westerners, even those who are sympathetic to Sri Aurobindo's teachings. Apparently, it was also a stumbling block for some of the original disciples, for Sri Aurobindo recalled in a letter of 1934 that there was "a time when the Mother was not fully recognised or accepted by some of those who were here from the beginning.''[22] But for virtually all of the disciples during the past several decades, the Mother represents the embodiment of the divine process for the present age. By Sri Aurobindo's own insistence, it is impossible to follow his yoga except through the Mother:

> The Mother's consciousness and mine are the same, the one Divine Consciousness in two, because that is necessary for the play. Nothing can be done without her knowledge and force, without her consciousness—if anybody really feels her consciousness, he should know that I am there behind it and if he feels me it is the same with hers.[23]

Sri Aurobindo's identification of the Mother's consciousness with his own, and the indispensability of the Mother for his yoga, may best be understood in the context of the traditional concept of *shakti* and in light of the Mother's own spiritual biography.

In Sri Aurobindo's Integral Yoga, the concept of *shakti* refers to *prakriti,* or world process, in its feminine aspect; in short, World-Mother. Just as Aurobindo Ghose the political revolutionary identified "Mother India" as the embodiment of *shakti,* Sri Aurobindo the prophet of the Supramental Age identified the Mother of the Sri Aurobindo Ashram (the former Mira Richard) as a manifestation of *shakti* in the form of the Divine Mother. In philosophical terms, *shakti* is the conscious force—rather like a Bergsonian *élan vital*—that carries the world process to ever higher stages of evolution; *shakti* raises the lower levels of reality by infusing them with the higher levels. *Shakti* refers to many aspects of the Divine, one of which is *mahashakti,* or the Divine Mother through which the yoga functions. As an expression of *shakti,* the Mother of the Sri Aurobindo Ashram manifests the conscious force of the universe in three ways:

> Transcendent, the original supreme *shakti,* she stands above the worlds and links the creation to the ever unmanifest mystery of the Supreme. Universal, the cosmic *mahashakti,* she creates all these beings and contains and enters, supports and embodies the power of these two vaster ways of her existence, makes

them living and near to us and mediates between the human personality and the divine Nature.[24]

In view of the lofty status and function of this concept, it is obviously significant that Sri Aurobindo, from the beginning of his spiritual collaboration with her, acknowledged Mira Richard as the Mother—as Mother of the Sri Aurobindo Ashram and as the embodiment of *shakti*.[25]

In light of the spiritual level which they each had attained by the time of their meeting in 1914, it is perhaps not surprising that they immediately saw in each other a unique and complementary aspect of the divine. Mira Richard had heard of Sri Aurobindo from her husband, Paul Richard, a French diplomat and spiritual seeker who, on the basis of his meeting with Sri Aurobindo in 1910, had described him as "the hero of tomorrow," the greatest among "the divine men of Asia."[26] When Mira met Sri Aurobindo four years later, on March 29, 1914, she saw in him the Lord Krishna (the reincarnation of Vishnu in the Bhagavadgita), of whom she had been conscious before going to India. As she wrote in her diary the next day:

> Little by little the horizon becomes precise, the path becomes clear. And we advance to an even greater certitude. It matters not if there are hundreds of beings plunged in densest ignorance. He whom we saw yesterday is on earth: his presence is enough to prove that a day will come when darkness shall be transformed into light, when Thy reign shall be indeed established upon earth.[27]

For Mira Richard, who was then thirty-six years old, this extraordinary encounter conformed to a spiritual capacity which had been in evidence from her youth. As Sri Aurobindo later explained: "The Mother was inwardly above the human even in childhood."[28] As an adolescent, Mira was extremely meditative and psychic; subsequently, she studied occultism in Algeria and then established a group of spiritual seekers who met in her home in Paris.[29] In 1912 she recorded that "the general aim to be attained is the advent of a progressive universal harmony . . . through the awakening in all and the manifestation by all of the inner Divinity which is One. In other words—to create unity by founding the Kingdom of God which is within us all."[30] As this and other passages indicate, the meeting of Sri Aurobindo and the Mother was the unification of two equally remarkable spiritual personalities.

After nine months of intense spiritual and literary activity, Paul and Mira Richard returned to France in January 1915; a year later they sailed for Japan, where they remained until 1920 when Mira sailed for Pondicherry in order to begin the spiritual mission which she shared with Sri Aurobindo until his death in 1950. In the tradition of the Indian spiritual consortship exemplified by Rama and Sita, Krishna and Radha, the Mother can be seen as the consort in a divinely inspired romance of the spirit. According to this symbolism, the collaboration of Sri Aurobindo and the Mother represents the union of Śiva-*shakti*, Indian-Western, and male-female polarities. Such a union signals what Sri Aurobindo refers to as "the Hour of God." According to Sri Aurobindo's vision, articulated in *Savitri:*

> But when the hour of the Divine draws near,
> The Mighty Mother shall take birth in Time
> And God be born into the human clay
> In forms made ready by your human lives.
> Then shall the Truth supreme be given to Men.[31]

Thus, Sri Aurobindo's elaborate account of the Mother, from his booklet of 1928 until the concluding lines of *Savitri* which he penned only days before he died, contends that her function is subsequent to his but no less important or necessary. When the Mother is explained apart from the spiritual framework established by Sri Aurobindo, the divine powers attributed to her cannot help but appear as the pious exaggerations of the disciples; whether these attributions be justified or not, they do not have their origin in the piety of the disciples but in the unequivocal statements of Sri Aurobindo. For her part, the Mother is equally insistent that, by virtue of his teaching and force, Sri Aurobindo is the proper focus for all spiritual aspirants. According to what Sri Aurobindo calls "the divine play," the possibility of the Mother depends upon Sri Aurobindo, and the manifestation of Sri Aurobindo depends upon the Mother. The exact nature of Sri Aurobindo, however, may be more a mystery to be lived with than a question to be answered.

Sri Aurobindo's spiritual force no more lends itself to exact definition than does a claim for the divinity of the Buddha, Krishna, or the Christ. Indeed, Sri Aurobindo sees his own mission as comparable in uniqueness and transformative power to these three avatars. When asked by one of his disciples whether he was an avatar, he defined his function as follows:

> I am seeking to manifest something of the Divine that I am conscious of and feel—I care a damn whether that constitutes me an avatar or something else. That is not a question which concerns me. By manifestation, of course, I mean the bringing out and spreading of that Consciousness so that others also may feel and enter into it and live in it.[32]

In reply to the same disciple's persistent questioning on his self-conception and on the nature of the avatar, Sri Aurobindo explained that his own powers were of value to others precisely because they had developed in accordance with a reliable spiritual discipline:

> I had no urge to spirituality in me, I developed spirituality. I was incapable of understanding metaphysics, I developed into a philosopher. I had no eye for painting—I developed it by yoga. I transformed my nature from what it was to what it was not. I did it by a special manner, not by a miracle and I did it to show what could be done and how it could be done. I did not do it out of any personal necessity of my own or by a miracle without any process. I say that if it is not so, then my yoga is useless and my life was a mistake—a mere absurd freak of nature without meaning or consequence. You all seem to think it a great compliment to me to say that what I have done has no meaning for anybody except for myself—it is the most damaging criticism on my work that could be made. I also did not do it by myself, if you mean by myself the Aurobindo that I was. He did

it by the help of Krishna and the divine *shakti*. I had help from human sources also.[33]

Thus the concept of the avatar—whether Rama, Krishna, Buddha, Caitanya, Ramakrishna, or Sri Aurobindo—refers to a Divine Consciousness in an instrumental personality "according to the rules of the game—though also sometimes to change the rules of the game." So the avatar comes into existence not as "a mere superfluous freak of nature," but as a "coherent part of the arrangement of the omnipotent Divine in nature."[34]

According to the Mother and the disciples, Sri Aurobindo's account of the arrangement of the Divine in nature, and his role in the arrangement, leaves no doubt about his status as an avatar:

> In the eternity of becoming each avatar is only the announcer, the forerunner of a more perfect future realisation.
>
> And yet men have always the tendency to deify the avatar of the past in opposition to the avatar of the future.
>
> Now again Sri Aurobindo has come announcing to the world the realisation of tomorrow; and again his message meets with the same opposition as of all those who preceded him.
>
> But tomorrow will prove the truth of what he revealed and his work will be done.[35]

Sri Aurobindo's announcement is the imminent descent of the Supermind, or the advent of the Supramental Age. All previous avatars, then, were on the mental or perhaps the overmental level; Sri Aurobindo is the prophet or avatar of the Supramental. As he has repeatedly explained, however, he would be the instrument of the overmental descent, but the Supermind would be brought into the earth consciousness by the Mother:

> Her embodiment is a chance for the earth consciousness to receive the Supramental into it and to undergo first the transformation necessary for that to be possible. Afterwards there will be a further transformation by the Supramental. . . .
>
> There is one divine force which acts in the universe and in the individual and is also beyond the individual and the universe. The Mother stands for all these, but she is working

here in the body to bring down something not yet expressed in this material world so as to transform life here—it is so that you should regard her as the divine *shakti* working here for that purpose. She is that in the body, but in her whole consciousness she is also identified with all the other aspects of the Divine.[36]

According to the Mother's announcement, the third transformation, the descent of the Supermind, took place on February 29, 1956. In April of the same year, the Mother announced: "The manifestation of the supramental upon earth is no longer a promise but a living fact, a reality. It is at work here, and one day will come when the most blind, the most unconscious, even the most unwilling shall be obliged to recognise it."[37] At the same time the Mother disclosed that "the supramental consciousness will enter into a phase of realising power in 1967."[38] The Mother clearly intended that this supramental consciousness be manifest in the creation of Auroville, the first planetary city, under construction in Pondicherry since 1968.

While it is certainly possible to appreciate, and cooperate with, Sri Aurobindo's and the Mother's teachings and works without accepting the claims made for this spiritual power, these works take on an added significance if they are seen as a higher stage of spiritual evolution. If we accept a Jamesian or pragmatic test of religious experience, according to its personal and historical contributions, Sri Aurobindo's and the Mother's legacy bears witness to the depth, and perhaps uniqueness, of their spiritual experience.

Yoga, Religion, and Utopia

Throughout his four decades of *sādhanā,* and thirty volumes of systematic writing and correspondence, Sri Aurobindo consistently distinguished his spiritual discipline from traditional religion. He repeatedly emphasized that his teaching was concerned with the spiritualization of the natural world:

> Our aim is not . . . to found a religion or a school of philosophy
> or a school of yoga, but to create a ground and a way which
> will bring down a greater truth beyond the mind but not inacces-
> sible to the human soul and consciousness. . . .
>
> The way of yoga followed here has a different purpose
> from others—for its aim is not only to rise out of the ordinary
> ignorant world-consciousness into the divine consciousness
> but to bring the supramental power of that divine consciousness
> down into the ignorance of the mind, life and body, to transform
> them, to manifest the Divine here and create a divine life
> in matter.[39]

But in the same place he admits that "this is an exceedingly difficult aim and difficult yoga," to many or most it will
seem impossible." Consequently, many who attempt this yoga
will reduce it to a more manageable task. One such reduction
would be to follow Sri Aurobindo's directives on a religious
level; another would be to participate in the social and historical
programs generated by this yoga without the requisite spiritual
discipline.

As the number of disciples increases, and variety of groups
and activities proliferates, Sri Aurobindo's warning against
a movement, whether religious or sociological, will assume
greater urgency. In 1934, decades before there was any serious
interest in his teachings outside of India, Sri Aurobindo
cautioned:

> A movement in the case of a work like mine means the founding
> of a school or a sect or some other damned nonsense. It means
> that hundreds or thousands of useless people join in and corrupt
> the work or reduce it to a pompous farce from which the
> Truth that was coming down recedes into secrecy and silence.
> It is what has happened to the "religions" and is the reason
> of their failure.[40]

What Sri Aurobindo and the Mother objected to in the religious
function was its dependence upon externals and its emphasis
on an other-worldly goal of the spiritual life, both of which
detract from the essential task of spiritualizing the natural
world. Just as Sri Aurobindo argues for an integral metaphysics
against both materialism and spiritualism, he also argues for

an integral yoga against other-worldly and merely externalized religious forms. In the following passage he distinguishes the spiritual from the religious:

> The spiritual life (*adhyātma-jīvana*), the religious life (*dharma-jīvana*) and the ordinary human life of which morality is a part are three quite different things and one must know which one desires and not confuse the three together. The ordinary life is that of the average human consciousness separated from its own true self and from the Divine and led by the common habits of the mind, life and body which are the laws of the Ignorance. The religious life is a movement of the same ignorant human consciousness, turning or trying to turn away from the earth towards the Divine, but as yet without knowledge and led by the dogmatic tenets and rules of some sect or creed which claims to have found the way out of the bonds of the earth-consciousness into some beatific Beyond. The religious life may be the first approach to the spiritual, but very often it is only a turning about in a round of rites, ceremonies and practices or set ideas and forms without any issue. The spiritual life, on the contrary, proceeds directly by a change of consciousness, a change from the ordinary consciousness, ignorant and separated from its true self and from God, to a greater consciousness in which one finds one's true being and comes first into direct and living contact and then into union with the Divine. For the spiritual seeker this change of consciousness is the one thing he seeks and nothing else matters.[41]

But since Sri Aurobindo and the Mother well knew that it is precisely the dogmas, rites, and institutional forms that make religion so persistent, they have warned the disciples against the lure of religious ideals and practices. Sri Aurobindo emphasized that "it is not his object to develop any one religion or to amalgamate the older religions or to found any religion—for any one of these things would lead away from his central purpose."[42] Similarly, the Mother has reminded the disciples that religion belongs to a previous mode of spirituality:

> Why do men cling to a religion?
> Religions are based on creeds which are spiritual experi-

ences brought down to a level where they become more easy
to grasp, but at the cost of their integral purity and truth.
    The time of religions is over.
    We have entered the age of universal spirituality, of
spiritual experience in its initial purity.[43]

Despite the efforts and example of Sri Aurobindo, the Mother,
and the more accomplished disciples, many will undoubtedly
follow the master's teachings on a religious level. In this
respect, the gap between Sri Aurobindo's Integral Yoga and
the religious tradition that it will probably generate has its
analogues in the highly external and formal religious traditions
that developed from the profound spirituality of Gotama and
Jesus.

    While some will adhere to the yoga for religious purposes,
others will acclaim Sri Aurobindo's and the Mother's work
as a purely sociological and historical legacy. The Mother
has sought to establish the spiritual basis of Auroville from
its earliest conception: the Auroville Charter, for example,
stipulates that an "Aurovillian must be a willing servitor of
the Divine Consciousness." Since "the earth is certainly not
ready to realise such an ideal," however, the Mother has
repeatedly issued reminders such as the following:

> One lives in Auroville in order to be free of moral and social
> conventions; but this liberty must not be a new slavery to
> the ego, its desires and its ambitions. The fulfillment of desires
> bars the route to the inner discovery which can only be attained
> in peace and the transparency of a perfect disinterestedness.[44]

    The prospect of a community "free of social and moral
conventions" will attract sufficient publicity and enthusiastic
followers to jeopardize the spiritual discipline presently in evidence at the Ashram and Auroville. Most observers grant
that the high quality of these communities will probably last
as long as they remain under the Mother's direction. The
urgency of the question of succession, a question invariably
raised by observers and largely ignored by the disciples,
depends upon the extent to which the disciples sustain Sri
Aurobindo's and the Mother's discipline and vision. Both posi-

tive and negative forecasts can find supporting evidence: while many of the disciples will continue to work creatively for the individual and collective goals established by the Mother, many others seem incapable of decisive action without assurance of the Mother's approval. If the implementation of Sri Aurobindo's and the Mother's teachings has been difficult even with the benefit of their physical presence and constant direction, it will of course be significantly more difficult when their spiritual experience and teachings have been filtered by the ravages of time and the limitations of the disciples. Like the yoga itself, the completion of Sri Aurobindo's and the Mother's legacy will be "an exceedingly difficult aim . . . ; to many or most it will seem impossible." That many or most will fall far short of Sri Aurobindo's and the Mother's goals should be expected—but an increasing number of people believe that those who accept the Mother's invitation to "the great adventure" may indeed participate in "the birth of a new world."

Notes

1. Erik Erikson, *Gandhi's Truth* (New York: W. W. Norton, 1969), p. 229.
2. For an introduction to these and other Indian thinkers, see V. S. Naravane, *Modern Indian Thought* (New York: Asia Publishing House, 1964); for selected writings of these thinkers, see Robert A. McDermott and V. S. Naravane, eds., *The Spirit of Modern India* (New York: T. Y. Crowell, 1974).
3. When Tagore visited Sri Aurobindo at Pondicherry in 1928, he greeted his fellow Bengali poet as the prophet and voice of a new vision:

> I felt that the utterance of the ancient Hindu Rishi spoke from him of that equanimity which gives the human soul its freedom of entrance into the All. I said to him, "You have the Word and we are waiting to accept it from you. India will speak through your voice to the world, 'Hearken to me.' "
>
> In her earlier forest home Sakuntala had her awakenment of life in the restlessness of her youth. In the later hermitage she attained the fulfillment of her life. Years ago I saw Aurobindo in the atmosphere of his earlier heroic youth and I sang to him, "Aurobindo, accept the salutation from Rabindranath."

Today I saw him in a deeper atmosphere of a reticent richness
of wisdom and again sang to him in silence, "Aurobindo, accept
the salutation from Rabindranath."

4. Curiously, Sri Aurobindo and Gandhi had no personal contact even
though Nehru and many other Nationalist leaders (e.g., Surendra Mohan
Ghose of Bengal) maintained contact with Sri Aurobindo throughout the
1930's and 1940's. For Sri Aurobindo's rejection of Gandhi's program,
specifically its insistence on nonviolence, see *On Himself,* XXVI, pp. 40–41,
438. (Unless otherwise cited, all of Sri Aurobindo's writings are published
by the Sri Aurobindo Ashram, Pondicherry, India. References to the Sri
Aurobindo Centenary Library, 1970–73, are cited by volume title, number,
and page.)

5. Sri Aurobindo and Radhakrishnan share many of the same philosophical sources and concerns, but the prominence of yoga—particularly his
profound spiritual realization—separates Sri Aurobindo's Integral
Philosophy from the Vedantist (or neo-Vedantist) system of Radhakrishnan.
Considering their respective efforts to combine Indian and Western
philosophies, it is curious that the two most prominent philosophers of
modern India had virtually no personal or philosophical contact. For Radhakrishnan's own writings, see Robert A. McDermott, ed., *Radhakrishnan:
Selected Writings on Philosophy, Religion and Culture* (New York: E. P.
Dutton, 1970).

6. Sri Aurobindo, *On Himself,* XXVI, epigraph.

7. Note that the Mother has been primarily responsible for the creation
of both the Ashram and Auroville, but that the theoretical basis for both
was clearly provided in Sri Aurobindo's writings, especially in *The Human
Cycle.*

8. In addition to such standard works as A. B. Purani, *The Life of
Sri Aurobindo* (1964), R. R. Diwakar, *Mahayogi Sri Aurobindo* (Bombay:
Bharatiya Vidya Bhavan, 1967), and Sisirkumar Mitra, *The Liberator*
(Bombay: Jaico Publishing House, 1970), the fullest account of Sri
Aurobindo's early life is K. R. Srinivas Iyengar, *Sri Aurobindo: A Biography
and a History,* 2 vols. (1972).

9. Saint Augustine *Confessions* vii. 9, 27.

10. "Uttarpara Speech," in *Karmayogin,* II, p. 3.

11. "Prison and Freedom," in *Kara Kahini* (1969), trans. Sisirkumar
Ghose, p. 3; see also *Writings in Bengali,* IV, pp. 298–305.

12. "The Ideal of the Karmayogin," in *Karmayogin,* II, p. 17. The
spiritual method and goal of this revolution, however, included a radical
political program which Sri Aurobindo later summarized as follows:

There were three sides to Sri Aurobindo's political ideas and activities.
First, there was the action with which he started, a secret revolutionary
propaganda and organisation of which the central object was the prep-

aration of an armed insurrection. Secondly, there was a public propaganda intended to convert the whole nation to the ideal of independence which was regarded, when he entered into politics, by the vast majority of Indians as unpractical and impossible, an almost insane chimera. It was thought that the British Empire was too powerful and India too weak, effectively disarmed and impotent even to dream of the success of such an endeavour. Thirdly, there was the organisation of the people to carry on a public and united opposition and undermining of the foreign rule through an increasing non-cooperation and passive resistance *(On Himself,* XXVI, p. 21).

13. Field of the Kurus near Delhi. As Gandhi and others have pointed out, "the battlefield of Kurukshetra only provides the occasion for the dialogue. The real Kurukshetra is the human heart."

14. In 1901, when he was twenty-eight, Sri Aurobindo married Mrinalini Bose, a pious Hindu girl barely half his age. As he became more deeply involved in politics and yoga, the obvious gap between them grew wider; in 1918, after being separated from her husband for more than ten years, Mrinalini was about to journey to Pondicherry when she contracted influenza and died.

15. Quoted in Purani, *op. cit.,* pp. 87–90; reprinted in *Cross Currents,* XXII (Winter 1972), 9–11.

16. Purani, *op, cit.,* p. 90; *Cross Currents,* p. 11.

17. "The Fifteenth of August, 1947," in *Sri Aurobindo and His Ashram* (1964), pp. 40–41; *Cross Currents,* pp. 44–45.

18. S. Radhakrishnan, *Indian Philosophy* (New York: Macmillan Company, 1962), I, p. 24; McDermott, ed., *Radhakrishnan,* p. 69.

19. Quoted in Diwakar, *op. cit.,* p. 174.

20. *The Life Divine,* XIX, p. 891.

21. "The Teaching of Sri Aurobindo," in *Sri Aurobindo and His Ashram,* p. 62.

22. *On Himself,* XXVI, p. 455.

23. *Ibid.*

24. *The Mother,* XXV, p. 20.

25. In reply to a disciple's question on this matter, Sri Aurobindo confirmed that his booklet "The Mother" (1928) does indeed refer to the Mother of the Sri Aurobindo Ashram *(The Mother,* XXV, p. 47).

26. Paul Richard, *Dawn Over Asia;* quoted in Srinivas Iyengar, *op. cit.,* p. 694.

27. *Prayers and Meditations of the Mother* (1948), pp. 88–89.

28. *The Mother,* XXV, p. 48.

29. Srinivas Iyengar, *op. cit.,* p. 696.

30. Quoted in *ibid.*

31. *Savitri,* XXIX, p. 705.

32. Nirodbaran, *Correspondence with Sri Aurobindo* (1969), p. 58.

33. *Ibid.*, p. 49.

34. *Ibid.*, p. 50.

35. *The Mother on Sri Aurobindo* (1961), p. 6.

36. *The Mother*, XXV, pp. 49–50.

37. Quoted in Mitra, *The Liberator*, p. 279; see also *Bulletin of the International Centre of Education* (hereafter: *Bull. I.C.E.*), November 1957, and *Gazette Aurovilienne*, Nos. 5–6, p. 13.

38. Quoted in Mitra, *op. cit.*, p. 285.

39. Quoted in *Bull. I.C.E.* (Special Issue of *Mother India)*, November–December 1968, p. 5.

40. Quoted in *Gazette Aurovilienne*, 1971, p. 1.

41. *Letters on Yoga*, XXII, p. 137.

42. "The Teaching of Sri Aurobindo," p. 62.

43. Quoted in *Bull. I.C.E.*, p. 6.

44. *Gazette Aurovilienne*, No. 4, p. 5.

AUROBINDO ON SRI AUROBINDO

by Sri Aurobindo

THE TEACHING OF Sri Aurobindo starts from that of the ancient
sages of India: that behind the appearances of the universe
there is the reality of a being and consciousness, a self of
all things, one and eternal. All beings are united in that one
self and spirit but divided by a certain separativity of consciousness, an ignorance of their true self and reality in the
mind, life, and body. It is possible by a certain psychological
discipline to remove this veil of separative consciousness and
become aware of the true Self, the divinity within us and
all.

Sri Aurobindo's teaching states that this one being and
consciousness is involved here in matter. Evolution is the
process by which it liberates itself; consciousness appears in
what seems to be inconscient, and once having appeared is
self-impelled to grow higher and higher and at the same time
to enlarge and develop toward a greater and greater perfection.
Life is the first step of this release of consciousness; mind
is the second. But the evolution does not finish with mind;
it awaits a release into something greater, a consciousness
which is spiritual and supramental. The next step of the evolution must be toward the development of Supermind and spirit
as the dominant power in the conscious being. For only then
will the involved divinity in things release itself entirely and
it become possible for life to manifest perfection.

But while the former steps in evolution were taken by
nature without a conscious will in the plant and animal life,
in man nature becomes able to evolve by a conscious will
in the instrument. It is not, however, by the mental will in
man that this can be wholly done, for the mind goes only
to a certain point and after that can only move in a circle.
A conversion has to be made, a turning of the consciousness
by which mind has to change into the higher principle. This

method is to be found through the ancient psychological discipline and practice of yoga. In the past, it has been attempted by a drawing away from the world and a disappearance into the height of the self or spirit. Sri Aurobindo teaches that a descent of the higher principle is possible which will not merely release the spiritual Self out of the world, but release it in the world, replace the mind's ignorance or its very limited knowledge by a supramental Truth-Consciousness which will be a sufficient instrument of the inner self, and make it possible for the human being to find himself dynamically as well as inwardly and grow out of his still animal humanity into a diviner race. The psychological discipline of yoga can be used to that end by opening all the parts of the being to a conversion or transformation through the descent and working of the higher, still-concealed supramental principle.

This, however, cannot be done at once or in a short time or by any rapid or miraculous transformation. Many steps have to be taken by the seeker before the supramental descent is possible. Man lives mostly in his surface mind, life, and body, but there is an inner being within him with greater possibilities to which he has to awake—for it is only a very restricted influence from it that he receives now and that pushes him to a constant pursuit of a greater beauty, harmony, power, and knowledge. The first process of yoga is therefore to open the ranges of this inner being and to live from there outward, governing his outward life by an inner light and force. In doing so he discovers in himself his true soul, which is not this outer mixture of mental, vital, and physical elements, but something of the reality behind them, a spark from the one divine fire. He has to learn to live in his soul and purify and orientate by its drive toward the truth the rest of the nature. There can follow afterwards an opening upward and descent of a higher principle of the being. But even then it is not at once the full supramental light and force. For there are several ranges of consciousness between the ordinary human mind and the supramental Truth-Consciousness. These intervening ranges have to be opened up and their power brought down into the mind, life, and body. Only afterwards can the full power of the Truth-Consciousness work in the nature. The process of this self-discipline or *sādhanā* is therefore long and difficult, but even a little of it is so much gained because it makes the ultimate release and perfection more possible.

There are many things belonging to older systems that are necessary on the way—an opening of the mind to a greater wideness and to the sense of the self and the infinite, an emergence into what has been called the cosmic consciousness, mastery over the desires and passions; an outward asceticism is not essential, but the conquest of desire and attachment and a control over the body and its needs, greeds, and instincts are indispensable. There is a combination of the principles of the old systems, the way of knowledge through the mind's discernment between reality and the appearance; the heart's way of devotion, love, and surrender; and the way of works, turning the will away from motives of self-interest to the truth and the service of a greater reality than the ego. For the whole being has to be trained so that it can respond and be transformed when it is possible for that greater light and force to work in the nature.

In this discipline the inspiration of the master and, in the difficult stages, his control and his presence are indispensable—for it would be impossible otherwise to go through it without much stumbling and error which would prevent all chance of success. The master is one who has risen to a higher consciousness and being and he is often regarded as its manifestation or representative. He not only helps by his teaching and still more by his influence and example, but by a power to communicate his own experience to others.

This is Sri Aurobindo's teaching and method of practice. It is not his object to develop any one religion or to amalgamate the older religions or to found any new religion—for any of these things would lead away from his central purpose. The one aim of his yoga is an inner self-development by which each one who follows it can in time discover the One Self in all and evolve a higher consciousness than the mental, a spiritual and supramental consciousness which will transform and divinize human nature.

CHRONOLOGY OF
SRI AUROBINDO'S LIFE

1872, August 15	Birth; fourth child of Dr. Krishnadhan Ghose, a surgeon, and Swarnalata Devi Ghose, who later suffered from hysteria; originally named Aravinda Ackroyd, but dropped Ackroyd while a student at Cambridge; "Sri," which has been part of his name at least since 1926, refers to his spiritual eminence.
1872–79	At Khulna, East Bengal, where his father was District Medical Officer.
1877–79	At Darjeeling, in the Loretto Convent School.
1879–84	At Manchester, England, in the charge of the Drewett family; educated at home by the Drewetts.
1884–90	At St. Paul's School, Cambridge.
1890–92	At King's College, Cambridge. Advocates Indian freedom in speeches to Indian Majlis, a student group. Writes poetry and pursues other literary activities.
1893, February	Returns to India, landing at Apollo Bunder, Bombay, and experiences a vast calm which lasts for several months. Begins employment in the service of the Maharaja of Baroda. Professor of English and French, and subsequently Vice-Principal of Baroda College.
1893, August 7	Series of political articles, "New Lamps for Old," in *Indu Prakash* (Bombay).
1898–99	Begins writing *Savitri*.
1900–1902	Begins political activity.
1901, April	Marriage to Mrinalini Bose, in Calcutta.
1902	Meets Sister Nevedita.
1902–3	Joins the secret society of Western India.
1903, April	Experiences "the vacant Infinite" at the "Hill of Sankaracharya" in Kashmir.
1904–5	Begins the practice of yoga.
1905	Partition of Bengal. "Bhavani Mandir" and "No Compromise," revolutionary pamphlets.
1906, February	Moves to Calcutta.

42

1906, March	Exercises general control over *Yugantar*, a revolutionary Bengali weekly, begun by his younger brother, Barindra.
1906, August	Assists Bipan Chandra Pal in founding *Bande Mataram*, a radical political newspaper, and subsequently the organ of the Nationalist Party in Bengal.
1906, December	Succeeds Bipan Chandra Pal as leader of the Nationalist Party in Bengal and editor of *Bande Mataram*.
1907, April	Several series of articles, including "The Doctrine of Passive Resistance" in *Bande Mataram*.
1907, August 16	Arrested on the charge of sedition for articles in *Bande Mataram*, and released on bail.
1907, August 23	Speech to the Bengal National College after his resignation as Principal.
1907, December	Leader of the Nationalists at the Bengal Provincial Congress and at the Surat Congress.
1908, January	Meets Vishnu Bhaskar Lele, a Mahastrian yogi, in Baroda. Following Lele's instructions, he silences his mind and experiences the spaceless and timeless Brahman.
1908, January 19	"The Present Situation," speech to the Bombay National Union.
1908, May 2	Arrested in connection with the Alipore Conspiracy Case. May 5, 1908, to May 6, 1909, an undertrial prisoner at the Alipore jail. Meditates on the Gita and practices yoga.
1909, May 6	Acquitted of the charges against him.
1909, May 30	Uttarpara Speech.
1909, June 19	Founds and manages *Karmayoga*, an English weekly.
1909, August 23	Founds and manages *Dharma*, a Bengali weekly.
1909, September	Leads the Nationalists at the Bengal Provincial Conference.
1910, February	Leaves Calcutta for Chandernagore.
1910, April 1–4	Sails to Pondicherry.
1910	Meets Paul Richard.
1914, March 29	Meets Mira Richard.
1914, August 15	First issue of *Arya*, the monthly journal in which he published all of his major works except *Savitri*. Continued publication until January 1921,

1920, April 24	Mira Richard returns to Pondichery after living in Japan for several years.
1926, November 24	"The Day of Siddhi" (day of victory): the descent of Krishna, or overmental consciousness, into the physical. Retires completely into concentrated *sādhanā*. The Mother takes charge of the disciples and establishes the Ashram.
1928	Publication of "The Mother."
1930–38	Daily correspondence with the *sadhaks* in the Ashram.
1939–40	Revision and publication of *The Life Divine* in book form.
1939, September—October	Composes more than thirty sonnets.
1940, September	Joint declaration of Sri Aurobindo and the Mother in support of the Allies; countering the dominant Indian position, works for the Allies throughout the war.
1942, March	Supports the Cripps Proposal of the British Government, seeking Indian cooperation for the war effort in Asia in return for increased self-government.
1942, December 2	Start of the Ashram School.
1947, August 15	India's Independence on Sri Aurobindo's seventy-fifth birthday.
1949, February 21	First issue of the *Bulletin of Physical Education* (later called the *Bulletin of the Sri Aurobindo International Centre of Education*), with Sri Aurobindo's Message (later published as *The Supramental Manifestation* and reprinted as *The Mind of Light*).
1950	Publication of Part One of *Savitri*.
1950, November	Kidney illness.
1950, December 5	Death. After being on view for five days, Sri Aurobindo's body is laid to rest in the courtyard of the Ashram.
1951	Publication of Parts Two and Three of *Savitri*.
1951, April 24	Start of the Sri Aurobindo International University Centre, later called the Sri Aurobindo International Centre of Education.
1956, February 29	Descent of the Supramental through the Mother.
1968, February 29	Foundation of Auroville.
1972, August 15	Sri Aurobindo's Birth Centenary.

PART ONE

MAN IN EVOLUTION

INTRODUCTION

The Destiny of Man

If the history of Western philosophy can be characterized as footnotes to Plato, it is-even safer to characterize the history of Indian philosophy as footnotes to the *ṛsis,* or sages, of the Vedic age. Although some of Sri Aurobindo's most basic ideas are as different from the Vedic *ṛsis* as Whitehead's are from Plato's, he clearly shares with the Indian philosophical tradition the vision of the unified reality or consciousness underlying the appearance of mind, life, and body. Centuries before Plato grappled with the relationship between the world of appearances and the reality that lay behind that world, the *ṛsis* of ancient India understood the world in separate realms—the empirical and transcendental. In the Bṛhadāraṇ-yaka Upanishad, for example, the sacrificer is instructed to recite the following verse:

> From the Unreal lead me to the Real,
> From Darkness lead me to Light,
> From Death lead me to Immortality (I. 3:28).

Sri Aurobindo's philosophical system, and the spiritual discipline whereby the unreal, darkness, and death are overcome, begins with the same kind of aspiration as yielded the extraordinary vision contained in the Vedas and Upanishads.

Stages of Evolution

The Life Divine systematically articulates the synthesis of matter and spirit by locating them both in the double movement of existence—involution and evolution. According to this scheme, man has been evolving, now self-consciously, from the lowest to the highest levels of existence; his latest evolutionary stage will integrate the physical, vital, and mental

47

in the synthesis made possible by the Supermind. Thus, the Supermind is the bridge between the lower and higher hemispheres of existence:

$$\left\{\begin{array}{l}\text{Existence (Sat)}\\\text{Consciousness-Force (Chit)}\\\text{Bliss (Ānanda)}\end{array}\right.$$

Supermind (perfect unity in diversity)

$$\left\{\begin{array}{l}\text{Mind (intellect and intuition)}\\\text{Life (vital, organic)}\\\text{Matter (physical, inconscient)}\end{array}\right.$$

Just as the lower three levels of consciousness need to be transformed by the higher three, the Sat-Chit-Ānanda is not fulfilled until it completely spiritualizes the entire realms of physical, vital, and mental existence. This transfer of the lower levels is possible because Sat-Chit-Ānanda, or pure Spirit, is from the beginning involved in every level of existence. Evolution, then, is ontologically subsequent to involution: first existence involves itself in its various levels, and then it is opened out by a series of natural and human transformations.

In accordance with his vision of philosophic and spiritual evolution from the Vedas to his own supramental prophecy, the opening chapters of Sri Aurobindo's metaphysical *magnum opus* show that the four goals of man's earliest "formula of Wisdom"—God, light, freedom, and immortality—can now be realized in man's individual and communal existence. This emphasis on man's aspirations runs throughout Sri Aurobindo's thought and legacy: the same "impulse toward perfection" that generated the Vedic experience of the Divine prepared the way for a series of increasingly advanced responses of the Divine in the world. These responses, in the form of avatars such as Rama, Krishna, and the Buddha, reveal the structure of existence and the levels through which humanity, in concert with its avatars, has evolved. But since these revelations fall unevenly on the mass of restless humanity, life remains a riddle in want of a solution.

Thus, the first point in *The Life Divine*, Sri Aurobindo's metaphysical treatise, is the two responses to the riddle of life between which man has vacillated throughout the centuries:

the "Materialist Denial," or rejection of the spiritual, so powerfully articulated in the modern West, and the "Ascetic Refusal," or rejection of the material, so characteristic of India. One of the tasks of *The Life Divine* is to transform these "two negations" into a wider and more positive account of the natural order. As he explains in the opening paragraph of "The Teaching of Sri Aurobindo," Sri Aurobindo accepts the basic insight of the ancient Indian sages that, although reality is One, it is "divided by a certain separativity of consciousness," or veil which separates each of us from "the true Self, the divinity within us and all." From this starting point, Sri Aurobindo develops a theory of reality that maintains the absolute Unity of the Vedic sages but at the same time affirms the reality and value of so-called appearances. As S. K. Maitra rightly asserts: "The fundamental idea upon which the whole structure of Sri Aurobindo's philosophy rests is that Matter as well as Spirit is to be looked upon as real."[*]

Revealingly, Sri Aurobindo contends that a narrow spiritualism, such as is expounded by the Advaita Vedānta so prominent in the history of Indian philosophy, is "more complete, more final, more perilous in its effects on individuals or collectivities that hear its potent call to the wilderness" than the materialist denial of the spiritual. While the spiritual emphasis takes account of the ascending movement, it unfortunately ignores the process by which the Spirit descends into the material. As the following section indicates, this dual process, also called Involution (Descent) and Evolution (Ascent), forms an essential ingredient of Sri Aurobindo's theory of reality.

According to Sri Aurobindo, the evolutionary process is real, novel, and delightful: real in that the process is no mere shadow or appearance, but a genuine component of reality-in-process; novel in that every transformation (specifically, from material to vital to mental to Supramental) need not have happened as or when it did, but did so because the natural and human orders were able to liberate the Spirit within the historical order; delightful in that *līlā*, or the divine process, constitutes the meaning of life, including every detail of human existence.

An Introduction to the Philosophy of Sri Aurobindo (1965), p. 1.

THE DESTINY OF MAN

The Human Aspiration*

She follows to the goal of those that are passing on beyond, she is the first in the eternal succession of the dawns that are coming, — Usha widens bringing out that which lives, awakening someone who was dead....What is her scope when she harmonises with the dawns that shone out before and those that now must shine? She desires the ancient mornings and fulfils their light; projecting forwards her illumination she enters into communion with the rest that are to come.

Kutsa Angirasa — Rig Veda.[1]

Threefold are those supreme births of this divine force that is in the world, they are true, they are desirable; he moves there wide-overt within the Infinite and shines pure, luminous and fulfilling.... That which is immortal in mortals and possessed of the truth, is a god and established inwardly as an energy working out in our divine powers.... Become high-uplifted, O Strength, pierce all veils, manifest in us the things of the Godhead.

Vamadeva — Rig Veda.[2]

THE earliest preoccupation of man in his awakened thoughts and, as it seems, his inevitable and ultimate preoccupation, — for it survives the longest periods of scepticism and returns after every banishment, — is also the highest which his thought can envisage. It manifests itself in the divination of Godhead, the impulse towards perfection, the search after pure Truth and unmixed Bliss, the sense of a secret immortality. The ancient dawns of human knowledge have left us their witness to this constant aspiration; today we see a humanity satiated but not satisfied by victorious analysis of the externalities of Nature preparing to return to its primeval longings. The earliest formula of Wisdom promises to be its last, — God, Light, Freedom, Immortality.

These persistent ideals of the race are at once the contradiction of its normal experience and the affirmation of higher and deeper experiences which are abnormal to humanity and only to be attained, in their organised entirety, by a revolution-

[1] I. 113. 8, 10.   [2] IV. 1. 7; IV. 2. 1; IV. 4. 5.

* *The Life Divine*, pp. 1–5.

50

ary individual effort or an evolutionary general progression. To know, possess and be the divine being in an animal and egoistic consciousness, to convert our twilit or obscure physical mentality into the plenary supramental illumination, to build peace and a self-existent bliss where there is only a stress of transitory satisfactions besieged by physical pain and emotional suffering, to establish an infinite freedom in a world which presents itself as a group of mechanical necessities, to discover and realise the immortal life in a body subjected to death and constant mutation, — this is offered to us as the manifestation of God in Matter and the goal of Nature in her terrestrial evolution. To the ordinary material intellect which takes its present organisation of consciousness for the limit of its possibilities, the direct contradiction of the unrealised ideals with the realised fact is a final argument against their validity. But if we take a more deliberate view of the world's workings, that direct opposition appears rather as part of Nature's profoundest method and the seal of her completest sanction.

For all problems of existence are essentially problems of harmony. They arise from the perception of an unsolved discord and the instinct of an undiscovered agreement or unity. To rest content with an unsolved discord is possible for the practical and more animal part of man, but impossible for his fully awakened mind, and usually even his practical parts only escape from the general necessity either by shutting out the problem or by accepting a rough, utilitarian and unillumined compromise. For essentially, all Nature seeks a harmony, life and matter in their own sphere as much as mind in the arrangement of its perceptions. The greater the apparent disorder of the materials offered or the apparent disparateness, even to irreconcilable opposition, of the elements that have to be utilised, the stronger is the spur, and it drives towards a more subtle and puissant order than can normally be the result of a less difficult endeavour. The accordance of active Life with a material of form in which the condition of activity itself seems to be inertia, is one problem of opposites that Nature has solved and seeks always to solve better with greater complexities; for its perfect solution would be the material immortality of a fully organised mind-supporting

animal body. The accordance of conscious mind and conscious
will with a form and a life in themselves not overtly self-conscious
and capable at best of a mechanical or sub-conscious will is
another problem of opposites in which she has produced aston-
ishing results and aims always at higher marvels; for there her
ultimate miracle would be an animal consciousness no longer
seeking but possessed of Truth and Light, with the practical
omnipotence which would result from the possession of a direct
and perfected knowledge. Not only, then, is the upward impulse
of man towards the accordance of yet higher opposites rational
in itself, but it is the only logical completion of a rule and an
effort that seem to be a fundamental method of Nature and the
very sense of her universal strivings.

We speak of the evolution of Life in Matter, the evolution
of Mind in Matter; but evolution is a word which merely states
the phenomenon without explaining it. For there seems to be
no reason why Life should evolve out of material elements or
Mind out of living form, unless we accept the Vedantic solution
that Life is already involved in Matter and Mind in Life because
in essence Matter is a form of veiled Life, Life a form of veiled
Consciousness. And then there seems to be little objection to a
farther step in the series and the admission that mental consciousness may itself be only a form and a veil of higher states
which are beyond Mind. In that case, the unconquerable impulse of man towards God, Light, Bliss, Freedom, Immortality
presents itself in its right place in the chain as simply the imperative impulse by which Nature is seeking to evolve beyond Mind,
and appears to be as natural, true and just as the impulse towards
Life which she has planted in certain forms of Matter or the
impulse towards Mind which she has planted in certain forms
of Life. As there, so here, the impulse exists more or less obscurely in her different vessels with an ever-ascending series in the
power of its will-to-be; as there, so here, it is gradually evolving
and bound fully to evolve the necessary organs and faculties.
As the impulse towards Mind ranges from the more sensitive
reactions of Life in the metal and the plant up to its full organisation in man, so in man himself there is the same ascending series,
the preparation, if nothing more, of a higher and divine life.

The animal is a living laboratory in which Nature has, it is said, worked out man. Man himself may well be a thinking and living laboratory in whom and with whose conscious co-operation she wills to work out the superman, the god. Or shall we not say, rather, to manifest God? For if evolution is the progressive manifestation by Nature of that which slept or worked in her, involved, it is also the overt realisation of that which she secretly is. We cannot, then, bid her pause at a given stage of her evolution, nor have we the right to condemn with the religionist as perverse and presumptuous or with the rationalist as a disease or hallucination any intention she may evince or effort she may make to go beyond. If it be true that Spirit is involved in Matter and apparent Nature is secret God, then the manifestation of the divine in himself and the realisation of God within and without are the highest and most legitimate aim possible to man upon earth.

Thus the eternal paradox and eternal truth of a divine life in an animal body, an immortal aspiration or reality inhabiting a mortal tenement, a single and universal consciousness representing itself in limited minds and divided egos, a transcendent, indefinable, timeless and spaceless Being who alone renders time and space and cosmos possible, and in all these the higher truth realisable by the lower term, justify themselves to the deliberate reason as well as to the persistent instinct or intuition of mankind. Attempts are sometimes made to have done finally with questionings which have so often been declared insoluble by logical thought and to persuade men to limit their mental activities to the practical and immediate problems of their material existence in the universe; but such evasions are never permanent in their effect. Mankind returns from them with a more vehement impulse of inquiry or a more violent hunger for an immediate solution. By that hunger mysticism profits and new religions arise to replace the old that have been destroyed or stripped of significance by a scepticism which itself could not satisfy because, although its business was inquiry, it was unwilling sufficiently to inquire. The attempt to deny or stifle a truth because it is yet obscure in its outward workings and too often represented by obscurantist superstition or a crude faith, is itself a kind of

obscurantism. The will to escape from a cosmic necessity because
it is arduous, difficult to justify by immediate tangible results,
slow in regulating its operations, must turn out eventually to
have been no acceptance of the truth of Nature but a revolt
against the secret, mightier will of the great Mother. It is better
and more rational to accept what she will not allow us as a race
to reject and lift it from the sphere of blind instinct, obscure
intuition and random aspiration into the light of reason and an
instructed and consciously self-guiding will. And if there is any
higher light of illumined intuition or self-revealing truth which is
now in man either obstructed and inoperative or works with
intermittent glancings as if from behind a veil or with occasional
displays as of the northern lights in our material skies, then there
also we need not fear to aspire. For it is likely that such is the
next higher state of consciousness of which Mind is only a form
and veil, and through the splendours of that light may lie the
path of our progressive self-enlargement into whatever highest
state is humanity's ultimate resting-place.

*

There is therefore no reason to put a limit to evolutionary
possibility by taking our present organisation or status of existence as final. The animal is a laboratory in which Nature has
worked out man; man may very well be a laboratory in which
she wills to work out superman, to disclose the soul as a divine
being, to evolve a divine nature.

(XXVII, p. 380)

Man in the Universe*

The Soul of man, a traveller, wanders in this cycle of Brahman, huge, a totality of lives, a totality of states, thinking itself different from the Impeller of the journey. Accepted by Him, it attains its goal of Immortality.

Swetaswatara Upanishad.[1]

THE progressive revelation of a great, a transcendent, a luminous Reality with the multitudinous relativities of this world that we see and those other worlds that we do not see as means and material, condition and field, this would seem then to be the meaning of the universe, — since meaning and aim it has and is neither a purposeless illusion nor a fortuitous accident. For the same reasoning which leads us to conclude that world-existence is not a deceptive trick of Mind, justifies equally the certainty that it is no blindly and helplessly self-existent mass of separate phenomenal existences clinging together and struggling together as best they can in their orbit through eternity, no tremendous self-creation and self-impulsion of an ignorant Force without any secret Intelligence within aware of its starting-point and its goal and guiding its process and its motion. An existence, wholly self-aware and therefore entirely master of itself, possesses the phenomenal being in which it is involved, realises itself in form, unfolds itself in the individual.

That luminous Emergence is the dawn which the Aryan forefathers worshipped. Its fulfilled perfection is that highest step of the world-pervading Vishnu which they beheld as if an eye of vision extended in the purest heavens of the Mind. For it exists already as an all-revealing and all-guiding Truth of things which watches over the world and attracts mortal man, first without the knowledge of his conscious mind, by the general march of Nature, but at last consciously by a progressive awakening and self-enlargement, to his divine ascension. The ascent to the divine Life is the human journey, the Work of works, the acceptable Sacrifice. This alone is man's real business in the world and the

[1] I. 6.

* *The Life Divine*, pp. 42–50.

55

justification of his existence, without which he would be only an insect crawling among other ephemeral insects on a speck of surface mud and water which has managed to form itself amid the appalling immensities of the physical universe.

This Truth of things that has to emerge out of the phenomenal world's contradictions is declared to be an infinite Bliss and self-conscious Existence, the same everywhere, in all things, in all times and beyond Time, and aware of itself behind all these phenomena by whose intensest vibrations of activity or by whose largest totality it can never be entirely expressed or in any way limited; for it is self-existent and does not depend for its being upon its manifestations. They represent it, but do not exhaust it; point to it, but do not reveal it. It is revealed only to itself within their forms. The conscious existence involved in the form comes, as it evolves, to know itself by intuition, by self-vision, by self-experience. It becomes itself in the world by knowing itself; it knows itself by becoming itself. Thus possessed of itself inwardly, it imparts also to its forms and modes the conscious delight of Sachchidananda. This becoming of the infinite Bliss-Existence-Consciousness in mind and life and body, — for independent of them it exists eternally, — is the transfiguration intended and the utility of individual existence. Through the individual it manifests in relation even as of itself it exists in identity.

The Unknowable knowing itself as Sachchidananda is the one supreme affirmation of Vedanta; it contains all the others or on it they depend. This is the one veritable experience that remains when all appearances have been accounted for negatively by the elimination of their shapes and coverings or positively by the reduction of their names and forms to the constant truth that they contain. For fulfilment of life or for transcendence of life, and whether purity, calm and freedom in the spirit be our aim or puissance, joy and perfection, Sachchidananda is the unknown, omnipresent, indispensable term for which the human consciousness, whether in knowledge and sentiment or in sensation and action, is eternally seeking.

The universe and the individual are the two essential appearances into which the Unknowable descends and through which it has to be approached; for other intermediate collectivities are born only of their interaction. This descent of the supreme Reality is in its nature a self-concealing; and in the descent there are successive levels, in the concealing successive veils. Necessarily, the revelation takes the form of an ascent; and necessarily also the ascent and the revelation are both progressive. For each successive level in the descent of the Divine is to man a stage in an ascension; each veil that hides the unknown God becomes for the God-lover and God-seeker an instrument of His unveiling. Out of the rhythmic slumber of material Nature unconscious of the Soul and the Idea that maintain the ordered activities of her energy even in her dumb and mighty material trance, the world struggles into the more quick, varied and disordered rhythm of Life labouring on the verges of self-consciousness. Out of Life it struggles upward into Mind in which the unit becomes awake to itself and its world, and in that awakening the universe gains the leverage it required for its supreme work, it gains self-conscious individuality. But Mind takes up the work to continue, not to complete it. It is a labourer of acute but limited intelligence who takes the confused materials offered by Life and, having improved, adapted, varied, classified according to its power, hands them over to the supreme Artist of our divine manhood. That Artist dwells in Supermind; for Supermind is Superman. Therefore our world has yet to climb beyond Mind to a higher principle, a higher status, a higher dynamism in which universe and individual become aware of and possess that which they both are and therefore stand explained to each other, in harmony with each other, unified.

The disorders of life and mind cease by discerning the secret of a more perfect order than the physical. Matter below life and mind contains in itself the balance between a perfect poise of tranquillity and the action of an immeasurable energy, but does not possess that which it contains. Its peace wears the dull mask of an obscure inertia, a sleep of unconsciousness or rather of a drugged and imprisoned consciousness. Driven by a force which is its real self but whose sense it cannot yet seize nor share, it has not the awakened joy of its own harmonious energies.

Life and mind awaken to the sense of this want in the form

of a striving and seeking ignorance and a troubled and baffled
desire which are the first steps towards self-knowledge and self-
fulfilment. But where then is the kingdom of their self-fulfilling?
It comes to them by the exceeding of themselves. Beyond life
and mind we recover consciously in its divine truth that which
the balance of material Nature grossly represented, — a tranquillity which is neither inertia nor a sealed trance of consciousness but the concentration of an absolute force and an absolute
self-awareness, and an action of immeasurable energy which is
at the same time an out-thrilling of ineffable bliss because its
every act is the expression, not of a want and an ignorant
straining, but of an absolute peace and self-mastery. In that
attainment our ignorance realises the light of which it was a
darkened or a partial reflection; our desires cease in the plenitude
and fulfilment towards which even in their most brute material
forms they were an obscure and fallen aspiration.

The universe and the individual are necessary to each other
in their ascent. Always indeed they exist for each other and
profit by each other. Universe is a diffusion of the divine All in
infinite Space and Time, the individual its concentration within
limits of Space and Time. Universe seeks in infinite extension
the divine totality it feels itself to be but cannot entirely realise;
for in extension existence drives at a pluralistic sum of itself
which can neither be the primal nor the final unit, but only a
recurring decimal without end or beginning. Therefore it creates
in itself a self-conscious concentration of the All through which
it can aspire. In the conscious individual Prakriti turns back to
perceive Purusha, World seeks after Self; God having entirely
become Nature, Nature seeks to become progressively God.

On the other hand, it is by means of the universe that the
individual is impelled to realise himself. Not only is it his foundation, his means, his field, the stuff of the divine Work; but also,
since the concentration of the universal Life which he is takes
place within limits and is not like the intensive unity of Brahman
free from all conception of bound and term, he must necessarily
universalise and impersonalise himself in order to manifest the
divine All which is his reality. Yet is he called upon to preserve,
even when he most extends himself in universality of conscious-

ness, a mysterious transcendent something of which his sense of personality gives him an obscure and egoistic representation. Otherwise he has missed his goal, the problem set to him has not been solved, the divine work for which he accepted birth has not been done.

The universe comes to the individual as Life, — a dynamism the entire secret of which he has to master and a mass of colliding results, a whirl of potential energies out of which he has to disengage some supreme order and some yet unrealised harmony. This is after all the real sense of man's progress. It is not merely a restatement in slightly different terms of what physical Nature has already accomplished. Nor can the ideal of human life be simply the animal repeated on a higher scale of mentality. Otherwise, any system or order which assured a tolerable well-being and a moderate mental satisfaction would have stayed our advance. The animal is satisfied with a modicum of necessity; the gods are content with their splendours. But man cannot rest permanently until he reaches some highest good. He is the greatest of living beings because he is the most discontented, because he feels most the pressure of limitations. He alone, perhaps, is capable of being seized by the divine frenzy for a remote ideal.

To the Life-Spirit, therefore, the individual in whom its potentialities centre is pre-eminently Man, the Purusha. It is the Son of Man who is supremely capable of incarnating God. This Man is the Manu, the thinker, the Manomaya Purusha, mental person or soul in mind of the ancient sages. No mere superior mammal is he, but a conceptive soul basing itself on the animal body in Matter. He is conscious Name or Numen accepting and utilising form as a medium through which Person can deal with substance. The animal life emerging out of Matter is only the inferior term of his existence. The life of thought, feeling, will, conscious impulsion, that which we name in its totality Mind, that which strives to seize upon Matter and its vital energies and subject them to the law of its own progressive transformation, is the middle term in which he takes his effectual station. But there is equally a supreme term which Mind in man searches after so that having found he may affirm it in his mental and bodily existence. This practical affirmation of something essentially superior to his present self is the basis of the divine life in the human being.

Awakened to a profounder self-knowledge than his first mental idea of himself, Man begins to conceive some formula and to perceive some appearance of the thing that he has to affirm. But it appears to him as if poised between two negations of itself. If, beyond his present attainment, he perceives or is touched by the power, light, bliss of a self-conscious infinite existence and translates his thought or his experience of it into terms convenient for his mentality, — Infinity, Omniscience, Omnipotence, Immortality, Freedom, Love, Beatitude, God, — yet does this sun of his seeing appear to shine between a double Night, — a darkness below, a mightier darkness beyond. For when he strives to know it utterly, it seems to pass into something which neither any one of these terms nor the sum of them can at all represent. His mind at last negates God for a Beyond, or at least it seems to find God transcending Himself, denying Himself to the conception. Here also, in the world, in himself, and around himself, he is met always by the opposites of his affirmation. Death is ever with him, limitation invests his being and his experience, error, inconscience, weakness, inertia, grief, pain, evil are constant oppressors of his effort. Here also he is driven to deny God, or at least the Divine seems to negate or to hide itself in some appearance or outcome which is other than its true and eternal reality.

And the terms of this denial are not, like that other and remoter negation, inconceivable and therefore naturally mysterious, unknowable to his mind, but appear to be knowable, known, definite, — and still mysterious. He knows not what they are, why they exist, how they came into being. He sees their processes as they affect and appear to him; he cannot fathom their essential reality.

Perhaps they are unfathomable, perhaps they also are really unknowable in their essence? Or, it may be, they have no essential reality, — are an illusion, Asat, non-being. The superior Negation appears to us sometimes as a Nihil, a Non-Existence; this inferior negation may also be, in its essence, a Nihil, a non-existence. But as we have already put away from us this evasion of the difficulty with regard to that higher, so also we discard it for this inferior Asat. To deny entirely its reality or to seek an escape from it as a mere disastrous illusion is to put away from us the problem and to shun our work. For Life, these things that seem to deny God, to be the opposites of Sachchidananda, are real, even if they turn out to be temporary. They and their opposites, good, knowledge, joy, pleasure, life, survival, strength, power, increase, are the very material of her workings.

It is probable indeed that they are the result or rather the inseparable accompaniments, not of an illusion, but of a wrong relation, wrong because it is founded on a false view of what the individual is in the universe and therefore a false attitude both towards God and Nature, towards self and environment. Because that which he has become is out of harmony both with what the world of his habitation is and what he himself should be and is to be, therefore man is subject to these contradictions of the secret Truth of things. In that case they are not the punishment of a fall, but the conditions of a progress. They are the first elements of the work he has to fulfil, the price he has to pay for the crown which he hopes to win, the narrow way by which Nature escapes out of Matter into consciousness; they are at once her ransom and her stock.

For out of these false relations and by their aid the true have to be found. By the Ignorance we have to cross over death. So too the Veda speaks cryptically of energies that are like women evil in impulse, wandering from the path, doing hurt to their Lord, which yet, though themselves false and unhappy, build up in the end "this vast Truth", the Truth that is the Bliss. It would be, then, not when he has excised the evil in Nature out of himself by an act of moral surgery or parted with life by an abhorrent recoil, but when he has turned Death into a more perfect life, lifted the small things of the human limitation into the great things of the divine vastness, transformed suffering into beatitude, converted evil into its proper good, translated error and falsehood into their secret truth that the sacrifice will be accomplished, the journey done and Heaven and Earth equalised join hands in the bliss of the Supreme.

Yet how can such contraries pass into each other? By what alchemy shall this lead of mortality be turned into that gold of divine Being? But if they are not in their essence contraries? If they are manifestations of one Reality, identical in substance? Then indeed a divine transmutation becomes conceivable.

We have seen that the Non-Being beyond may well be an inconceivable existence and perhaps an ineffable Bliss. At least the Nirvana of Buddhism which formulated one most luminous effort of man to reach and to rest in this highest Non-Existence, represents itself in the psychology of the liberated yet upon earth as an unspeakable peace and gladness; its practical effect is the extinction of all suffering through the disappearance of all egoistic idea or sensation and the nearest we can get to a positive conception of it is that it is some inexpressible Beatitude (if the name or any name can be applied to a peace so void of contents) into which even the notion of self-existence seems to be swallowed up and disappear. It is a Sachchidananda to which we dare no longer apply even the supreme terms of Sat, of Chit and of Ananda. For all terms are annulled and all cognitive experience is overpassed.

On the other hand, we have hazarded the suggestion that since all is one Reality, this inferior negation also, this other contradiction or non-existence of Sachchidananda is none other than Sachchidananda itself. It is capable of being conceived by the intellect, perceived in the vision, even received through the sensations as verily that which it seems to deny, and such would it always be to our conscious experience if things were not falsified by some great fundamental error, some possessing and compelling Ignorance, Maya or Avidya. In this sense a solution might be sought, not perhaps a satisfying metaphysical solution for the logical mind, — for we are standing on the border-line of the unknowable, the ineffable and straining our eyes beyond, — but a sufficient basis in experience for the practice of the divine life.

To do this we must dare to go below the clear surfaces of things on which the mind loves to dwell, to tempt the vast and obscure, to penetrate the unfathomable depths of consciousness and identify ourselves with states of being that are not our own.

Human language is a poor help in such a search, but at least we may find in it some symbols and figures, return with some just expressible hints which will help the light of the soul and throw upon the mind some reflection of the ineffable design.

★

The ordinary man lives in his own personal consciousness knowing things through his mind and senses as they are touched by a world which is outside him, outside his consciousness. When the consciousness subtilises, it begins to come into contact with things in a much more direct way, not only with their forms and outer impacts but with what is inside them, but still the range may be small. But the consciousness can also widen and begin to be first in direct contact with a universe of range of things in the world, then to contain them as it were, — as it is said to see the world in oneself, — and to be in a way identified with it. To see all things in the self and the self in all things — to be aware of one being everywhere, aware directly of the different planes, their forces, their beings — that is universalisation.

(XXII, p. 317)

Man A Transitional Being*

MAN is a transitional being; he is not final. For in man and high beyond him ascend the radiant degrees that climb to a divine supermanhood. There lies our destiny and the liberating key to our aspiring but troubled and limited mundane existence.

We mean by man mind imprisoned in a living body. But mind is not the highest possible power of consciousness; for mind is not in possession of Truth, but only its ignorant seeker. Beyond mind is a supramental or gnostic power of consciousness that is in eternal possession of Truth. This supermind is at its source the dynamic consciousness, in its nature at once and inseparably infinite wisdom and infinite will of the divine Knower and Creator. Supermind is superman; a gnostic supermanhood is the next distinct and triumphant evolutionary step to be reached by earthly nature.

The step from man to superman is the next approaching achievement in the earth's evolution. It is inevitable because it is at once the intention of the inner Spirit and the logic of Nature's process.

The appearance of a human possibility in a material and animal world was the first glint of some coming divine Light, the first far-off promise of a godhead to be born out of Matter. The appearance of the superman in the human world will be the fulfilment of this divine promise. Out of the material consciousness in which our mind works as a chained slave is emerging the disk of a secret sun of Power and Joy and Knowledge. The supermind will be the formed body of that radiant effulgence.

Supermanhood is not man climbed to his own natural zenith, not a superior degree of human greatness, knowledge, power, intelligence, will, character, genius, dynamic force, saintliness, love, purity or perfection. Supermind is something beyond

* *The Hour of God*, pp. 7–12.

mental man and his limits; it is a greater consciousness than the highest consciousness proper to human nature.

Man is a mental being whose mentality works here involved, obscure and degraded in a physical brain. Even in the highest of his kind it is baulked of its luminous possibilities of supreme force and freedom by this dependence, shut off even from its own divine powers, impotent to change our life beyond certain narrow and precarious limits; it is an imprisoned and checked force, most often nothing but a servitor or caterer of interests or a purveyor of amusement to the life and the body. But divine superman will be a gnostic spirit. Supermind in him will lay hands on the mental and physical instruments and, standing above and yet penetrating our lower already manifested parts, it will transform mind, life and body.

Mind is the highest force in man. But mind in man is an ignorant, clouded and struggling power. And even when most luminous it is possessed only of a thin, reflected and pallid light. A supermind free, master, expressive of divine glories will be the superman's central instrument. Its untrammelled movement of self-existent knowledge, spontaneous power and untainted delight will impress the harmony of the life of the gods on the earthly existence.

Man in himself is little more than an ambitious nothing. He is a littleness that reaches to a wideness and a grandeur that are beyond him, a dwarf enamoured of the heights. His mind is a dark ray in the splendours of the universal Mind. His life is a striving, exulting, suffering, an eager passion-tossed and sorrow-stricken or a blindly and dumbly longing petty moment of the universal Life. His body is a labouring perishable speck in the material universe. This cannot be the end of the mysterious upward surge of Nature. There is something beyond, something that mankind shall be; it is seen now only in broken glimpses through rifts in the great wall of limitations that deny its possibility and existence. An immortal soul is somewhere within him and gives out some sparks of its presence; above an eternal spirit overshadows him and upholds the soul-continuity of his nature. But this greater spirit is obstructed from descent by the hard lid of his constructed personality; and that inner luminous soul is wrapped, stifled, oppressed in dense outer coatings. In all but a few the soul is seldom active, in most hardly perceptible. The soul and spirit in man seem rather to exist above and behind his nature than to be a part of his external and visible reality. They are in course of birth rather than born in Matter; they are for human consciousness possibilities rather than things realised and present.

Man's greatness is not in what he is, but in what he makes possible. His glory is that he is the closed place and secret workshop of a living labour in which supermanhood is being made ready by a divine Craftsman. But he is admitted too to a yet greater greatness and it is this that, allowed to be unlike the lower creation, he is partly an artisan of this divine change; his conscious assent, his consecrated will and participation are needed that into his body may descend the glory that will replace him. His aspiration is earth's call to the supramental creator.

If earth calls and the Supreme answers, the hour can be even now for that immense and glorious transformation.

But what shall be the gain to be won for the Earth-consciousness we embody by this unprecedented ascent from mind to supermind and what the ransom of the supramental change? To what end should man leave his safe human limits for this hazardous adventure?

First consider what was gained when Nature passed from the brute inconscience and inertia of what seems inanimate Matter to the vibrant awakening of sensibility of plant range. Life was gained; the gain was the first beginnings of a mite groping and involved, reaching a consciousness that stretches out dumbly for growth, towards sense vibration, to a preparation for vital yearnings, a living joy and beauty. The plant achieved a first form of life but could not possess it, because this first organised life-consciousness had feeling and seeking but blind, dumb, deaf, chained to the soil and was involved in its own nerve and tissue; it could not get out of them, could not get behind its nerve self as does the vital mind of the animal; still less could it turn down from above upon it to know and realise and control its own motions as does the observing and thinking mind in man. This was an imprisoned gain, for there was still a gross oppression of the first Inconscience which had covered up with the brute phenomenon of Matter and of Energy of Matter all signs of the Spirit. Nature could in no wise stop here, because she held much in her that was still occult, potential, unexpressed, unorganised, latent; the evolution had perforce to go farther. The animal had to replace the plant at the head and top of Nature.

And what then was gained when Nature passed from the obscurity of the plant kingdom to the awakened sense, desire and emotion and the free mobility of animal life? The gain was liberated sense and feeling and desire and courage and cunning and the contrivance of the objects of desire, passion and action and hunger and battle and conquest and the sex-call and play and pleasure, and all the joy and pain of the conscious living creature. Not only the life of the body which the animal has in common with the plant but a life-mind that appeared for the first time in the earth-story and grew from form to more organised form till it reached in the best the limit of its own formula.

The animal achieved a first form of mind, but could not possess it, because this first organised mind-consciousness was enslaved to a narrow scope, tied to the full functioning of the physical body and brain and nerve, tied to serve the physical life and its desires and needs and passions, limited to the insistent uses of the vital urge, to material longing and feeling and action, bound in its own inferior instrumentation, its spontaneous combinings of association and memory and instinct. It could not get away from them, could not get behind them as man's intelligence gets behind them to observe them; still less could it turn down on them from above as do human reason and will to control, enlarge, re-order, exceed, sublimate.

At each capital step of Nature's ascent there is a reversal of consciousness in the evolving spirit. As when a climber turns on a summit to which he has laboured and looks down with an exalted and wider power of vision on all that was once above or on a level with him but is now below his feet, the evolutionary being not only transcends his past self, his former now exceeded status, but commands from a higher grade of self-experience and vision, with a new apprehending feeling or a new comprehending sight and effectuating power in a greater system of values, all that was once his own consciousness but is now below him and belongs to an inferior creation. This reversal is the sign of a decisive victory and the seal of a radical progress in Nature.

The new consciousness attained in the spiritual evolution is always higher in grade and power, always larger, more comprehensive, wider in sight and feeling, richer and finer in faculties, more complex, organic, dominating than the consciousness that was once our own but is now left behind us. There are greater breadth and space, heights before impassable, unexpected depths and intimacies. There is a luminous expansion that is the very sign-manual of the Supreme upon his work.

Mark that each of the great radical steps forward already taken by Nature has been infinitely greater in its change, incalculably vaster in its consequences than its puny predecessor. There is a miraculous opening to an always richer and wider expression, there is a new illuminating of the creation and a dynamic heightening of its significances. There is in this world we live in no equality of all on a flat level, but a hierarchy of ever-increasing precipitous superiorities pushing their mountain shoulders upwards towards the Supreme.

Because man is a mental being, he naturally imagines that mind is the one great leader and actor and creator or the indispensable agent in the universe. But this is an error; even for knowledge mind is not the only or the greatest possible instrument, the one aspirant and discoverer. Mind is a clumsy interlude between Nature's vast and precise subconscient action and the vaster infallible superconscient action of the Godhead.

There is nothing mind can do that cannot be better done in the mind's immobility and thought-free stillness.

When mind is still, then Truth gets her chance to be heard in the purity of the silence.

Truth cannot be attained by the Mind's thought but only by identity and silent vision. Truth lives in the calm wordless Light of the eternal spaces; she does not intervene in the noise and cackle of logical debate.

Thought in the mind can at most be Truth's brilliant and transparent garment; it is not even her body. Look through the robe, not at it and you may see some hint of her form. There can be a thought-body of Truth, but that is the spontaneous supramental Thought and Word that leap fully formed out of the Light, not any difficult mental counterfeit and patchwork. The Supramental Thought is not a means of arriving at Truth, but a way of expressing her; for Truth in the Supermind is self-found or self-existent. It is an arrow from the Light, not a bridge to reach it.

Cease inwardly from thought and word, be motionless within you, look upward into the light and outward into the vast cosmic consciousness that is around you. Be more and more one with the brightness and the vastness. Then will Truth dawn on you from above and flow in you from all around you.

But only if the mind is no less intense in its purity than its silence. For in an impure mind the silence will soon fill with misleading lights and false voices, the echo or sublimation of its own vain conceits and opinions or the response to its secret pride, vanity, ambition, lust, greed or desire. The Titans and the Demons will speak to it more readily than the divine Voices.

Silence is indispensable, but also there is needed wideness. If the mind is not silent, it cannot receive the lights and voices of the supernal Truth or receiving mixes with them its own flickering tongues and blind pretentious babble. Active, arrogant, noisy it distorts and disfigures what it receives. If it is not wide, it cannot house the effective power and creative force of the Truth. Some light may play there but it becomes narrow, confined and sterile: the Force that is descending is cabined and thwarted and withdraws again to its vast heights from this rebellious foreign plane. Or even if something comes down and remains it is a pearl in the mire; for no change takes place in the nature or else there is formed only a thin intensity that points narrowly upward to the summits, but can hold little and diffuse less upon the world around it.

STAGES OF EVOLUTION

Involution and Evolution*

THE Western idea of evolution is the state-
ment of a process of formation, not an explanation of our being.
Limited to the physical and biological data of Nature, it does not
attempt except in a summary or a superficial fashion to discover
its own meaning, but is content to announce itself as the general
law of a quite mysterious and inexplicable energy. Evolution
becomes a problem in motion which is satisfied to work up with
an automatic regularity its own puzzle, but not to work it out,
because, since it is only a process, it has no understanding of itself, and, since it is a blind perpetual automatism of mechanical
energy, it has neither an origin nor an issue. It began perhaps or
is always beginning; it will stop perhaps in time or is always
somewhere stopping and going back to its beginnings, but there is
no why, only a great turmoil and fuss of a how to its beginning
and its cessation; for there is in its acts no fountain of spiritual
intention, but only the force of an unresting material necessity.
The ancient idea of evolution was the fruit of a philosophical
intuition, the modern is an effort of scientific observation. Each
as enounced misses something, but the ancient got at the spirit of
the movement where the modern is content with a form and the
most external machinery. The Sankhya thinker gave us the psychological elements of the total evolutionary process, analysed
mind and sense and the subtle basis of matter and divined some
of the secrets of the executive energy, but had no eye for the detail
of the physical labour of Nature. He saw in it too not only the
covering active evident Force, but the concealed sustaining spiritual entity, though by an excess of the analytic intellect, obsessed
with its love of trenchant scissions and symmetrical oppositions,
he set between meeting Soul and Force an original and eternal
gulf or line of separation. The modern scientist strives to make a
complete scheme and institution of the physical method which he
has detected in its minute workings, but is blind to the miracle
each step involves or content to lose the sense of it in the satisfied

* *The Supramental Manifestation*, pp. 232–44.

70

observation of a vast ordered phenomenon. But always the marvel of the thing remains, one with the inexplicable wonder of all existence, — even as it is said in the ancient Scripture,

> *āścaryavat paśyati kaścid enam*
> *āścaryavad vadati tathaiva cānyaḥ.*
> *āścaryavaccainam anyaḥ śṛṇoti*
> *śrutvāpyenam veda na caiva kaścit.*

"One looks on it and sees a miracle, another speaks of it as a miracle, as a miracle another hears of it, but what it is, for all the hearing, none knoweth."

We know that an evolution there is, but not what evolution is; that remains still one of the initial mysteries of Nature.

For evolution, as is the habit with the human reason's accounts and solutions of the deep and unfathomable way of the Spirit in things, raises more questions than it solves; it does not do away with the problem of creation for all its appearance of solid orderly fact, any more than the religious affirmation of an external omnipotent Creator could do it or the Illusionist's mystic Maya, *aghaṭana-ghaṭana-paṭiyasī*, very skilful in bringing about the impossible, some strange existent non-existent Power with an idea in That which is beyond and without ideas, self-empowered to create an existent non-existent world, existent because it very evidently is, non-existent because it is a patched up consistency of dreamful unreal transiences. The problem is only prolonged, put farther back, given a subtle and orderly, but all the more challengingly complex appearance. But, even when our questioning is confined to the one issue of evolution alone, the difficulty still arises of the essential significance of the bare outward facts observed, what is meant by evolution, what is it that evolves, from what and by what force of necessity? The scientist is content to affirm an original matter or substance, atomic, electric, etheric or whatever it may finally turn out to be, which by the very nature of its own inherent energy or of an energy acting in it and on it, — the two things are not the same, and the distinction, though it may seem immaterial in the beginning of the process, is of a considerable ultimate consequence, — produces owing to some unexplained law, constant system of results or other unalterable principle a number of different basic forms and powers of matter or different sensible and effective movements of energy: these come into being, it seems, when the minute original particles of matter meet together in variously disposed quantities, measures and combinations, and all the rest is a varying, developing, mounting movement of organised energy and its evolutionary consequences, *pariṇāma*, which depend on this crude constituting basis. All that is or may be a correct statement of phenomenal fact, — but we must not forget that the fundamental theory of science has been going of late through a considerable commotion of an upsetting and a rapid rearrangement, — but it carries us no step farther towards the principal, the all-important thing that we want to know. The way in which man sees and experiences the universe, imposes on his reason the necessity of a one original eternal substance of which all things are the forms and a one eternal original energy of which all movement of action and consequence is the variation. But the whole question is, what is the reality of this substance and what is the essential nature of this energy?

Then, even if we suppose the least explicable part of the action to be an evolutionary development of the immaterial from Matter, still is that development a creation or a liberation, a birth of what did not exist before or a slow bringing out of what already existed in suppressed fact or in eternal potentiality? And the interest of the question becomes acute, its importance incalculable when we come to the still unexplained phenomenon of life and mind. Is life a creation out of inanimate substance or the appearance of a new, a suddenly or slowly resultant power out of the brute material energy, and is conscious mind a creation out of inconscient or subconscious life, or do these powers and godheads appear because they were always there though in a shrouded and by us unrecognizable condition of their hidden or suppressed idea and activity, Nomen and Numen? And what of the soul and of man? Is soul a new result or creation of our mentalised life, — even so many regard it, because it clearly appears as a self-conscient, bright, distinguishable power only when thinking life has reached some high pitch of its intensity, — or is it not a permanent entity, the original mystery that now unveils its hidden form, the eternal companion of the energy we call Nature, her secret inhabitant or her very spirit and reality? And is man a biological creation of a brute energy which has somehow unexpectedly and quite inexplicably managed to begin to feel and think, or is he in his real self that inner Being and Power which is the whole sense of the evolution and the master of Nature? Is Nature only the force of self-expression, self-formation, self-creation of a secret spirit, and man however hedged in his present capacity, the first being in Nature in whom that power begins to be consciently self-creative in the front of the action, in this outer chamber of physical being, there set to work and bring out by an increasingly self-conscious evolution what he can of all its human significance or its divine possibility? That is the clear conclusion we must arrive at in the end, if we once admit as the key of the whole movement, the reality of this whole mounting creation a spiritual evolution.

The word evolution carries with it in its intrinsic sense, in the idea at its root the necessity of a previous involution. We must, if a hidden spiritual being is the secret of all the action of Nature, give its full power to that latent value of the idea. We are bound then to suppose that all that evolves already existed involved, passive or otherwise active, but in either case concealed from us in the shell of material Nature. The Spirit which manifests itself here in a body, must be involved from the beginning in the whole of matter and in every knot, formation and particle of matter; life, mind and whatever is above mind must be latent, inactive or concealed active powers in all the operations of material energy. The only alternative would be to drive in between the two sides of our being the acute Sankhya scission; but that divides too much Spirit and Nature. Nature would be an inert and mechanical thing, but she would set to her work activised by some pressure on her of the Spirit. Spirit would be Being conscious and free in its own essence from the natural activity, but would phenomenally modify or appear to modify its consciousness in response to some reaction of Nature. One would reflect the movements of the active Power, the other would enlighten her activities with the consciousness of the self-aware immortal being. In that case the scientific evolutionary view of Nature as a vast mechanical energy, life, mind and natural soul action its scale of developing operations would have a justification. Our consciousness would only be a luminous translation of the self-driven unresting mechanical activity into responsive notes of experience of the consenting spiritual witness. But the disabling difficulty in this notion is the quite opposite character of our own highest seeing; for in the end and as the energy of the universal force mounts up the gradients of its own possibilities, Nature becomes always more evidently a power of the Spirit and all her mechanism only figures of its devising mastery. The power of the Flame cannot be divided from the Flame; where the Flame is, there is the power, and where the power is there is the fiery Principle. We have to come back to the idea of a Spirit present in the universe and, if the process of its works of power and its appearance is in the steps of an evolution, there imposes itself the necessity of a previous involution.

This Spirit in things is not apparent from the beginning, but self-betrayed in an increasing light of manifestation. We see the compressed powers of Nature start released from their original involution, disclose in a passion of work the secrets of their infinite capacity, press upon themselves and on the supporting inferior principle to subject its lower movement on which they are forced to depend into a higher working proper to their own type and feel their proper greatness in the greatness of their self-revealing effectuations. Life takes hold of matter and breathes into it the numberless figures of its abundant creative force, its subtle and variable patterns, its enthusiasm of birth and death and growth and act and response, its will of more and more complex organisation of experience, its quivering search and feeling out after a self-consciousness of its own pleasure and pain and understanding gust of action; mind seizes on life to make it an instrument for the wonders of will and intelligence; soul possesses and lifts mind through the attraction of beauty and good and wisdom and greatness towards the joy of some half-seen ideal highest existence; and in all this miraculous movement and these climbing greatnesses each step sets its foot on a higher rung and opens to a clearer, larger and fuller scope and view of the always secret and always self-manifesting spirit in things. The eye fixed on the physical evolution has only the sight of a mechanical grandeur and subtlety of creation; the evolution of life opening to mind, the evolution of mind opening to the soul of its own light and action, the evolution of soul out of the limited powers of mind to a resplendent blaze of the infinites of spiritual being are the more significant things, give us greater and subtler reaches of the self-disclosing Secrecy. The physical evolution is only an outward sign, the more and more complex and subtle development of a supporting structure, the growing exterior metre mould of form which is devised to sustain in matter the rising intonations of the spiritual harmony. The spiritual significance finds us as the notes rise; but not till we get to the summit of the scale can we command the integral meaning of that for which all these first formal measures were made the outward lines, the sketch or the crude notation. Life itself is only a coloured vehicle, physical birth a convenience for the greater and greater births of the Spirit.

The spiritual process of evolution is then in some sense a creation, but a self-creation, not a making of what never was, but a bringing out of what was implicit in the Being. The Sanskrit word for creation signifies a loosing forth, a letting out into the workings of Nature. The Upanishad in a telling figure applies the image of the spider which brings its web out of itself and creates the structure in which it takes its station. That is applied in the ancient Scripture not to the evolution of things out of Matter, but to an original bringing of temporal becoming out of the eternal infinity; Matter itself and this material universe are only such a web or indeed no more than a part of it brought out from the spiritual being of the Infinite. But the same truth, the same law holds good of all that we see of the emergence of things from involution in the material energy. We might almost speak here of a double evolution. A Force inherent in the Infinite brings out of it eternally the structure of its action in a universe of which the last descending scale is based upon an involution of all the powers of the Spirit into an inconscient absorption in her self-oblivious passion of form and structural working. Thence comes an ascent and progressive liberation of power after power till the Spirit self-disclosed and set free by knowledge and mastery of its works repossesses the eternal fullness of its being which envelopes then and carries in its grasp the manifold and unified splendours of its nature. At any rate, the spiritual process of which our human birth is a step and our life is a portion, appears as the bringing out of a greatness, *asya mahimānam*, which is secret, inherent and self-imprisoned, absorbed in the form and working of things. Our world-action figures an evolution, an outrolling of a manifold Power gathered and coiled up in the crude intricacy of Matter. The upward progress of the successive births of things is a rise into waking and larger and larger light of a consciousness shut into the first hermetic cell of sleep of the eternal Energy.

There is a parallel in the Yogic experience of the Kundalini, eternal Force coiled up in the body in the bottom root vessel or chamber, *mulādhāra*, pedestal, earth-centre of the physical nervous system. There she slumbers coiled up like a python and filled full of all that she holds gathered in her being, but when she is struck by the freely coursing breath, by the current of Life which enters into search for her, she awakes and rises flaming up the ladder of the spinal cord and forces open centre after centre of the involved dynamic secrets of consciousness till at the summit she finds, joins and becomes one with the Spirit. Thus she passes from an involution in inconscience through a series of opening glories of her powers into the greatest eternal superconscience of the Spirit. This mysterious evolving Nature in the world around us follows even such a course. Inconscient being is not so much a matrix as a chamber of materialised energy in which are gathered up all the powers of the Spirit; they are there, but work in the conditions of the material energy, involved, we say, and therefore not apparent as themselves because they have passed into a form of working subnormal to their own right scale where the characteristics by which we recognise and think we know them are suppressed into a minor and an undetected force of working. As Nature rises in the scale, she liberates them into their recognisable scales of energy, discloses the operations by which they can feel themselves and their greatness. At the

highest summit she rises into the self-knowledge of the Spirit
which informed her action, but because of its involution or concealment in the forms of its workings could not be known in the
greatness of its reality. Spirit and Nature discovering the secret
of her energies become one at the top of the spiritual evolution
by a soul in Nature which awakens to the significance of its own
being in the liberation of the highest truths it comes to know
that its births were the births, the assumptions of form of an
eternal Spirit, to know itself as that and not a creature of Nature
and rises to the possession of the revealed, full and highest power
of its own real and spiritual nature. That liberation, because liberation is self-possession, comes to us as the crown of a spiritual
evolution.

We must consider all the packed significance of this involution. The Spirit involved in material energy is there with all its
powers; life, mind and a greater supramental power are involved
in Matter. But what do we mean when we say that they are involved, and do we mean that all these things are quite different
energies cut off from each other by an essential separateness,
but rolled up together in an interaction, or do we mean that
there is only one Being with its one energy, varying shades of the
light of its power differentiated in the spectrum of Nature?
When we say that Life is involved in Matter or in material Force,
for of that Force Matter seems after all to be only a various self-
spun formation, do we not mean that all this universal working,
even in what seems to us its inconscient inanimate action, is a
life-power of the Spirit busy with formation, and we do not
recognise it because it is there in a lower scale in which the characteristics by which we recognise life are not evident or are only
slightly evolved in the dullness of the material covering? Material energy would be then Life packed into the density of Matter
and feeling out in it for its own intenser recognisable power
which it finds within itself in the material concealment and liberates into action. Life itself would be an energy of a secret mind,
a mind imprisoned in its own forms and quivering out in the nervous seekings of life for its intenser recognisable power of consciousness which it discovers within the vital and material sup-
pression and liberates into sensibility. No doubt, practically,

these powers work upon each other as different energies, but in essence they would be one energy and their interaction the power of the Spirit working by its higher on its lower forces, depending on them at first, but yet turning in the scale of its ascent to overtop and master them. Mind too might only be an inferior scale and formulation derived from a much greater and supramental consciousness, and that consciousness too with its greater light and will a characteristic originating power of spiritual being, the power which secret in all things, in mind, in life, in matter, in the plant and the metal and the atom, assures constantly by its inevitable action the idea and harmony of the universe. And what is the Spirit itself but infinite existence, eternal, immortal being, but always a conscious self-aware being, — and that is the difference between the materialist's mechanical monism and the spiritual theory of the universe, — which here expresses itself in a world finite to our conceptions whose every movement yet bears witness to the Infinite? And this world is because the Spirit has the delight of its own infinite existence and the delight of its own infinite self-variation; birth is because all consciousness carries with it power of its own being and all power of being is self-creative and must have the joy of its self-creation. For creation means nothing else than a self-expression; and the birth of the soul in the body is nothing but a mode of its own self-expression. Therefore all things here are expression, form, energy, action of the Spirit; matter itself is but form of Spirit, life but power of being of the Spirit, mind but working out of consciousness of the Spirit. All Nature is a display and a play of God, power and action and self-creation of the one spiritual Being. Nature presents to Spirit at once the force, the instrument, the medium, the obstacle, the result of his powers, and all these things, obstacles as well as instrument, are the necessary elements for a gradual and developing creation.

But if the Spirit has involved its eternal greatness in the material universe and is there evolving its powers by the virtue of a secret self-knowledge, is disclosing them in a grandiose succession under the self-imposed difficulties of a material form of being, is disengaging them from a first veiling absorbed inconscience of Nature, there is no difficulty in thinking or seeing that this soul shaped into humanity is a being of that Being, that this also has risen out of material involution by increasing self-expression in a series of births of which each grade is a new ridge of the ascent opening to higher powers of the Spirit and that it is still arising and will not be for ever limited by the present walls of its birth but may, if we will, be born into a divine humanity. Our humanity is the conscious meeting-place of the finite and the infinite and to grow more and more towards that Infinite even in this physical birth is our privilege. This Infinite, this Spirit who is housed within us but not bound or shut in by mind or body, is our own self and to find and be our self was, as the ancient sages knew, always the object of our human striving, for it is the object of the whole immense working of Nature. But it is by degrees of the self-finding that Nature enlarges to her spiritual reality. Man himself is a doubly involved being; most of himself in mind and below is involved in a subliminal conscience or a subconscience; most of himself above mind is involved in a spiritual superconscience. When he becomes conscient in the superconscience, the heights and the depths of his being will be illumined by another light of knowledge than the flickering lamp of the reason can now cast into a few corners; for then the master of the field will enlighten this whole wonderful field of his being, as the sun illumines the whole system it has created out of its own glories. Then only he can know the reality even of his own mind and life and body. Mind will be changed into a greater consciousness, his life will be a direct power and action of the Divinity, his very body no longer this first gross lump of breathing clay, but a very image and body of spiritual being. That transfiguration on the summit of the mountain, divine birth, *divya janma*, is that to which all these births are a long series of laborious steps. An involution of spirit in matter is the beginning, but a spiritual assumption of divine birth is the fullness of the evolution.

East and West have two ways of looking at life which are opposite sides of one reality. Between the pragmatic truth on which the vital thought of modern Europe enamoured of the vigour of life, all the dance of God in Nature, puts so vehement and exclusive a stress and the eternal immutable Truth to which the Indian mind enamoured of calm and poise loves to turn with an equal passion for an exclusive finding, there is no such divorce and quarrel as is now declared by the partisan mind, the separating reason, the absorbing passion of an exclusive will of realisation. The one eternal immutable Truth is the Spirit and without the Spirit the pragmatic truth of a self-creating universe would have no origin or foundation; it would be barren of significance, empty of inner guidance, lost in its end, a firework display shooting up into the void only to fall away and perish in mid-air. But neither is the pragmatic truth a dream of the non-existent, an illusion or a long lapse into some futile delirium of creative imagination; that would be to make the eternal Spirit a drunkard or a dreamer, the fool of his own gigantic self-hallucinations. The truths of universal existence are of two kinds, truths of the Spirit which are themselves eternal and immutable, and these are the great things that cast themselves out into becoming and there constantly realise their powers and significances, and the play of the consciousness with them, the discords, the musical variations, soundings of possibility, progressive notations, reversions, perversions, mounting conversions into a greater figure of harmony; and of all these things the Spirit has made, makes always his universe. But it is himself that he makes in it, himself that is the creator and the energy of creation and the cause and the method and the result of the working, the mechanist and the machine, the music and the musician, the poet and the poem, supermind, mind and life and matter, the soul and Nature.

An original error pursues us in our solutions of our problem. We are perplexed by the appearance of an antinomy; we set soul against Nature, the spirit against his creative energy. But Soul and Nature, Purusha and Prakriti, are two eternal lovers who possess their perpetual unity and enjoy their constant difference, and in the unity abound in the passion of the multitudinous play of their difference, and in every step of the difference abound in the secret sense or the overt consciousness of unity. Nature takes the Soul into herself so that he falls asleep in a trance of union with her absorbed passion of creation and she too seems then to be asleep in the whirl of her own creative energy; and that is the involution in Matter. Above, it may be, the Soul takes

Nature into himself so that she falls asleep in a trance of oneness with the absorbed self-possession of the Spirit and he too seems to be asleep in the deep of his own self-locked immobile being. But still above and below and around and within all this beat and rhythm is the eternity of the Spirit who has thus figured himself in soul and Nature and enjoys with a perfect awareness all that he creates in himself by this involution and evolution. The soul fulfils itself in Nature when it possesses in her the consciousness of that eternity and its power and joy and transfigures the natural becoming with the fullness of the spiritual being. The constant self-creation which we call birth finds there the perfect evolution of all that it held in its own nature and reveals its own utmost significance. The complete soul possesses all its self and all Nature.

Therefore all this evolution is a growing of the Self in material Nature to the conscious possession of its own spiritual being. It begins with form — apparently a form of Force — in which a Spirit is housed and hidden; it ends in a Spirit which consciously directs its own force and creates or assumes its own forms for the free joy of its being in Nature. Nature holding her own Self and Spirit involved and suppressed within herself, an imprisoned master of existence subjected to her ways of birth and action, — yet are these ways his and this Spirit the condition of her being and the law of her workings, — commences the evolution: the Spirit holding Nature conscious in himself, complete by his completeness, liberated by his liberation, perfected in his perfection, crowns the evolution. All our births are the births of this Spirit and self which has become or put forth a soul in Nature. To be is the object of our existence, — there is no other end or object, for the consciousness and bliss of being is the whole beginning and middle and end, as it is that which is without beginning or end. But this means in the steps of the evolution to grow more and more until we grow into our own fullness of self; all birth is a progressive self-finding, a means of self-realisation. To grow in knowledge, in power, in delight, love and oneness, towards the infinite light, capacity and bliss of spiritual existence, to universalise ourselves till we are one with all being, and to exceed constantly our present limited self till it opens fully to the transcendence in which the universal lives and to base upon it all our becoming, that is the full evolution of what now lies darkly wrapped or works half-evolved in Nature.

*

Because this infinite Spirit and eternal Divinity is here concealed in the process of material Nature, the evolution of a power beyond Mind is not only possible, but inevitable. If all were result of cosmic Chance there need be no necessity of its appearance, even as there was no necessity for any embarrassing emergence of a stumbling and striving vital consciousness in the mechanical whirl of Matter. And if all were the works of a mechanical Force, then too mind need not have unexpectedly appeared as a superior mechanism labouring to deal with Nature's grosser first machine and supermind would be still more a superfluity and a luminous insolence. Or, if a limited experimenting external Creator were the inventor of this universe, there would be no reason why he should not stop short at mind, content with the ingenuity of his labour. But since the Divinity is involved here and is emerging, it is inevitable that all his powers or degrees of power should emerge one after the other till the whole glory is embodied and visible.

(XVII, p. 20)

The Sevenfold Chord of Being*

In the ignorance of my mind, I ask of these steps of the Gods that are set within. The all-knowing Gods have taken the Infant of a year and they have woven about him seven threads to make this weft.

Rig Veda.[1]

WE HAVE now, by our scrutiny of the seven great terms of existence which the ancient seers fixed on as the foundation and sevenfold mode of all cosmic existence, discerned the gradations of evolution and involution and arrived at the basis of knowledge towards which we were striving. We have laid down that the origin, the continent, the initial and the ultimate reality of all that is in the cosmos is the triune principle of transcendent and infinite Existence, Consciousness and Bliss which is the nature of divine being. Consciousness has two aspects, illuminating and effective, state and power of self-awareness and state and power of self-force, by which Being possesses itself whether in its static condition or in its dynamic movement; for in its creative action it knows by omnipotent self-consciousness all that is latent within it and produces and governs the universe of its potentialities by an omniscient self-energy. This creative action of the All-Existent has its nodus in the fourth, the intermediate principle of Supermind or Real-Idea, in which a divine Knowledge one with self-existence and self-awareness and a substantial Will which is in perfect unison with that knowledge, because it is itself in its substance and nature that self-conscious self-existence dynamic in illumined action, develop infallibly the movement and form and law of things in right accordance with their self-existent Truth and in harmony with the significances of its manifestation.

The creation depends on and moves between the biune principle of unity and multiplicity; it is a manifoldness of idea and force and form which is the expression of an original unity, and it

[1] I. 164. 5.
* *The Life Divine*, pp. 262–70.

is an eternal oneness which is the foundation and reality of the multiple worlds and makes their play possible. Supermind therefore proceeds by a double faculty of comprehensive and apprehensive knowledge; proceeding from the essential oneness to the resultant multiplicity, it comprehends all things in itself as itself the One in its manifold aspects and it apprehends separately all things in itself as objects of its will and knowledge. While to its original self-awareness all things are one being, one consciousness, one will, one self-delight and the whole movement of things a movement one and indivisible, it proceeds in its action from the unity to the multiplicity and from multiplicity to unity, creating an ordered relation between them and an appearance but not a binding reality of division, a subtle unseparating division, or rather a demarcation and determination within the indivisible. The Supermind is the divine Gnosis which creates, governs and upholds the worlds: it is the secret Wisdom which upholds both our Knowledge and our Ignorance.

We have discovered also that Mind, Life and Matter are a triple aspect of these higher principles working, so far as our universe is concerned, in subjection to the principle of Ignorance, to the superficial and apparent self-forgetfulness of the One in its play of division and multiplicity. Really, these three are only subordinate powers of the divine quaternary: Mind is a subordinate power of Supermind which takes its stand in the standpoint of division, actually forgetful here of the oneness behind though able to return to it by reillumination from the supramental; Life is similarly a subordinate power of the energy aspect of Sachchidananda, it is Force working out form and the play of conscious energy from the standpoint of division created by Mind; Matter is the form of substance of being which the existence of Sachchidananda assumes when it subjects itself to this phenomenal action of its own consciousness and force.

In addition, there is a fourth principle which comes into manifestation at the nodus of mind, life and body, that which we call the soul; but this has a double appearance, in front the desire-soul which strives for the possession and delight of things, and, behind and either largely or entirely concealed by the desire-soul, the true psychic entity which is the real repository of the experiences of the spirit. And we have concluded that this fourth human principle is a projection and an action of the third divine principle of infinite Bliss, but an action in the terms of our consciousness and under the conditions of soul-evolution in this world. As the existence of the Divine is in its nature an infinite consciousness and the self-power of that consciousness, so the nature of its infinite consciousness is pure and infinite Bliss; self-possession and self-awareness are the essence of its self-delight. The cosmos also is a play of this divine self-delight and the delight of that play is entirely possessed by the Universal; but in the individual owing to the action of ignorance and division it is held back in the subliminal and the superconscient being; on our surface it lacks and has to be sought for, found and possessed by the development of the individual consciousness towards universality and transcendence.

We may, therefore, if we will, pose eight[1] principles instead of seven, and then we perceive that our existence is a sort of refraction of the divine existence, in inverted order of ascent and descent, thus ranged, —

Existence	Matter
Consciousness-Force	Life
Bliss	Psyche
Supermind	Mind.

The Divine descends from pure existence through the play of Consciousness-Force and Bliss and the creative medium of Supermind into cosmic being; we ascend from Matter through a developing life, soul and mind and the illuminating medium of Supermind towards the divine being. The knot of the two, the higher and the lower hemisphere[2], is where mind and Supermind meet with a veil between them. The rending of the veil is the condition of the divine life in humanity; for by that rending, by the illumining descent of the higher into the nature of the lower being and the forceful ascent of the lower being into the nature of the higher, mind can recover its divine light in the all-comprehending

---

[1] The Vedic Seers speak of the seven Rays, but also of eight, nine, ten or twelve.
[2] *Parārdha* and *Aparārdha*.

Supermind, the soul realise its divine self in the all-possessing all-blissful Ananda, life repossess its divine power in the play of omnipotent Conscious-Force and Matter open to its divine liberty as a form of the divine Existence. And if there be any goal to the evolution which finds here its present crown and head in the human being, other than an aimless circling and an individual escape from the circling, if the infinite potentiality of this creature, who alone here stands between Spirit and Matter with the power to mediate between them, has any meaning other than an ultimate awakening from the delusion of life by despair and disgust of the cosmic effort and its complete rejection, then even such a luminous and puissant transfiguration and emergence of the Divine in the creature must be that high-uplifted goal and that supreme significance.

But before we can turn to the psychological and practical conditions under which such a transfiguration may be changed from an essential possibility into a dynamic potentiality, we have much to consider; for we must discern not only the essential principles of the descent of Sachchidananda into cosmic existence, which we have already done, but the large plan of its order here and the nature and action of the manifested power of Conscious-Force which reigns over the conditions under which we now exist. At present, what we have first to see is that the seven or the eight principles we have examined are essential to all cosmic creation and are there, manifested or as yet unmanifested, in ourselves, in this "Infant of a year" which we still are, — for we are far yet from being the adults of evolutionary Nature. The higher Trinity is the source and basis of all existence and play of existence, and all cosmos must be an expression and action of its essential reality. No universe can be merely a form of being which has sprung up and outlined itself in an absolute nullity and void and remains standing out against a non-existent emptiness. It must be either a figure of existence within the infinite Existence who is beyond all figure or it must be itself the All-Existence. In fact, when we unify our self with cosmic being, we see that it is really both of these things at once; that is to say, it is the All-Existent figuring Himself out in an infinite series of rhythms in His own conceptive extension of Himself as Time and

Space. Moreover we see that this cosmic action or any cosmic action is impossible without the play of an infinite Force of Existence which produces and regulates all these forms and movements; and that Force equally presupposes or is the action of an infinite Consciousness, because it is in its nature a cosmic Will determining all relations and apprehending them by its own mode of awareness, and it could not so determine and apprehend them if there were no comprehensive Consciousness behind that mode of cosmic awareness to originate as well as to hold, fix and reflect through it the relations of Being in the developing formation or becoming of itself which we call a universe.

Finally, Consciousness being thus omniscient and omnipotent, in entire luminous possession of itself, and such entire luminous possession being necessarily and in its very nature Bliss, for it cannot be anything else, a vast universal self-delight must be the cause, essence and object of cosmic existence. "If there were not," says the ancient seer, "this all-encompassing ether of Delight of existence in which we dwell, if that delight were not our ether, then none could breathe, none could live." This self-bliss may become subconscient, seemingly lost on the surface, but not only must it be there at our roots, all existence must be essentially a seeking and reaching out to discover and possess it, and in proportion as the creature in the cosmos finds himself, whether in will and power or in light and knowledge or in being and wideness or in love and joy itself, he must awaken to something of the secret ecstasy. Joy of being, delight of realisation by knowledge, rapture of possession by will and power or creative force, ecstasy of union in love and joy are the highest terms of expanding life because they are the essence of existence itself in its hidden roots as on its yet unseen heights. Wherever, then, cosmic existence manifests itself, these three must be behind and within it.

But infinite Existence, Consciousness and Bliss need not throw themselves out into apparent being at all or, doing so, it would not be cosmic being, but simply an infinity of figures without fixed order or relation, if they did not hold or develop and bring out from themselves this fourth term of Supermind, of the divine Gnosis. There must be in every cosmos a power of

Knowledge and Will which out of infinite potentiality fixes
determined relations, develops the result out of the seed, rolls
out the mighty rhythms of cosmic Law and views and governs
the worlds as their immortal and infinite Seer and Ruler[1]. This
power indeed is nothing else than Sachchidananda Himself; it
creates nothing which is not in its own self-existence, and for
that reason all cosmic and real Law is a thing not imposed from
outside, but from within, all development is self-development,
all seed and result are seed of a Truth of things and result of
that seed determined out of its potentialities. For the same
reason no Law is absolute, because only the infinite is absolute,
and everything contains within itself endless potentialities
quite beyond its determined form and course, which are only
determined through a self-limitation by Idea proceeding from
an infinite liberty within. This power of self-limitation is necessarily inherent in the boundless All-Existent. The Infinite would
not be the Infinite if it could not assume a manifold finite-
ness; the Absolute would not be the Absolute if it were denied
in knowledge and power and will and manifestation of being a
boundless capacity of self-determination. This Supermind then
is the Truth or Real-Idea, inherent in all cosmic force and existence, which is necessary, itself remaining infinite, to determine
and combine and uphold relation and order and the great lines
of the manifestation. In the language of the Vedic Rishis, as infinite Existence, Consciousness and Bliss are the three highest
and hidden Names of the Nameless, so this Supermind is the
fourth Name[2] — fourth to That in its descent, fourth to us in
our ascension.

But Mind, Life and Matter, the lower trilogy, are also indispensable to all cosmic being, not necessarily in the form or
with the action and conditions which we know upon earth or in
this material universe, but in some kind of action, however luminous, however puissant, however subtle. For Mind is essentially
that faculty of Supermind which measures and limits, which

---

[1] The Seer, the Thinker, He who becomes everywhere, the Self-existent. — *Isha Upanishad.* 8.
[2] *Turiyam svid,* "a certain Fourth", also called *turiyam dhāma,* the fourth placing or
poise of existence.

fixes a particular centre and views from that the cosmic movement and its interactions. Granted that in a particular world, plane or cosmic arrangement, mind need not be limited, or rather that the being who uses mind as a subordinate faculty need not be incapable of seeing things from other centres or standpoints or even from the real Centre of all or in the vastness of a universal self-diffusion, still if he is not capable of fixing himself normally in his own firm standpoint for certain purposes of the divine activity, if there is only the universal self-diffusion or only infinite centres without some determining or freely limiting action for each, then there is no cosmos but only a Being musing within Himself infinitely as a creator or poet may muse freely, not plastically, before he proceeds to the determining work of creation. Such a state must exist somewhere in the infinite scale of existence, but it is not what we understand by a cosmos. Whatever order there may be in it, must be a sort of unfixed, unbinding order such as Supermind might evolve before it had proceeded to the work of fixed development, measurement and interaction of relations. For that measurement and interaction Mind is necessary, though it need not be aware of itself as anything but a subordinate action of Supermind nor develop the interaction of relations on the basis of a self-imprisoned egoism such as we see active in terrestrial Nature.

Mind once existent, Life and Form of substance follow; for life is simply the determination of force and action, of relation and interaction of energy from many fixed centres of consciousness, — fixed, not necessarily in place or time, but in a persistent coexistence of beings or soul-forms of the Eternal supporting a cosmic harmony. That life may be very different from life as we know or conceive it, but essentially it would be the same principle at work which we see here figured as vitality, — the principle to which the ancient Indian thinkers gave the name of Vayu or Prana, the life-stuff, the substantial will and energy in the cosmos working out into determined form and action and conscious dynamis of being. Substance too might be very different from our view and sense of material body, much more subtle, much less rigidly binding in its law of self-division and mutual resistance, and body or form might be an instru-

ment and not a prison, yet for the cosmic interaction some
determination of form and substance would always be necessary,
even if it be only a mental body or something yet more luminous, subtle and puissantly and freely responsive than the freest
mental body.

It follows that wherever Cosmos is, there, even if only one
principle be initially apparent, even if at first that seem to be
the sole principle of things and everything else that may appear
afterwards in the world seem to be no more than its forms and
results and not in themselves indispensable to cosmic existence,
such a front presented by being can only be an illusory mask
or appearance of its real truth. Where one principle is manifest in Cosmos, there all the rest must be not merely present
and passively latent, but secretly at work. In any given world
its scale and harmony of being may be openly in possession of
all seven at a higher or lower degree of activity; in another
they may be all involved in one which becomes the initial or
fundamental principle of evolution in that world, but evolution
of the involved there must be. The evolution of the sevenfold
power of being, the realisation of its septuple Name, must be
the destiny of any world which starts apparently from the involution of all in one power[1]. Therefore the material universe
was bound in the nature of things to evolve from its hidden
life apparent life, from its hidden mind apparent mind, and it
must in the same nature of things evolve from its hidden Supermind apparent Supermind and from the concealed Spirit within
it the triune glory of Sachchidananda. The only question is
whether the earth is to be a scene of that emergence or the
human creation on this or any other material scene, in this or
any other cycle of the large wheelings of Time, its instrument
and vehicle. The ancient seers believed in this possibility for
man and held it to be his divine destiny; the modern thinker
does not even conceive of it or, if he conceived, would deny
or doubt. If he sees a vision of the Superman, it is in the figure
of increased degrees of mentality or vitality; he admits no other

---

[1] In any given world there need not be an involution but only a subordination of the
other principles to one or their inclusion in one; then evolution is not a necessity of that
world-order.

emergence, sees nothing beyond these principles, for these have traced for us up till now our limit and circle. In this progressive world, with this human creature in whom the divine spark has been kindled, real wisdom is likely to dwell with the higher aspiration rather than with the denial of aspiration or with the hope that limits and circumscribes itself within those narrow walls of apparent possibility which are only our intermediate house of training. In the spiritual order of things, the higher we project our view and our aspiration, the greater the Truth that seeks to descend upon us, because it is already there within us and calls for its release from the covering that conceals it in manifested Nature.

*

The aim of the yoga is to open the consciousness to the Divine and to live in the inner consciousness more and more while acting from it on the external life, to bring the inmost psychic into the front and by the power of the psychic to purify and change the being so that it may become ready for transformation and be in union with the Divine Knowledge, Will and Love. Secondly, to develop the yogic consciousness, i.e., to universalise the being in all the planes, become aware of the cosmic being and cosmic forces and be in union with the Divine on all the planes up to the overmind. Thirdly, to come into contact with the transcendent Divine beyond the overmind through the supramental consciousness, supramentalise the consciousness and the nature and make oneself an instrument for the realisation of the dynamic Divine Truth and its transforming descent into the earth-nature.

(XXIII, p. 509)

EVOLUTION AND REBIRTH

The Philosophy of Rebirth*

> An end have these bodies of an embodied soul that is eternal;...it is not born nor dies nor is it that having been it will not be again. It is unborn, ancient, everlasting; it is not slain with the slaying of the body. As a man casts from him his worn-out garments and takes others that are new, so the embodied being casts off its bodies and joins itself to others that are new. Certain is the death of that which is born and certain is the birth of that which dies....
>
> *Gita.*[1]

> There is a birth and growth of the self. According to his actions the embodied being assumes forms successively in many places; many forms gross and subtle he assumes by force of his own qualities of nature....
>
> *Swetaswatara Upanishad.*[2]

BIRTH is the first spiritual mystery of the physical universe, death is the second which gives its double point of perplexity to the mystery of birth; for life, which would otherwise be a self-evident fact of existence, becomes itself a mystery by virtue of these two which seem to be its beginning and its end and yet in a thousand ways betray themselves as neither of these things, but rather intermediate stages in an occult processus of life. At first sight birth might seem to be a constant outburst of life in a general death, a persistant circumstance in the universal lifelessness of Matter. On a closer examination it begins to be more probable that life is something involved in Matter or even an inherent power of the Energy that creates Matter, but able to appear only when it gets the necessary conditions for the affirmation of its characteristic phenomena and for an appropriate self-organisation. But in the birth of life there is something more that participates in the emergence, — there is an element which is no longer material, a strong upsurging of some flame of soul, a first evident vibration of the spirit.

All the known circumstances and results of birth presuppose an unknown before, and there is a suggestion of universality, a will of persistence of life, an inconclusiveness in death which seem

---

[1] II. 18, 20, 22, 27.   [2] V. 11, 12.
* *The Life Divine*, pp. 742–64.

to point to an unknown hereafter. What were we before birth and what are we after death, are the questions, the answer of the one depending upon that of the other, which the intellect of man has put to itself from the beginning without even now resting in any final solution. The intellect indeed can hardly give the final answer: for that must in its very nature lie beyond the data of the physical consciousness and memory, whether of the race or the individual, yet these are the sole data which the intellect is in the habit of consulting with something like confidence. In this poverty of materials and this incertitude it wheels from one hypothesis to another and calls each in turn a conclusion. Moreover, the solution depends upon the nature, source and object of the cosmic movement, and as we determine these, so we shall have to conclude about birth and life and death, the before and the hereafter.

The first question is whether the before and the after are purely physical and vital or in some way, and more predominantly, mental and spiritual. If Matter were the principle of the universe, as the materialist alleges, if the truth of things were to be found in the first formula arrived at by Bhrigu, son of Varuna, when he meditated upon the eternal Brahman, "Matter is the Eternal, for from Matter all beings are born and by Matter all beings exist and to Matter all beings depart and return", then no farther questioning would be possible. The before of our bodies would be a gathering of their constituents out of various physical elements through the instrumentality of the seed and food and under the influence perhaps of occult but always material energies, and the before of our conscious being a preparation by heredity or by some other physically vital or physically mental operation in universal Matter specialising its action and building the individual through the bodies of our parents, through seed and gene and chromosome. The after of the body would be a dissolution into the material elements and the after of the conscious being a relapse into Matter with some survival of the effects of its activity in the general mind and life of humanity: this last quite illusory survival would be our only chance of immortality. But since the universality of Matter can no longer be held as giving any sufficient explanation of the existence of Mind,

— and indeed Matter itself can no longer be explained by Matter alone, for it does not appear to be self-existent, — we are thrown back from this easy and obvious solution to other hypotheses.

One of these is the old religious myth and dogmatic mystery of a God who creates constantly immortal souls out of his own being or else by his "breath" or life-power entering, it is to be presumed, into material Nature or rather into the bodies he creates in it and vivifying them internally with a spiritual principle. As a mystery of faith this can hold and need not be examined, for the mysteries of faith are intended to be beyond question and scrutiny; but for reason and philosophy it lacks convincingness and does not fit into the known order of things. For it involves two paradoxes which need more justification before they can even be accorded any consideration; first, the hourly creation of beings who have a beginning in time but no end in time, and are, moreover, born by the birth of the body but do not end by the death of the body; secondly, their assumption of a ready-made mass of combined qualities, virtues, vices, capacities, defects, temperamental and other advantages and handicaps, not made by them at all through growth, but made for them by arbitrary fiat, — if not by law of heredity, — yet for which and for the perfect use of which they are held responsible by their Creator.

We may maintain, — provisionally, at least, — certain things as legitimate presumptions of the philosophic reason and fairly throw the burden of disproving them on their denier. Among these postulates is the principle that that which has no end must necessarily have had no beginning; all that begins or is created has an end by cessation of the process that created and maintains it or the dissolution of the materials of which it is compounded or the end of the function for which it came into being. If there is an exception to this law, it must be by a descent of spirit into matter animating matter with divinity or giving matter its own immortality; but the spirit itself which so descends is immortal, not made or created. If the soul was created to animate the body, if it depended on the body for its coming into existence, it can have no reason or basis for existence after the disappearance of the body. It is naturally to be supposed that the breath or power given for the animation of the body would return at its final dissolution to its Maker. If, on the contrary, it still persists as an immortal embodied being, there must be a subtle or psychic body in which it continues, and it is fairly certain that this psychic body and its inhabitant must be pre-existent to the material vehicle: it is irrational to suppose that they were created originally to inhabit that brief and perishable form; an immortal being cannot be the outcome of so ephemeral an incident in creation. If the soul remains but in a disembodied condition, then it can have had no original dependence on a body for its existence; it must have subsisted as an unembodied spirit before birth even as it persists in its disembodied spiritual entity after death.

Again, we can assume that where we see in Time a certain stage of development, there must have been a past to that development. Therefore, if the soul enters this life with a certain development of personality, it must have prepared it in other precedent lives here or elsewhere. Or, if it only takes up a ready-made life and personality not prepared by it, prepared perhaps by a physical, vital and mental heredity, it must itself be something quite independent of that life and personality, something which is only fortuitously connected with the mind and body and cannot therefore be really affected by what is done or developed in this mental and bodily living. If the soul is real and immortal, not a constructed being or figure of being, it must also be eternal, beginningless in the past even as endless in the future; but, if eternal, it must be either a changeless self unaffected by life and its terms or a timeless Purusha, an eternal and spiritual Person manifesting or causing in time a stream of changing personality. If it is such a Person, it can only manifest this stream of personality in a world of birth and death by the assumption of successive bodies, — in a word, by constant or by repeated rebirth into the forms of Nature.

But the immortality or eternity of the soul does not at once impose itself, even if we reject the explanation of all things by eternal Matter. For we have also the hypothesis of the creation of a temporary or apparent soul by some power of the original Unity from which all things began, by which they live and into which they cease. On one side, we can erect upon the foundation

of certain modern ideas or discoveries the theory of a cosmic
Inconscient creating a temporary soul, a consciousness which
after a brief play is extinguished and goes back into the Inconscient. Or there may be an eternal Becoming, which manifests
itself in a cosmic Life-force with the appearance of Matter as one
objective end of its operations and the appearance of Mind as the
other subjective end, the interaction of these two phenomena of
Life-force creating our human existence. On the other side, we
have the old theory of a sole-existing Superconscient, an eternal
unmodifiable Being which admits or creates by Maya an illusion
of individual soul-life in this world of phenomenal Mind and
Matter, both of them ultimately unreal, — even if they have or
assume a temporary and phenomenal reality, — since one unmodifiable and eternal Self or Spirit is the only entity. Or we
have the Buddhist theory of a Nihil or Nirvana and, somehow
imposed upon that, an eternal action or energy of successive
becoming, Karma, which creates the illusion of a persistent self
or soul by a constant continuity of associations, ideas, memories,
sensations, images. In their effect upon the life-problem all these
three explanations are practically one; for even the Superconscient is for the purposes of the universal action an equivalent of
the Inconscient; it can be aware only of its own unmodifiable
self-existence: the creation of a world of individual beings by
Maya is an imposition on this self-existence; it takes place, perhaps, in a sort of self-absorbed sleep of consciousness, *suṣupti*,[1]
out of which yet all active consciousness and modification of
phenomenal becoming emerge, just as in the modern theory our
consciousness is an impermanent development out of the Inconscient. In all three theories the apparent soul or spiritual
individuality of the creature is not immortal in the sense of eternity, but has a beginning and an end in Time, is a creation by
Maya or by Nature-Force or cosmic Action out of the Inconscient or Superconscient, and is therefore impermanent in its
existence. In all three rebirth is either unnecessary or else illusory; it is either the prolongation by repetition of an illusion,
or it is an additional revolving wheel among the many wheels of

[1] Prajna of the Mandukya Upanishad, the Self situated in deep sleep, is the lord and creator of things.

the complex machinery of the Becoming, or it is excluded since a single birth is all that can be asked for by a conscious being fortuitously engendered as part of an inconscient creation.

In these views, whether we suppose the one Eternal Existence to be a vital Becoming or an immutable and unmodifiable spiritual Being or a nameless and formless Non-being, that which we call the soul can be only a changing mass or stream of phenomena of consciousness which has come into existence in the sea of real or illusory becoming and will cease to exist there, — or, it may be, it is a temporary spiritual substratum, a conscious reflection of the Superconscient Eternal which by its presence supports the mass of phenomena. It is not eternal, and its only immortality is a greater or less continuity in the Becoming. It is not a real and always existent Person who maintains and experiences the stream or mass of phenomena. That which supports them, that which really and always exists, is either the one eternal Becoming or the one eternal and impersonal Being or the continual stream of Energy in its workings. For a theory of this kind it is not indispensable that a psychic entity always the same should persist and assume body after body, form after form, until it is dissolved at last by some process annulling altogether the original impetus which created this cycle. It is quite possible that as each form is developed, a consciousness develops corresponding to the form, and as the form dissolves, the corresponding consciousness dissolves with it; the One which forms all, alone endures for ever. Or, as the body is gathered out of the general elements of Matter and begins its life with birth and ends with death, so the consciousness may be developed out of the general elements of mind and equally begin with birth and end with death. Here too, the One who supplies by Maya or otherwise the force which creates the elements, is the sole reality that endures. In none of these theories of existence is rebirth an absolute necessity or an inevitable result of the theory.[1]

[1] In the Buddhist theory rebirth is imperative because Karma compels it; not a soul, but Karma is the link of an apparently continuing consciousness, — for the consciousness changes from moment to moment: there is this apparent continuity of consciousness, but there is no real immortal soul taking birth and passing through the death of the body to be reborn in another body.

As a matter of fact, however, we find a great difference; for the old theories affirm, the modern denies rebirth as a part of the universal process. Modern thought starts from the physical body as the basis of our existence and recognises the reality of no other world except this material universe. What it sees here is a mental consciousness associated with the life of the body, giving in its birth no sign of previous individual existence and leaving in its end no sign of subsequent individual existence. What was before birth is the material energy with its seed of life, or at best an energy of life-force, which persists in the seed transmitted by the parents and gives, by its mysterious infusion of past developments into that trifling vehicle, a particular mental and physical stamp to the new individual mind and body thus strangely created. What remains after death is the same material energy or life-force persisting in the seed transmitted to the children and active for the farther development of the mental and physical life carried with it. Nothing is left of us except what we so transmit to others or what the Energy which shaped the individual by its pre-existent and its surrounding action, by birth and by environment, may take as the result of his life and works into its subsequent action; whatever may help by chance or by physical law to build the mental and vital constituents and environment of other individuals, that alone can have any survival. Behind both the mental and the physical phenomena there is perhaps a universal Life of which we are individualised, evolutionary and phenomenal becomings. This universal Life creates a real world and real beings, but the conscious personality in these beings is not, or at least it need not be, the sign or the shape of consciousness of an eternal nor even of a persistent soul or supraphysical Person: there is nothing in this formula of existence compelling us to believe in a psychic entity that outlasts the death of the body. There is here no reason and little room for the admission of rebirth as a part of the scheme of things.

But what if it were found with the increase of our knowledge, as certain researches and discoveries seem to presage, that the dependence of the mental being or the psychic entity in us on the body is not so complete as we at first naturally conclude it to be from the study of the data of physical existence and the physical universe alone? What if it were found that the human personality survives the death of the body and moves between other planes and this material universe? The prevalent modern idea of a temporary conscious existence would then have to broaden itself and admit a Life that has a wider range than the physical universe and admit too a personal individuality not dependent on the material body. It might have practically to readopt the ancient idea of a subtle form or body inhabited by a psychic entity. A psychic or soul entity, carrying with it the mental consciousness, or, if there be no such original soul, then the evolved and persistent mental individual would continue after death in this subtle persistent form, which must have been either created for it before this birth or by the birth itself or during the life. For either a psychic entity pre-exists in other worlds in a subtle form and comes from there with it to its brief earthly sojourn, or the soul develops here in the material world itself, and with it a psychic body is developed in the course of Nature and persists after death in other worlds or by reincarnation here. These would be the two possible alternatives.

An evolving universal Life may have developed on earth the growing personality that has now become ourselves, before it entered a human body at all; the soul in us may have evolved in lower life-shapes before man was created. In that case, our personality has previously inhabited animal forms, and the subtle body would be a plastic formation carried from birth to birth but adapting itself to whatever physical shape the soul inhabits. Or the evolving Life may be able to build a personality capable of survival, but only in the human form when that is created. This would happen by the force of a sudden growth of mental consciousness, and at the same time a sheath of subtle mind-substance might develop and help to individualise this mental consciousness and would then function as an inner body, just as the gross physical form by its organisation at once individualises and houses the animal mind and life. On the former supposition, we must admit that the animal too survives the dissolution of the physical body and has some kind of soul formation which after death occupies other animal forms on earth and finally a human body. For there is little likelihood that the animal soul passes beyond earth and enters other planes of life than the physical and constantly returns here until it is ready for the human incarnation; the animal's conscious individualisation does not seem sufficient to bear such a transfer or to adapt itself to an other-worldly existence. On the second supposition, the power thus to survive the death of the physical body in other states of existence would only arrive with the human stage of the evolution. If, indeed, the soul is not such a constructed personality evolved by Life, but a persistent unevolving reality with a terrestrial life and body as its necessary field, the theory of re-birth in the sense of Pythagorean transmigration would have to be admitted. But if it is a persistent evolving entity capable of passing beyond the terrestrial stage, then the Indian idea of a passage to other worlds and a return to terrestrial birth would become possible and highly probable. But it would not be inevit-able; for it might be supposed that the human personality, once capable of attaining to other planes, need not return from them: it would naturally, in the absence of some greater compelling reason, pursue its existence upon the higher plane to which it had arisen; it would have finished with the terrestrial life-evolution. Only if faced with actual evidence of a return to earth, would a larger supposition be compulsory and the admission of a repeated rebirth in human forms become inevitable.

But even then the developing vitalistic theory need not spiri-tualise itself, need not admit the real existence of a soul or its immortality or eternity. It might regard the personality still as a phenomenal creation of the universal Life by the interaction of life-consciousnes sand physical form and force, but with a wider, more variable and subtler action of both upon each other and another history than it had at first seen to be possible. It might even arrive at a sort of vitalistic Buddhism, admitting Karma, but admitting it only as the action of a universal Life-force; it would admit as one of its results the continuity of the stream of personality in rebirth by mental association, but might deny any real self for the individual or any eternal being other than this ever-active vital Becoming. On the other hand, it might, obeying a turn of thought which is now beginning to gain a little in strength, admit a universal Self or cosmic Spirit as the primal reality and Life as its power or agent and so arrive at a form of spiritualised vital Monism. In this theory too a law of rebirth would be possible but not inevitable; it might be a phenomenal fact, an actual law of life, but it would not be a logical result of the theory of being and its inevitable consequence.

Adwaita of the Mayavada, like Buddhism, started with the already accepted belief, — part of the received stock of an antique knowledge, — of supraphysical planes and worlds and a commerce between them and ours which determined a passage from earth and, though this seems to have been a less primitive discovery, a return to earth of the human personality. At any rate their thought had behind it an ancient perception and even experience, or at least an age-long tradition, of a before and after for the personality which was not confined to the experience of the physical universe; for they based themselves on a view of self and world which already regarded a supraphysical consciousness as the primary phenomenon and physical being as only a secondary and dependent phenomenon. It was around these data that they had to determine the nature of the eternal Reality and the origin of the phenomenal becoming. Therefore they admitted the passage of the personality from this to other worlds and its return into form of life upon earth; but the rebirth thus admitted was not in the Buddhistic view a real rebirth of a real spiritual Person into the forms of material existence. In the later Adwaita view the spiritual reality was there, but its apparent individuality and therefore its birth and rebirth were part of a cosmic illusion, a deceptive but effective construction of universal Maya.

In Buddhistic thought the existence of the Self was denied, and rebirth could only mean a continuity of the ideas, sensations and actions which constituted a fictitious individual moving between different worlds, — let us say, between differently organised planes of idea and sensation; for, in fact, it is only the conscious continuity of the flux that creates a phenomenon of self and a phenomenon of personality. In the Adwaitic Mayavada there was the admission of a Jivatman, an individual self, and even of a real self of the individual;[1] but this concession to our normal language and ideas ends by being only apparent. For it turns out that there is no real and eternal individual, no "I" or "you", and therefore there can be no real self of the individual, even no true universal self, but only a Self apart from the universe, ever unborn, ever unmodified, ever unaffected by the mutations of phenomena. Birth, life, death, the whole mass of individual and cosmic experience, become in the last resort no more than an illusion or a temporary phenomenon; even bondage and release can be only such an illusion, a part of temporal phenomena: they amount only to the conscious continuity of the illusory experiences of the ego, itself a creation of the great Illusion, and the cessation of the continuity and the consciousness into the superconsciousness of That which alone was, is and ever will be, or rather which has nothing to do with Time, is for ever unborn, timeless and ineffable.

Thus while in the vitalistic view of things there is a real universe and a real though brief temporary becoming of individual life which, even though there is no ever-enduring Purusha, yet gives a considerable importance to our individual experience and actions, — for these are truly effective in a real becoming, — in the Mayavada theory these things have no real importance or true effect, but only something like a dream-consequence. For even release takes place only in the cosmic dream or hallucination by the recognition of the illusion and the cessation of the individualised mind and body; in reality, there is no one bound and no one released, for the sole-existent Self is untouched by these illusions of the ego. To escape from the all-destroying sterility which would be the logical result, we have to lend a practical reality, however false it may be eventually, to this dream-consequence and an immense importance to our bondage and individual release, even though the life of the individual is phenomenal only and to the one real Self both the bondage and the release are and cannot but be non-existent. In this compulsory concession to the tyrannous falsehood of Maya the sole

---

[1] The Self in this view is one, it cannot be many or multiply itself; there cannot therefore be any true individual, only at most a one Self omnipresent and animating each mind and body with the idea of an "I".

true importance of life and experience must lie in the measure in which they prepare for the negation of life, for the self-elimination of the individual, for the end of the cosmic illusion.

This, however, is an extreme view and consequence of the monistic thesis, and the older Adwaita Vedantism starting from the Upanishads does not go so far. It admits an actual and temporal becoming of the Eternal and therefore a real universe; the individual too assumes a sufficient reality, for each individual is in himself the Eternal who has assumed name and form and supports through him the experiences of life turning on an ever-circling wheel of birth in the manifestation. The wheel is kept in motion by the desire of the individual, which becomes the effective cause of rebirth and by the mind's turning away from the knowledge of the eternal self to the preoccupations of the temporal becoming. With the cessation of this desire and of this ignorance, the Eternal in the individual draws away from the mutations of individual personality and experience into his timeless, impersonal and immutable being.

But this reality of the individual is quite temporal; it has no enduring foundation, not even a perpetual recurrence in Time. Rebirth, though a very important actuality in this account of the universe, is not an inevitable consequence of the relation between individuality and the purpose of the manifestation. For the manifestation seems to have no purpose except the will of the Eternal towards world-creation and it can end only by that will's withdrawal: this cosmic will could work itself out without any machinery of rebirth and the individual's desire maintaining it; for his desire can be only a spring of the machinery, it could not be the cause or the necessary condition of cosmic existence, since he is himself in this view a result of the creation and not in existence prior to the Becoming. The will to creation could then accomplish itself through a temporary assumption of individuality in each name and form, a single life of many impermanent individuals. There would be a self-shaping of the one consciousness in correspondence with the type of each created being, but it could very well begin in each individual body with the appearance of the physical form and end with its cessation. Individual would follow individual as wave follows wave, the sea remaining always the same;[1] each formation of conscious being would surge up from the universal, roll for its allotted time and then sink back into the Silence. The necessity for this purpose of an individualised consciousness persistently continuous, assuming name after name and form after form and moving between different planes backward and forward, is not apparent and, even as a possibility, does not strongly impose itself; still less is there any room for an evolutionary progress inevitably pursued from form to higher form such as must be supposed by a theory of rebirth that affirms the involution and evolution of the Spirit in Matter as the significant formula of our terrestrial existence.

It is conceivable that so the Eternal may have actually chosen to manifest or rather to conceal himself in the body; he may have willed to become or to appear as an individual passing from birth to death and from death to new life in a cycle of persistent and recurrent human and animal existence. The One Being personalised would pass through various forms of becoming at fancy or according to some law of the consequences of action, till the close came by an enlightenment, a return to Oneness, a withdrawal of the Sole and Identical from that particular individualisation. But such a cycle would have no original or final determining Truth which would give it any significance. There is nothing for which it would be necessary; it would be purely a play, a Lila. But if it is once admitted that the Spirit has involved itself in the Inconscience and is manifesting itself in the individual being by an evolutionary gradation, then the whole process assumes meaning and consistence; the progressive ascent of the individual becomes a key-note of this cosmic significance, and the rebirth of the soul in the body becomes a natural and unavoidable consequence of the truth of the Becoming and its inherent law. Rebirth is an indispensable machinery for the

---

[1] Dr. Schweitzer in his book on Indian thought asserts that this was the real sense of the Upanishadic teachings and rebirth was a later invention. But there are numerous important passages in almost all the Upanishads positively affirming rebirth and, in any case, the Upanishads admit the survival of the personality after death and its passage into other worlds which is incompatible with this interpretation. If there is survival in other worlds and also a final destiny of liberation into the Brahman for souls embodied here, rebirth imposes itself, and there is no reason to suppose that it was a later theory. The writer has evidently been moved by the associations of Western philosophy to read a merely pantheistic sense into the more subtle and complex thought of the ancient Vedanta.

working out of a spiritual evolution; it is the only possible effective condition, the obvious dynamic process of such a manifestation in the material universe.

Our explanation of the evolution in Matter is that the universe is a self-creative process of a supreme Reality whose presence makes spirit the substance of things, — all things are there as the spirit's powers and means and forms of manifestation. An infinite existence, an infinite consciousness, an infinite force and will, an infinite delight of being is the Reality secret behind the appearances of the universe; its divine Supermind or Gnosis has arranged the cosmic order, but arranged it indirectly through the three subordinate and limiting terms of which we are conscious here, Mind, Life and Matter. The material universe is the lowest stage of a downward plunge of the manifestation, an involution of the manifested being of this triune Reality into an apparent nescience of itself, that which we now call the Inconscient; but out of this nescience the evolution of that manifested being into a recovered self-awareness was from the very first inevitable. It was inevitable because that which is involved must evolve; for it is not only there as an existence, a force hidden in its apparent opposite, and every such force must in its inmost nature be moved to find itself, to realise itself, to release itself into play, but it is the reality of that which conceals it, it is the self which the Nescience has lost and which therefore it must be the whole secret meaning, the constant drift of its action to seek for and recover. It is through the conscious individual being that this recovery is possible; it is in him that the evolving consciousness becomes organised and capable of awaking to its own Reality. The immense importance of the individual being, which increases as he rises in the scale, is the most remarkable and significant fact of a universe which started without consciousness and without individuality in an undifferentiated Nescience. This importance can only be justified if the Self as individual is no less real than the Self as cosmic Being or Spirit and both are powers of the Eternal. It is only so that can be explained the necessity for the growth of the individual and his discovery of himself as a condition for the discovery of the cosmic Self and Consciousness and of the supreme Reality. If we adopt this solution, this is the first result,

the reality of the persistent individual; but from that first consequence the other result follows, that rebirth of some kind is no
longer a possible machinery which may or may not be accepted,
it becomes a necessity, an inevitable outcome of the root nature
of our existence.

For it is no longer sufficient to suppose an illusory or temporary individual, created in each form by the play of consciousness; individuality can no longer be conceived as an accompani-
ment of play of consciousness in figure of body which may or may
not survive the form, may or may not prolong its false continuity
of self from form to form, from life to life, but which certainly
need not do it. In this world what we seem at first to see is individual replacing individual without any continuity, the form
dissolving, the false or transient individuality dissolving with it,
while the universal Energy or some universal Being alone remains
for ever; that might very well be the whole principle of cosmic
manifestation. But if the individual is a persistent reality, an eternal portion or power of the Eternal, if his growth of consciousness is the means by which the Spirit in things discloses its being,
the cosmos reveals itself as a conditioned manifestation of the play
of the eternal One in the being of Sachchidananda with the
eternal Many. Then, secure behind all the changings of our
personality, upholding the stream of its mutations, there must be
a true Person, a real spiritual Individual, a true Purusha. The
One extended in universality exists in each being and affirms
himself in this individuality of himself. In the individual he
discloses his total existence by oneness with all in the universality. In the individual he discloses too his transcendence as the
Eternal in whom all the universal unity is founded. This trinity
of self-manifestation, this prodigious Lila of the manifold Identity, this magic of Maya or protean miracle of the conscious truth
of being of the Infinite, is the luminous revelation which emerges
by a slow evolution from the original Inconscience.

If there were no need of self-finding but only an eternal
enjoyment of this play of the being of Sachchidananda, — and
such an eternal enjoyment is the nature of certain supreme states
of conscious existence, — then evolution and rebirth need not
have come into operation. But there has been an involution of

this unity into the dividing Mind, a plunge into self-oblivion by which the ever-present sense of the complete oneness is lost, and the play of separative difference, — phenomenal, because the real unity in difference remains unabridged behind, — comes into the forefront as a dominant reality. This play of difference has found its utmost term of the sense of division by the precipitation of the dividing Mind into a form of body in which it becomes conscious of itself as a separate ego. A dense and solid basis has been laid for this play of division in a world of separative forms of Matter by an involution of the active self-conscience of Sach-chidananda into a phenomenal Nescience. It is this foundation in Nescience that makes the division secure because it imperative-ly opposes a return to the consciousness of unity; but still, though effectively obstructive, it is phenomenal and terminable because within it, above it, supporting it is the all-conscient Spirit and the apparent Nescience turns out to be only a concen-tration, an exclusive action of consciousness tranced into self-forgetfulness by an abysmal plunge into the absorption of the formative and creative material process. In a phenomenal universe so created, the separative form becomes the foundation and the starting-point of all its life-action; therefore the indi-vidual Purusha in working out its cosmic relations with the One has in this physical world to base himself upon the form, to assume a body; it is the body that he must make his own foundation and the starting-point for his development of the life and mind and spirit in the physical existence. That assump-tion of body we call birth, and in it only can take place here the development of self and the play of relations between the indi-vidual and the universal and all other individuals; in it only can there be the growth by a progressive development of our con-scious being towards a supreme recovery of unity with God and with all in God: all the sum of what we call Life in the physical world is a progress of the soul and proceeds by birth into the body and has that for its fulcrum, its condition of action and its condition of evolutionary persistence.

Birth then is a necessity of the manifestation of the Purusha on the physical plane; but his birth, whether the human or any other, cannot be in this world-order an isolated accident or a sudden excursion of a soul into physicality without any preparing past to it or any fulfilling hereafter. In a world of involution and evolution, not of physical form only, but of conscious being through life and mind to spirit, such an isolated assumption of life in the human body could not be the rule of the individual soul's existence; it would be a quite meaningless and inconsequential arrangement, a freak for which the nature and system of things here have no place, a contrary violence which would break the rhythm of the Spirit's self-manifestation. The intrusion of such a rule of individual soul-life into an evolutionary spiritual progression would make it an effect without cause and a cause without effect; it would be a fragmentary present without a past or a future. The life of the individual must have the same rhythm of significance, the same law of progression as the cosmic life; its place in that rhythm cannot be a stray purposeless intervention, it must be an abiding instrumentation of the cosmic purpose. Neither in such an order can we explain an isolated advent, a one birth of the soul in the human body which would be its first and last experience of the kind, by a previous existence in other worlds with a future before it in yet other fields of experience. For here life upon earth, life in the physical universe is not and cannot be a casual perch for the wanderings of the soul from world to world; it is a great and slow development needing, as we now know, incalculable spaces of Time for its evolution. Human life is itself only a term in a graded series, through which the secret Spirit in the universe develops gradually his purpose and works it out finally through the enlarging and ascending individual soul-consciousness in the body. This ascent can only take place by rebirth within the ascending order; an individual visit coming across it and progressing on some other line elsewhere could not fit into the system of this evolutionary existence.

Nor is the human soul, the human individual, a free wanderer capriciously or lightly hastening from field to field according to its unfettered choice or according to its free and spontaneously variable action and result of action. That is a radiant thought of pure spiritual liberty which may have its truth in planes beyond or in an eventual release, but is not true at first of the earth-life, of life in the physical universe. The human birth in this world is on its spiritual side a complex of two elements, a spiritual Person and a soul of personality; the former is man's eternal being, the latter is his cosmic and mutable being. As the spiritual impersonal person he is one in his nature and being with the freedom of Sachchidananda who has here consented to or willed his involution in the Nescience for a certain round of soul-experience, impossible otherwise, and presides secretly over its evolution. As the soul of personality he is himself part of that long development of the soul-experience in the forms of Nature; his own evolution must follow the laws and the lines of the universal evolution. As a spirit he is one with the Transcendence which is immanent in the world and comprehensive of it; as a soul he is at once one with and part of the universality of Sachchidananda self-expressed in the world: his self-expression must go through the stages of the cosmic expression, his soul-experience follow the revolutions of the wheel of Brahman in the universe.

The universal Spirit in things involved in the Nescience of the physical universe evolves its nature-self in a succession of physical forms up the graded series of Matter, Life, Mind and Spirit. It emerges first as a secret soul in material forms quite subject on the surface to the nescience; it develops as a soul still secret but about to emerge in vital forms that stand on the borders between nescience and the partial light of consciousness which is our ignorance; it develops still farther as the initially conscient soul in the animal mind and, finally, as the more outwardly conscious, but not yet fully conscient soul in man: the consciousness is there throughout in our occult parts of being, the development is in the manifesting Nature. This evolutionary development has a universal as well as an individual aspect: the Universal develops the grades of its being and the ordered variation of the universality of itself in the series of its evolved forms of being; the individual soul follows the line of this cosmic series and manifests what is prepared in the universality of the Spirit. The universal Man, the cosmic Purusha in humanity, is developing in the human race the power that has grown into humanity from below it and shall yet grow to Supermind and

Spirit and become the Godhead in man who is aware of his true and integral self and the divine universality of his nature. The individual must have followed this line of development; he must have presided over a soul-experience in the lower forms of life before he took up the human evolution: as the One was capable of assuming in its universality these lower forms of the plant and animal, so must the individual, now human, have been capable of assuming them in his previous stages of existence. He now appears as a human soul, the Spirit accepting the inner and outer form of humanity, but he is not limited by this form any more than he was limited by the plant or animal forms previously assumed by him; he can pass on from it to a greater self-expression in a higher scale of Nature.

To suppose otherwise would be to suppose that the spirit which now presides over the human soul-experience was originally formed by a human mentality and the human body, exists by that and cannot exist apart from it, cannot ever go below or above it. In fact, it would then be reasonable to suppose that it is not immortal but has come into existence by the appearance of the human mind and body in the evolution and would disappear by their disappearance. But body and mind are not the creators of the spirit, the spirit is the creator of the mind and body; it develops these principles out of its being, it is not developed into being out of them, it is not a compound of their elements or a resultant of their meeting. If it appears to evolve out of mind and body, that is because it gradually manifests itself in them and not because it is created by them or exists by them; as it manifests, they are revealed as subordinate terms of its being and are to be finally taken up out of their present imperfection and transformed into visible forms and instruments of the spirit. Our conception of the spirit is of something which is not constituted by name and form, but assumes various forms of body and mind according to the various manifestations of its soul-being. This it does here by a successive evolution; it evolves successive forms and successive strata of consciousness: for it is not bound always to assume one form and no other or to possess one kind of mentality which is its sole possible subjective manifestation. The soul is not bound by the formula of mental humanity: it did not begin with that and will not end with it; it had a pre-human past, it has a superhuman future.

What we see of Nature and of human nature justifies this view of a birth of the individual soul from form to form until it reaches the human level of manifested consciousness which is its instrument for rising to yet higher levels. We see that Nature develops from stage to stage and in each stage takes up its past and transforms it into stuff of its new development. We see too that human nature is of the same make; all the earth-past is there in it. It has an element of matter taken up by life, an element of life taken up by mind, an element of mind which is being taken up by spirit: the animal is still present in its humanity; the very nature of the human being presupposes a material and a vital stage which prepared his emergence into mind and an animal past which moulded a first element of his complex humanity. And let us not say that this is because material Nature developed by evolution his life and his body and his animal mind, and only afterwards did a soul descend into the form so created: there is a certain truth behind this idea, but not the truth which that formula would suggest. For that supposes a gulf between soul and body, between soul and life, between soul and mind, which does not exist; there is no body without soul, no body that is not itself a form of soul: Matter itself is substance and power of spirit and could not exist if it were anything else, for nothing can exist which is not substance and power of Brahman; and if Matter, then still more clearly and certainly Life and Mind must be that and ensouled by the presence of the Spirit. If Matter and Life had not already been ensouled, man could not have appeared or only as an intervention or an accident, not as a part of the evolutionary order.

We arrive then necessarily at this conclusion that human birth is a term at which the soul must arrive in a long succession of rebirths and that it has had for its previous and preparatory terms in the succession the lower forms of life upon earth; it has passed through the whole chain that life.has strung in the physical universe on the basis of the body, the physical principle. Then the farther question arises whether, humanity once attained, this succession of rebirths still continues and, if so, how, by what series or by what alternations. And, first, we have to ask whether the soul, having once arrived at humanity, can go back to the animal life.and body, a retrogression which the old popular theories of transmigration have supposed to be an ordinary movement. It seems impossible that it should so go back with any entirety, and for this reason that the transit from animal to human life means a decisive conversion of consciousness, quite as decisive as the conversion of the vital consciousness of the plant into the mental consciousness of the animal. It is surely impossible that a conversion so decisive made by Nature should be reversed by the soul and the decision of the spirit within her come, as it were, to naught. It could only be possible for human souls, supposing such to exist, in whom the conversion was not decisive, souls that had developed far enough to make, occupy or assume a human body, but not enough to ensure the safety of this assumption, not enough to remain secure in its achievement and faithful to the human type of consciousness. Or at most there might be, supposing certain animal propensities to be vehement enough to demand a separate satisfaction quite of their own kind, a sort of partial rebirth, a loose holding of an animal form by a human soul, with an immediate subsequent reversion to its normal progression. The movement of Nature is always sufficiently complex for us not to deny dogmatically such a possibility, and, if it be a fact, then there may exist this modicum of truth behind the exaggerated popular belief which assumes an animal rebirth of the soul once lodged in man to be quite as normal and possible as a human reincarnation. But whether the animal reversion is possible or not, the normal law must be the recurrence of birth in new human forms for a soul that has once become capable of humanity.

But why a succession of human births and not one alone? For the same reason that has made the human birth itself a culminating point of the past succession, the previous upward series, — it must be so by the very necessity of the spiritual evolution. For the soul has not finished what it has to do by merely developing into humanity; it has still to develop that humanity into its higher possibilities. Obviously, the soul that lodges in a Caribbee or an untaught primitive or an Apache of Paris or an American gangster, has not yet exhausted the necessity of human birth, has not developed all its possibilities or the whole meaning of humanity, has not worked out all the sense of Sachchidananda in the universal Man; neither has the soul lodged in a vitalistic European occupied with dynamic production and vital pleasure or in an Asiatic peasant engrossed in the ignorant round of the domestic and economic life. We may reasonably doubt whether even a Plato or a Shankara marks the crown and therefore the end of the outflowering of the spirit in man. We are apt to suppose that these may be the limit, because these and others like them seem to us the highest point which the mind and soul of man can reach, but that may be the illusion of our present possibility. There may be a higher or at least a larger possibility which the Divine intends yet to realise in man, and, if so, it is the steps built by these highest souls which were needed to compose the way up to it and to open the gates. At any rate this present highest point at least must be reached before we can write finis on the recurrence of the human birth for the individual. Man is there to move from the ignorance and from the little life which he is in his mind and body to the knowledge and the large divine life which he can compass by the unfolding of the spirit. At least the opening out of the spirit in him, the knowledge of his real self and the leading of the spiritual life must be attained before he can go definitively and for ever otherwhere. There may too be beyond this initial culmination a greater flowering of the spirit in the human life of which we have as yet only the first intimations; the imperfection of Man is not the last word of Nature, but his perfection too is not the last peak of the Spirit.

This possibility becomes a certitude if the present leading principle of the mind as man has developed it, the intellect, is not its highest principle. If mind itself has other powers as yet only imperfectly possessed by the highest types of the human individual, then a prolongation of the line of evolution and consequently of the ascending line of rebirth to embody them is inevitable. If Supermind also is a power of consciousness concealed here in the evolution, the line of rebirth cannot stop even there; it cannot cease in its ascent before the mental has been replaced by the supramental nature and an embodied supramental being becomes the leader of terrestrial existence.

This then is the rational and philosophical foundation for a belief in rebirth; it is an inevitable logical conclusion if there exists at the same time an evolutionary principle in the Earth-Nature and a reality of the individual soul born into evolutionary Nature. If there is no soul, then there carr be a mechanical evolution without necessity or significance and birth is only part of this curious but senseless machinery. If the individual is only a temporary formation beginning and ending with the body, then evolution can be a play of the All-Soul or Cosmic Existence mounting through a progression of higher and higher species towards its own utmost possibility in this Becoming or to its highest conscious principle; rebirth does not exist and is not needed as a mechanism of that evolution. Or, if the All-Existence expresses itself in a persistent but illusory individuality, rebirth becomes a possibility or an illusory fact, but it has no evolutionary necessity and is not a spiritual necessity; it is only a means of accentuating and prolonging the illusion up to its utmost time-limit. If there is an individual soul or Purusha not dependent on the body but inhabiting and using it for its purpose, then rebirth begins to be possible, but it is not a necessity if there is no evolution of the soul in Nature: the presence of the individual soul in an individual body may be a passing phenomenon, a single experience without a past here or a future; its past and its future may be elsewhere. But if there is an evolution of consciousness in an evolutionary body and a soul inhabiting the body, a real and conscious individual, then it is evident that it is the progressive experience of that soul in Nature which takes the form of this evolution of consciousness: rebirth is self-evidently a necessary part, the sole possible machinery of such an evolution. It is as necessary as birth itself; for without it birth would be an initial step without a sequel, the starting of a journey without its farther steps and arrival. It is rebirth that gives to the birth of an incomplete being in a body its promise of completeness and its spiritual significance.

PART TWO

INTEGRAL YOGA

INTRODUCTION

On the Gita

Interpretations of the eighteen-chapter, ninety-page reply of Krishna, the God-man charioteer, to Arjuna, the beleaguered warrior of ancient India, are frequently more revealing of the interpreter than of the Gita itself. Sri Aurobindo's *Essays on the Gita* is faithful to the text and intent of the Gita, in that, like the Gita itself, it transforms an ethical problem by a spiritual solution.

In "The Gist of the Karmayoga" in *Essays on the Gita,* Sri Aurobindo explains that the first six chapters of the Gita offer a theory of *karmayoga* as a solution to the problem of action on the ethical level, but the solution to the larger problem of God and man can be solved only by the revelation of Krishna in the remaining chapters. Thus, a true understanding of *karmayoga* requires a transcendence from the ethical to the spiritual levels of existence. Ultimately, the yoga of divine works presupposes the yoga of divine love.

So, the message of the Gita according to Sri Aurobindo offers neither a simple affirmation nor deprecation of social and political action, but rather a transformation of all action by surrender to the needs of the Divine working in creation. On the basis of his own political involvement and his study of historical evolution, Sri Aurobindo was convinced that at the present stage of evolution neither individuals nor history can escape the kind of dilemma Arjuna faced in the first chapter of the Gita. Sri Aurobindo explains that the Gita rightfully admits to the value of *ahiṃsā* (nonviolence) "as part of the ethical-spiritual ideal"; it also "recognises the ascetic renunciation as a way of spiritual salvation." But according to Sri Aurobindo's reading, it goes beyond the Gandhian ideal of *ahiṃsā* and the traditional ideal of renunciation. In this respect, Sri Aurobindo's interpretation of the Gita conforms to—as, indeed, it helped to form—his system of Integral Yoga.

Integral Yoga

As is evident in both *Essays on the Gita* and *The Synthesis of Yoga*, Sri Aurobindo accepts the four yogas that vie for prominence in the Gita—*jñāna* (knowledge), *karma* (action), *bhakti* (devotion or love), and *dhyāna'* (contemplation)—but he insists that these yogas, both individually and collectively, fail to deal effectively with the natural and historical processes. Whereas the traditional yogas lead to individual liberation, Sri Aurobindo's Integral Yoga binds the process of individual liberation to the larger demands of time. In this sense, *dharma* (duty) cannot be eternally fixed, but is constantly transformed by avatars such as Rama, Krishna, and Buddha. Consistent with this belief that man is at present in a period of radical transition—from a mental to a supramental existence—the meaning of the Gita must not be limited to the spiritual needs of the individual. Sri Aurobindo's reading of the Gita in the light of his Integral Yoga emphasizes that spiritual aspiration must strive to transform the spiritual, mental, vital, and physical orders of existence. In a letter to a disciple, Sri Aurobindo offers the following forceful summary of his position:

> I do not mean by work action done in the ego and the ignorance, for the satisfaction of the ego and in the drive of rajasic desire. There can be no *karmayoga* without the will to get rid of ego, *rajas* and desire, which are the seals of ignorance.
>
> I do not mean philanthropy or the service of humanity or all the rest of the things—moral or idealistic—which the mind of man substitutes for the deeper truth of works.
>
> I mean by work action done for the Divine and more and more in union with the Divine—for the Divine alone and nothing else. Naturally that is not easy at the beginning, any more than deep meditation and luminous knowledge are easy or even true love and *bhakti* are easy. But like the others it has to be begun in the right spirit and attitude, with the right will in you, then all the rest will come.
>
> Works done in this spirit are quite as effective as *bhakti* or contemplation. One gets by the rejection of desire, *rajas* and ego a quietude and purity into which the Peace ineffable can descend; one gets by the dedication of one's will to the

Divine, by the merging of one's will in the Divine Will the death of ego and the enlarging into the cosmic consciousness or else the uplifting into what is above the cosmic; one experiences the separation of *purusha* from *prakriti* and is liberated from the shackles of the outer nature; one becomes aware of one's inner being and sees the outer as an instrument; one feels the universal force doing one's works and the Self or *purusha* watching or witness but free; one feels all one's works taken from one and done by the universal or supreme Mother or by the Divine Power controlling and acting from behind the heart. By constant referring of all one's will and works to the Divine, love and adoration grow, the psychic being comes forward. By the reference to the Power above, we can come to feel it above and its descent and the opening to an increasing consciousness and knowledge. Finally, works, *bhakti* and knowledge go together and self-perfection becomes possible—what we call the transformation of the nature.

These results certainly do not come all at once; they come more or less slowly, more or less completely according to the condition and growth of the being. There is no royal road to the divine realisation.

This is the *karmayoga* laid down in the Gita as I have developed it for the integral spiritual life. It is founded not on speculation and reasoning but on experience. It does not exclude meditation and certainly does not exclude *bhakti,* for the self-offering to the Divine, the consecration of all oneself to the Divine which is the essence of this *karmayoga* are essentially a movement of *bhakti.* Only it does exclude a life-fleeing exclusive meditation or an emotional *bhakti* shut up in its own inner dream taken as the whole movement of the yoga. One may have hours of pure absorbed meditation or of the inner motionless adoration and ecstasy, but they are not the whole of the integral yoga.*

Letters on Yoga, XXIII, pp. 528–29.

ON THE GITA

The Gist of the Karmayoga*

THE first six chapters of the Gita form a sort of preliminary block of the teaching; all the rest, all the other twelve chapters are the working out of certain unfinished figures in this block which here are seen only as hints behind the large-size execution of the main motives, yet are in themselves of capital importance and are therefore reserved for a yet larger treatment on the other two faces of the work. If the Gita were not a great written Scripture which must be carried to its end, if it were actually a discourse by a living teacher to a disciple which could be resumed in good time, when the disciple was ready for farther truth, one could conceive of his stopping here at the end of the sixth chapter and saying, "Work this out first, there is plenty for you to do to realise it and you have the largest possible basis; as difficulties arise, they will solve themselves or I will solve them for you. But at present live out what I have told you; work in this spirit." True, there are many things here which cannot be properly understood except in the light thrown on them by what is to come after. In order to clear up immediate difficulties and obviate possible misunderstandings, I have had myself to anticipate a good deal, to bring in repeatedly, for example, the idea of the Purushottama, for without that it would have been impossible to clear up certain obscurities about the Self and action and the Lord of action, which the Gita deliberately accepts so that it may not disturb the firmness of the first steps by reaching out prematurely to things too great as yet for the mind of the human disciple.

Arjuna, himself, if the Teacher were to break off his discourse here, might well object: "You have spoken much of the destruction of desire and attachment, of equality, of the conquest of the senses and the stilling of the mind, of passionless and impersonal action, of the sacrifice of works, of the inner as pre-

* *Essays on the Gita*, pp. 236–46.

ferable to the outer renunciation, and these things I understand
intellectually, however difficult they may appear to me in practice.
But you have also spoken of rising above the Gunas, while yet
one remains in action, and you have not told me how the Gunas
work, and unless I know that, it will be difficult for me to detect
and rise above them. Besides, you have spoken of Bhakti as the
greatest element in Yoga, yet you have talked much of works and
knowledge, but very little or nothing of Bhakti. And to whom
is Bhakti, this greatest thing, to be offered? Not to the still impersonal Self, certainly, but to you, the Lord. Tell me, then,
what you are, who, as Bhakti is greater even than this self-
knowledge, are greater than the immutable Self, which is yet itself greater than mutable Nature and the world of action, even as
knowledge is greater than works. What is the relation between
these three things? between works and knowledge and divine
love? between the soul in Nature and the immutable Self and
that which is at once the changeless Self of all and the Master of
knowledge and love and works, the supreme Divinity who is
here with me in this great battle and massacre, my charioteer
in the chariot of this fierce and terrible action?" It is to answer
these questions that the rest of the Gita is written, and in a complete intellectual solution they have indeed to be taken up
without delay and resolved. But in actual *sādhanā* one has to
advance from stage to stage, leaving many things, indeed the
greatest things to arise subsequently and solve themselves fully
by the light of the advance we have made in spiritual experience.
The Gita follows to a certain extent this curve of experience and
puts first a sort of large preliminary basis of works and knowledge which contains an element leading up to Bhakti and to a
greater knowledge, but not yet fully arriving. The six chapters
present us with that basis.

We may then pause to consider how far they have carried
the solution of the original problem with which the Gita started.
The problem in itself, it may be useful again to remark, need not
necessarily have led up to the whole question of the nature of
existence and of the replacement of the normal by the spiritual
life. It might have been dealt with on a pragmatical or an
ethical basis or from an intellectual or an ideal standpoint or by

a consideration of all of these together; that in fact would have been our modern method of solving the difficulty. By itself it raises in the first instance just this question, whether Arjuna should be governed by the ethical sense of personal sin in slaughter or by the consideration equally ethical of his public and social duty, the defence of the Right, the opposition demanded by conscience from all noble natures to the armed forces of injustice and oppression? That question has been raised in our own time and the present hour, and it can be solved, as we solve it now, by one or other of very various solutions, but all from the standpoint of our normal life and our normal human mind. It may be answered as a question between the personal conscience and our duty to the society and the State, between an ideal and a practical morality, between "soul-force" and the recognition of the troublesome fact that life is not yet at least all soul and that to take up arms for the right in a physical struggle is sometimes inevitable. All these solutions are, however, intellectual, temperamental, emotional; they depend upon the individual standpoint and are at the best our own proper way of meeting the difficulty offered to us, proper because suitable to our nature and the stage of our ethical and intellectual evolution, the best we can, with the light we have, see and do; it leads to no final solution. And this is so because it proceeds from the normal mind which is always a tangle of various tendencies of our being and can only arrive at a choice or an accommodation between them, between our reason, our ethical being, our dynamic needs, our life-instincts, our emotional being and those rarer movements which we may perhaps call soul-instincts or psychical preferences. The Gita recognises that from this standpoint there can be no absolute, only an immediate practical solution and, after offering to Arjuna from the highest ideals of his age just such a practical solution, which he is in no mood to accept and indeed is evidently not intended to accept, it proceeds to quite a different standpoint and to quite another answer.

The Gita's solution is to rise above our natural being and normal mind, above our intellectual and ethical perplexities into another consciousness with another law of being and therefore another standpoint for our action; where personal desire and personal emotions no longer govern it; where the dualities fall away; where the action is no longer our own and where therefore the sense of personal virtue and personal sin is exceeded; where the universal, the impersonal, the divine spirit works out through us its purpose in the world; where we are ourselves by a new and divine birth changed into being of that Being, consciousness of that Consciousness, power of that Power, bliss of that Bliss, and, living no longer in our lower nature, have no works to do of our own, no personal aim to pursue of our own, but if we do works at all, — and that is the one real problem and difficulty left, — do only the divine works, those of which our outward nature is only a passive instrument and no longer the cause, no longer provides the motive; for the motive-power is above us in the will of the Master of our works. And this is presented to us as the true solution, because it goes back to the real truth of our being and to live according to the real truth of our being is evidently the highest solution and the sole entirely true solution of the problems of our existence. Our mental and vital personality is a truth of our natural existence, but a truth of the ignorance, and all that attaches itself to it is also truth of that order, practically valid for the works of the ignorance, but no longer valid when we get back to the real truth of our being. But how can we actually be sure that this is the truth? We cannot so long as we remain satisfied with our ordinary mental experience; for our normal mental experience is wholly that of this lower nature full of the ignorance. We can only know this greater truth by living it, that is to say, by passing beyond the mental into the spiritual experience, by Yoga. For the living out of spiritual experience until we cease to be mind and become spirit, until, liberated from the imperfections of our present nature, we are able to live entirely in our true and divine being is what in the end we mean by Yoga.

This upward transference of our centre of being and the consequent transformation of our whole existence and consciousness, with a resultant change in the whole spirit and motive of our action, the action often remaining precisely the same in all its outward appearances, makes the gist of the Gita's Karmayoga. Change your being, be reborn into the spirit and by that new birth proceed with the action to which the Spirit within has appointed you, may be said to be the heart of its message. Or again, put otherwise, with a deeper and more spiritual import, — make the work you have to do here your means of inner spiritual rebirth, the divine birth, and, having become divine, do still divine works as an instrument of the Divine for the leading of the peoples. Therefore there are here two things which have to be clearly laid down and clearly grasped, the way to the change, to this upward transference, this new divine birth, and the nature of the work or rather the spirit in which it has to be done, since the outward form of it need not at all change, although really its scope and aim become quite different. But these two things are practically the same, for the elucidation of one elucidates the other. The spirit of our action arises from the nature of our being and the inner foundation it has taken, but also this nature is itself affected by the trend and spiritual effect of our action; a very great change in the spirit of our works changes the nature of our being and alters the foundation it has taken; it shifts the centre of conscious force from which we act. If life and action were entirely illusory, as some would have it, if the Spirit had nothing to do with works or life, this would not be so; but the soul in us develops itself by life and works and, not indeed so much the action itself, but the way of our soul's inner force of working determines its relations to the Spirit. This is, indeed, the justification of Karmayoga as a practical means of the higher self-realisation.

We start from this foundation that the present inner life of man, almost entirely dependent as it is upon his vital and physical nature, only lifted beyond it by a limited play of mental energy, is not the whole of his possible existence, not even the whole of his present real existence. There is within him a hidden Self, of which his present nature is either only an outer appearance or is a partial dynamic result. The Gita seems throughout to admit its dynamic reality and not to adopt the severer view of the extreme Vedantists that it is only an appearance, a view which strikes at the very roots of all works and action. Its way of formulating this element of its philosophical thought, — it might be done in a different way, — is to admit the Sankhya distinction between the Soul and Nature, the power that knows, supports and informs and the power that works, acts, provides all the variations of instrument, medium and process. Only it takes the free and immutable Soul of the Sankhyas, calls it in Vedantic language the one immutable omnipresent Self or Brahman, and distinguishes it from this other soul involved in Nature, which is our mutable and dynamic being, the multiple soul of things, the basis of variation and personality. But in what then consists this action of Nature?

It consists in a power of process, Prakriti, which is the interplay of three fundamental modes of its working, three qualities, Gunas. And what is the medium? It is the complex system of existence created by a graded evolution of the instruments of Prakriti, which, as they are reflected here in the soul's experience of her workings, we may call successively the reason and the ego, the mind, the senses and the elements of material energy which are the basis of its forms. These are all mechanical, a complex engine of Nature, *yantra*; and from our modern point of view we may say that they are all involved in material energy and manifest themselves in it as the soul in Nature becomes aware of itself by an upward evolution of each instrument, but in the inverse order to that which we have stated, matter first, then sensation, then mind, next reason, last spiritual consciousness. Reason, which is at first only preoccupied with the workings of Nature, may then detect their ultimate character, may see them only as a play of the three Gunas in which the soul is entangled, may distinguish between the soul and these workings; then the soul gets a chance of disentangling itself and of going back to its original freedom and immutable existence. In Vedantic language, it sees the spirit, the being; it ceases to identify itself with the instruments and workings of Nature, with its becoming; it identifies itself with its true Self and being and recovers its immutable spiritual self-existence. It is then from this spiritual self-existence, according to the Gita, that it can freely and as the master of its being, the Ishwara, support the action of its becoming.

Looking only at the psychological facts on which these philosophical distinctions are founded, — philosophy is only a way of formulating to ourselves intellectually in their essential significance the psychological and physical facts of existence and their relation to any ultimate reality that may exist, — we may say that there are two lives we can lead, the life of the soul engrossed in the workings of its active nature, identified with its psychological and physical instruments, limited by them, bound by its personality, subject to Nature, and the life of the Spirit, superior to these things, large, impersonal, universal, free, unlimited, transcendent, supporting with an infinite equality its natural being and action, but exceeding them by its freedom and infinity. We may live in what is now our natural being or we may live in our greater and spiritual being. This is the first great distinction on which the Karmayoga of the Gita is founded.

The whole question and the whole method lie then in the liberation of the soul from the limitations of our present natural being. In our natural life the first dominating fact is our subjection to the forms of material Nature, the outward touches of things. These present themselves to our life through the senses, and the life through the senses immediately returns upon these objects to seize upon them and deal with them, desires, attaches itself, seeks for results. The mind in all its inner sensations, reactions, emotions, habitual ways of perceiving, thinking and feeling obeys this action of the senses; the reason too carried away by the mind gives itself up to this life of the senses, this life in which the inner being is subject to the externality of things and cannot for a moment really get above it or outside the circle of its action upon us and its psychological results and reactions within us. It cannot get beyond them because there is the principle of ego by which the reason differentiates the sum of the action of Nature upon our mind, will, sense, body from her action in other minds, wills, nervous organisms, bodies; and life to us means only the way she affects our ego and the way our ego replies to her touches. We know nothing else, we seem to be nothing else; the soul itself seems then only a separate mass of mind, will, emotional and nervous reception and reaction. We may enlarge our ego, identify ourselves with the family, clan, class, country, nation, humanity even, but still the ego remains in all these disguises the root of our actions, only it finds a larger satisfaction of its separate being by these wider dealings with external things.

What acts in us is still the will of the natural being seizing upon the touches of the external world to satisfy the different phases of its personality, and the will in this seizing is always a will of desire and passion and attachment to our works and their results, the will of Nature in us; our personal will, we say, but our ego personality is a creation of Nature, it is not and cannot be our free self, our independent being. The whole is the action of the modes of Nature. It may be a tamasic action, and then we have an inert personality subject to and satisfied with the mechanical round of things, incapable of any strong effort at a freer action and mastery. Or it may be the rajasic action, and then we have the restless active personality which throws itself upon Nature and tries to make her serve its needs and desires, but does not see that its apparent mastery is a servitude, since its needs and desires are those of Nature, and while we are subject to them, there can be for us no freedom. Or it may be a sattwic action, and then we have the enlightened personality which tries to live by reason or to realise some preferred ideal of good, truth or beauty; but this reason is still subject to the appearances of Nature and these ideals are only changing phases of our personality in which we find in the end no sure rule or permanent satisfaction. We are still carried on a wheel of mutation, obeying in our circlings through the ego some Power within us and within all this, but not ourselves that Power or in union and communion with it. Still there is no freedom, no real mastery.

Yet freedom is possible. For that we have to get first away into ourselves from the action of the external world upon our senses; that is to say, we have to live inwardly and be able to hold back the natural running of the senses after their external objects. A mastery of the senses, an ability to do without all that they hanker after, is the first condition of the true soul life; only so can we begin to feel that there is a soul within us which is other than the mutations of mind in its reception of the touches of outward things, a soul which in its depths goes back to something self-existent, immutable, tranquil, self-possessed, grandiose, serene and august, master of itself and unaffected by the eager runnings of our external nature. But this cannot be done so long as we are subject to desire. For it is desire, the principle of all our superficial life, which satisfies itself with the life of the senses and finds its whole account in the play of the passions. We must get rid then of desire and, that propensity of our natural being destroyed, the passions which are its emotional results will fall into quietude; for the joy and grief of possession and of loss, success and failure, pleasant and unpleasant touches, which entertain them, will pass out of our souls. A calm equality will then be gained. And since we have still to live and act in the world and our nature in works is to seek for the fruits of our works, we must change that nature and do works without attachment to their fruits, otherwise desire and all its results remain. But how can we change this nature of the doer of works in us? By dissociating works from ego and personality, by seeing through the reason that all this is only the play of the Gunas of Nature, and by dissociating our soul from the play, by making it first of all the observer of the workings of Nature and leaving those works to the Power that is really behind them, the something in Nature which is greater than ourselves, not our personality, but the Master of the universe. But the mind will not permit all this; its nature is to run out after the senses and carry the reason and will with it. Then we must learn to still the mind. We must attain that absolute peace and stillness in which we become aware of the calm, motionless, blissful Self within us which is eternally untroubled and unaffected by the touches of things, is sufficient to itself and finds there alone its eternal satisfaction.

This Self is our self-existent being. It is not limited by our personal existence. It is the same in all existences, pervasive, equal to all things, supporting the whole universal action with its infinity, but unlimited by all that is finite, unmodified by the changings of Nature and personality. When this Self is revealed within us, when we feel its peace and stillness, we can grow into that; we can transfer the poise of our soul from its lower immergence in Nature and draw it back into the Self. We can do this by the force of the things we have attained, calm, equality, passionless impersonality. For as we grow in these things, carry them to their fullness, subject all our nature to them, we are growing into this calm, equal, passionless, impersonal, all-pervading Self. Our senses fall into that stillness and receive the touches of the world on us with a supreme tranquillity; our mind falls into stillness and becomes the calm universal witness; our ego dissolves itself into this impersonal existence. All things we see in this self which we have become in ourself; and we see this self in all; we become one being with all beings in the spiritual basis of their existence. By doing works in this selfless tranquillity and impersonality, our works cease to be ours, cease to bind or trouble us with their reactions. Nature and her Gunas weave the web of her works, but without affecting our griefless self-existent tranquillity. All is given up into that one equal and universal Brahman.

But here there are two difficulties. First, there seems to be an antinomy between this tranquil and immutable Self and the action of Nature. How then does the action at all exist or how can it continue once we have entered into the immutable Self-existence? Where in that is the will to works which would make the action of our nature possible? If we say with the Sankhya that the will is in Nature and not in the Self, still there must be a motive in Nature and the power in her to draw the soul into its workings by interest, ego and attachment, and when these things cease to reflect themselves in the soul consciousness, her power ceases and the motive of works ceases with it. But the Gita does not accept this view, which seems indeed to necessitate the existence of many Purushas and not one universal Purusha, otherwise the separate experience of the soul and its separate liberation while millions of others are still involved, would not be intelligible. Nature is not a separate principle, but the power of the Supreme going forth in cosmic creation. But if the Supreme is only this immutable Self and the individual is only something that has gone forth from him in the Power, then the moment it returns and takes its poise in the self, everything must cease except the supreme unity and the supreme calm. Secondly, even if in some mysterious way action still continues, yet since the Self is equal to all things, it cannot matter whether works are done or, if they are done, it cannot matter what work is done. Why then this insistence on the most violent and disastrous form of action, this chariot, this battle, this warrior, this divine charioteer?

The Gita answers by presenting the Supreme as something greater even than the immutable Self, more comprehensive, one who is at once this Self and the Master of works in Nature. But he directs the works of Nature with the eternal calm, the equality, the superiority to works and personality which belong to the immutable. This, we may say, is the poise of being from which he directs works, and by growing into this we are growing into his being and into the poise of divine works. From this he goes forth as the Will and Power of his being in Nature, manifests himself in all existences, is born as Man in the world, is there in the heart of all men, reveals himself as the Avatar, the divine birth in man; and as man grows into his being, it is into the divine birth that he grows. Works must be done as a sacrifice to this Lord of our works, and we must by growing into the Self realise our oneness with him in our being and see our personality as a partial manifestation of him in Nature. One with him in being, we grow one with all beings in the universe and do divine works, not as ours, but as his workings through us, for the maintenance and leading of the peoples.

This is the essential thing to be done, and once this is done, the difficulties which present themselves to Arjuna will disappear. The problem is no longer one of our personal action, for that which makes our personality becomes a thing temporal and subordinate, the question is then only one of the workings of the divine Will through us in the universe. To understand that we must know what this supreme Being is in himself and in Nature, what the workings of Nature are and what they lead to, and the intimate relation between the soul in Nature and this supreme Soul, of which Bhakti with knowledge is the foundation. The elucidation of these questions is the subject of the rest of the Gita.

The Core of the Gita's Meaning*

W HAT then is the message of the Gita and
what its working value, its spiritual utility to the human mind of
the present day after the long ages that have elapsed since it was
written and the great subsequent transformations of thought and
experience? The human mind moves always forward, alters its
viewpoint and enlarges its thought substance, and the effect of
these changes is to render past systems of thinking obsolete or,
when they are preserved, to extend, to modify and subtly or
visibly to alter their value. The vitality of an ancient doctrine
consists in the extent to which it naturally lends itself to such a
treatment; for that means that whatever may have been the limitations or the obsolescences of the form of its thought, the truth
of substance, the truth of living vision and experience on which
its system was built is still sound and retains a permanent validity
and significance. The Gita is a book that has worn extraordinarily
well and it is almost as fresh and still in its real substance quite
as new, because always renewable in experience, as when it first
appeared in or was written into the frame of the Mahabharata.
It is still received in India as one of the great bodies of doctrine
that most authoritatively govern religious thinking and its teaching acknowledged as of the highest value if not wholly accepted
by almost all shades of religious belief and opinion. Its influence
is not merely philosophic or academic but immediate and living,
an influence both for thought and action, and its ideas are
actually at work as a powerful shaping factor in the revival and
renewal of a nation and a culture. It has even been said recently
by a great voice that all we need of spiritual truth for the spiritual
life is to be found in the Gita. It would be to encourage the superstition of the book to take too literally that utterance. The truth
of the spirit is infinite and cannot be circumscribed in that
manner. Still it may be said that most of the main clues are there

* *Essays on the Gita*, pp. 543–52.

131

and that after all the later developments of spiritual experience and discovery we can still return to it for a large inspiration and guidance. Outside India too it is universally acknowledged as one of the world's great scriptures, although in Europe its thought is better understood than its secret of spiritual practice. What is it then that gives this vitality to the thought and the truth of the Gita?

The central interest of the Gita's philosophy and Yoga is its attempt, the idea with which it sets out, continues and closes, to reconcile and even effect a kind of unity between the inner spiritual truth in its most absolute and integral realisation and the outer actualities of man's life and action. A compromise between the two is common enough, but that can never be a final and satisfactory solution. An ethical rendering of spirituality is also common and has its value as a law of conduct; but that is a mental solution which does not amount to a complete practical reconciliation of the whole truth of spirit with the whole truth of life and it raises as many problems as it solves. One of these is indeed the starting-point of the Gita; it sets out with an ethical problem raised by a conflict in which we have on one side the Dharma of the man of action, a prince and warrior and leader of men, the protagonist of a great crisis, of a struggle on the physical plane, the plane of actual life, between the powers of right and justice and the powers of wrong and injustice, the demand of the destiny of the race upon him that he shall resist and give battle and establish, even though through a terrible physical struggle and a giant slaughter, a new era and reign of truth and right and justice, and on the other side the ethical sense which condemns the means and the action as a sin, recoils from the price of individual suffering and social strife, unsettling and disturbance and regards abstention from violence and battle as the only way and the one right moral attitude. A spiritualised ethics insists on Ahinsa, on non-injuring and non-killing, as the highest law of spiritual conduct. The battle, if it is to be fought out at all, must be fought on the spiritual plane and by some kind of non-resistance or refusal of participation or only by soul resistance, and if this does not succeed on the external plane, if the force of injustice conquers, the individual will still have preserved his virtue and vindicated by his example the highest ideal. On the other hand, a more insistent extreme of the inner spiritual direction, passing beyond this struggle between social duty and an absolutist ethical ideal, is apt to take the ascetic turn and to point away from life and all its aims and standards of action towards another and celestial or supracosmic state in which alone beyond the perplexed vanity and illusion of man's birth and life and death there can be a pure spiritual existence. The Gita rejects none of these things in their place, — for it insists on the performance of the social duty, the following of the Dharma for the man who has to take his share in the common action, accepts Ahinsa as part of the highest spiritual-ethical ideal and recognises the ascetic renunciation as a way of spiritual salvation. And yet it goes boldly beyond all these conflicting positions; greatly daring, it justifies all life to the spirit as a significant manifestation of the one Divine Being and asserts the compatibility of a complete human action and a complete spiritual life lived in union with the Infinite, consonant with the highest Self, expressive of the perfect Godhead.

All the problems of human life arise from the complexity of our existence, the obscurity of its essential principle and the secrecy of the inmost power that makes out its determinations and governs its purpose and its processes. If our existence were of one piece, solely material-vital or solely mental or solely spiritual, or even if the others were entirely or mainly involved in one of these or were quite latent in our subconscient or our superconscient parts, there would be nothing to perplex us; the material and vital law would be imperative or the mental would be clear to its own pure and unobstructed principle or the spiritual self-existent and self-sufficient to spirit. The animals are aware of no problems; a mental god in a world of pure mentality would admit none or would solve them all by the purity of a mental rule or the satisfaction of a rational harmony; a pure spirit would be above them and self-content in the infinite. But the existence of man is a triple web, a thing mysteriously physical-vital, mental and spiritual at once, and he knows not what are the true relations of these things, which the real reality of his life and his nature, whither the attraction of his destiny and where the sphere of his perfection.

Matter and life are his actual basis, the thing from which
he starts and on which he stands and whose requirement and
law he has to satisfy if he would exist at all on earth and in the
body. The material and vital law is a rule of survival, of struggle,
of desire and possession, of self-assertion and the satisfaction of
the body, the life and the ego. All the intellectual reasoning in
the world, all the ethical idealism and spiritual absolutism of
which the higher faculties of man are capable, cannot abolish the
reality and claim of our vital and material base or prevent the
race from following under the imperative compulsion of Nature
its aims and the satisfaction of its necessities or from making its
important problems a great and legitimate part of human destiny
and human interest and endeavour. And the intelligence of
man even, failing to find any sustenance in spiritual or ideal
solutions that solve everything else but the pressing problems of
our actual human life, often turns away from them to an exclusive acceptance of the vital and material existence and the
reasoned or instinctive pursuit of its utmost possible efficiency,
well-being and organised satisfaction. A gospel of the will to live
or the will to power of a rationalised vital and material perfection becomes the recognised Dharma of the human race and all
else is considered either a pretentious falsity or a quite subsidiary
thing, a side issue of a minor and dependent consequence.

Matter and life, however, in spite of their insistence and great
importance are not all that man is, nor can he wholly accept
mind as nothing but a servant of the life and body admitted to
certain pure enjoyments of its own as a sort of reward for its
service or regard it as no more than an extension and flower of
the vital urge, an ideal luxury contingent upon the satisfaction of
the material life. The mind much more intimately than the body
and the life is the man, and the mind as it develops insists more
and more on making the body and the life an instrument —
an indispensable instrument and yet a considerable obstacle,
otherwise there would be no problem — for its own characteristic satisfactions and self-realisation. The mind of man is not only
a vital and physical, but an intellectual, aesthetic, ethical, psychic,
emotional and dynamic intelligence, and in the sphere of each of
its tendencies its highest and strongest nature is to strain towards

some absolute of them which the frame of life will not allow it to capture wholly and embody and make here entirely real. The mental absolute of our aspiration remains as a partly grasped shining or fiery ideal which the mind can make inwardly very present to itself, inwardly imperative on its effort, and can even effectuate partly, but not compel all the facts of life into its image. There is thus an absolute, a high imperative of intellectual truth and reason sought for by our intellectual being; there is an absolute, an imperative of right and conduct aimed at by the ethical conscience; there is an absolute, an imperative of love, sympathy, compassion, oneness yearned after by our emotional and psychic nature; there is an absolute, an imperative of delight and beauty quivered to by the aesthetic soul; there is an absolute, an imperative of inner self-mastery and control of life laboured after by the dynamic will; all these are there together and impinge upon the absolute, the imperative of possession and pleasure and safe embodied existence insisted on by the vital and physical mind. And the human intelligence, since it is not able to realise entirely any of these things, much less all of them together, erects in each sphere many standards and Dharmas, standards of truth and reason, of right and conduct, of delight and beauty, of love, sympathy and oneness, of self-mastery and control, of self-preservation and possession and vital efficiency and pleasure, and tries to impose them on life. The absolute shining ideals stand far above and beyond our capacity and rare individuals approximate to them as best they can: the mass follow or profess to follow some less magnificent norm, some established possible and relative standard. Human life as a whole undergoes the attraction and yet rejects the ideal. Life resists in the strength of some obscure infinite of its own and wears down or breaks down any established mental and moral order. And this must be either because the two are quite different and disparate though meeting and interacting principles or because mind has not the clue to the whole reality of life. The clue must be sought in something greater, an unknown something above the mentality and morality of the human creature.

The mind itself has the vague sense of some surpassing factor of this kind and in the pursuit of its absolutes frequently strikes

against it. It glimpses a state, a power, a presence that is near
and within and inmost to it and yet immeasurably greater and
singularly distant and above it; it has a vision of something
more essential, more absolute than its own absolutes, intimate,
infinite, one, and it is that which we call God, Self or Spirit.
This then the mind attempts to know, enter, touch and seize
wholly, to approach it or become it, to arrive at some kind of
unity or lose itself in a complete identity with that mystery,
āścaryam. The difficulty is that this spirit in its purity seems
something yet farther than the mental absolutes from the actualities of life, something not translatable by mind into its own
terms, much less into those of life and action. Therefore we have
the intransigent absolutists of the spirit who reject the mental
and condemn the material being and yearn after a pure spiritual
existence happily purchased by the dissolution of all that we are
in life and mind, a Nirvana. The rest of spiritual effort is for these
fanatics of the Absolute a mental preparation or a compromise,
a spiritualising of life and mind as much as possible. And because
the difficulty most constantly insistent on man's mentality in
practice is that presented by the claims of his vital being, by life
and conduct and action, the direction taken by this preparatory
endeavour consists mainly in a spiritualising of the ethical
supported by the psychical mind — or rather it brings in the spiritual power and purity to aid these in enforcing their absolute
claim and to impart a greater authority than life allows to the
ethical ideal of right and truth of conduct or the psychic ideal of
love and sympathy and oneness. These things are helped to some
highest expression, given their broadest luminous basis by an
assent of the reason and will to the underlying truth of the absolute oneness of the spirit and therefore the essential oneness of all
living creatures. This kind of spirituality linked on in some way
to the demands of the normal mind of man, persuaded to the
acceptance of useful social duty and current law of social conduct, popularised by cult and ceremony and image is the outward
substance of the world's greater religions. These religions have
their individual victories, call in some ray of a higher light, impose some shadow of a larger spiritual or semi-spiritual rule,
but cannot effect a complete victory, end flatly in a compromise

and in the act of compromise are defeated by life. Its problems remain and even recur in their fiercest forms — even such as this grim problem of Kurukshetra. The idealising intellect and ethical mind hope always to eliminate them, to discover some happy device born of their own aspiration and made effective by their own imperative insistence, which will annihilate this nether untoward aspect of life; but it endures and is not eliminated. The spiritualised intelligence on the other hand offers indeed by the voice of religion the promise of some victorious millennium hereafter, but meanwhile half-convinced of terrestrial impotence, persuaded that the soul is a stranger and intruder upon earth, declares that after all not here in the life of the body or in the collective life of mortal man but in some immortal Beyond lies the heaven or the Nirvana where alone is to be found the true spiritual existence.

It is here that the Gita intervenes with a restatement of the truth of the Spirit, of the Self, of God and of the world and Nature. It extends and remoulds the truth evolved by a later thought from the ancient Upanishads and ventures with assured steps on an endeavour to apply its solving power to the problem of life and action. The solution offered by the Gita does not disentangle all the problem as it offers itself to modern mankind; as stated here to a more ancient mentality, it does not meet the insistent pressure of the present mind of man for a collective advance, does not respond to its cry for a collective life that will at last embody a greater rational and ethical and, if possible, even a dynamic spiritual ideal. Its call is to the individual who has become capable of a complete spiritual existence; but for the rest of the race it prescribes only a gradual advance, to be wisely effected by following out faithfully with more and more of intelligence and moral purpose and with a final turn to spirituality the law of their nature. Its message touches the other smaller solutions but, even when it accepts them partly, it is to point them beyond themselves to a higher and more integral secret into which as yet only the few individuals have shown themselves fit to enter.

The Gita's message to the mind that follows after the vital and material life is that all life is indeed a manifestation of the

universal Power in the individual, a derivation from the Self, a
ray from the Divine, but actually it figures the Self and the
Divine veiled in a disguising Maya, and to pursue the lower life
for its own sake is to persist in a stumbling path and to en-
throne our nature's obscure ignorance and not at all to find the
true truth and complete law of existence. A gospel of the will
to live, the will to power, of the satisfaction of desire, of the glori-
fication of mere force and strength, of the worship of the ego and
its vehement acquisitive self-will and tireless self-regarding intellect is the gospel of the Asura and it can lead only to some
gigantic ruin and perdition. The vital and material man must
accept for his government a religious and social and ideal
Dharma by which, while satisfying desire and interest under right
restrictions, he can train and subdue his lower personality and
scrupulously attune it to a higher law both of the personal and
the communal life.

The Gita's message to the mind occupied with the pursuit of
intellectual, ethical and social standards, the mind that insists
on salvation by the observance of established Dharmas, the
moral law, social duty and function or the solutions of the
liberated intelligence, is that this is indeed a very necessary stage,
the Dharma has indeed to be observed and, rightly observed, can
raise the stature of the spirit and prepare and serve the spiritual
life, but still it is not the complete and last truth of existence.
The soul of man has to go beyond to some more absolute Dharma
of man's spiritual and immortal nature. And this can only be
done if we repress and get rid of the ignorant formulations of
the lower mental elements and the falsehood of egoistic personality, impersonalise the action of the intelligence and will, live in
the identity of the one self in all, break out of all ego-moulds into
the impersonal spirit. The mind moves under the limiting compulsion of the triple lower nature, it erects its standards in obedience to the tamasic, rajasic or at highest the sattwic qualities;
but the destiny of the soul is a divine perfection and liberation
and that can only be based in the freedom of our highest self, can
only be found by passing through its vast impersonality and universality beyond mind into the integral light of the immeasurable
Godhead and supreme Infinite who is beyond all Dharmas.

The Gita's message to those, absolutist seekers of the Infinite, who carry impersonality to an exclusive extreme, entertain an intolerant passion for the extinction of life and action and would have as the one ultimate aim and ideal an endeavour to cease from all individual being in the pure silence of the ineffable Spirit, is that this is indeed one path of journey and entry into the Infinite, but the most difficult, the ideal of inaction a dangerous thing to hold up by precept or example before the world, this way, though great, yet not the best way for man and this knowledge, though true, yet not the integral knowledge. The Supreme, the all-conscious Self, the Godhead, the Infinite is not solely a spiritual existence remote and ineffable; he is here in the universe at once hidden and expressed through man and the gods and through all beings and in all that is. And it is by finding him not only in some immutable silence but in the world and its beings and in all self and in all Nature, it is by raising to an integral as well as to a highest union with him all the activities of the intelligence, the heart, the will, the life that man can solve at once his inner riddle of Self and God and the outer problem of his active human existence. Made Godlike, God-becoming, he can enjoy the infinite breadth of a supreme spiritual consciousness that is reached through works no less than through love and knowledge. Immortal and free, he can continue his human action from that highest level and transmute it into a supreme and all-embracing divine activity, — that indeed is the ultimate crown and significance here of all works and living and sacrifice and the world's endeavour.

This highest message is first for those who have the strength to follow after it, the master men, the great spirits, the God-knowers, God-doers, God-lovers who can live in God and for God and do their work joyfully for him in the world, a divine work uplifted above the restless darkness of the human mind and the false limitations of the ego. At the same time, and here we get the gleam of a larger promise which we may even extend to the hope of a collective turn towards perfection, — for if there is hope for man, why should there not be hope for mankind? — the Gita declares that all can if they will, even to the lowest and sinfullest among men, enter into the path of this

Yoga. And if there is a true self-surrender and an absolute
unegoistic faith in the indwelling Divinity, success is certain in
this path. The decisive turn is needed; there must be an abiding
belief in the Spirit, a sincere and insistent will to live in the
Divine, to be in self one with him and in Nature — where too we
are an eternal portion of his being — one with his greater spiritual Nature, God-possessed in all our members and Godlike.

The Gita in the development of its idea raises many issues,
such as the determinism of Nature, the significance of the universal manifestation and the ultimate status of the liberated soul,
questions that have been the subject of unending and inconclu-
sive debate. It is not necessary in this series of essays of which
the object is a scrutiny and positive affirmation of the substance
of the Gita and a disengaging of its contribution to the abiding
spiritual thought of humanity and its kernel of living practice,
to enter far into these discussions or to consider where we
may differ from its standpoint or conclusions, make any reserves
in our assent or even, strong in later experience, go beyond its
metaphysical teaching or its Yoga. It will be sufficient to close
with a formulation of the living message it still brings for man
the eternal seeker and discoverer to guide him through the
present circuits and the possible steeper ascent of his life up to
the luminous heights of his spirit.

*

It is not a fact that the Gita gives the whole base of Sri
Aurobindo's message; for the Gita seems to admit the cessation of birth in the world as the ultimate aim or at least the
ultimate culmination of yoga; it does not bring forward the
idea of spiritual evolution or the idea of the higher planes and the
supramental Truth-Consciousness and the bringing down of that
consciousness as the means of the complete transformation of
earthly life.

(XXII, p. 69)

INTEGRAL YOGA

The Four Aids*

Y OGA-SIDDHI, the perfection that comes from the practice of Yoga, can be best attained by the combined working of four great instruments. There is, first, the knowledge of the truths, principles, powers and processes that govern the realisation — *śāstra*. Next comes a patient and persistent action on the lines laid down by the knowledge, the force of our personal effort — *utsāha*. There intervenes, third, uplifting our knowledge and effort into the domain of spiritual experience, the direct suggestion, example and influence of the Teacher — *guru*. Last comes the instrumentality of Time — *kāla*; for in all things there is a cycle of their action and a period of the divine movement.

The supreme Shastra of the integral Yoga is the eternal Veda secret in the heart of every thinking and living being. The lotus of the eternal knowledge and the eternal perfection is a bud closed and folded up within us. It opens swiftly or gradually, petal by petal, through successive realisations, once the mind of man begins to turn towards the Eternal, once his heart, no longer compressed and confined by attachment to finite appearances, becomes enamoured, in whatever degree, of the Infinite. All life, all thought, all energising of the faculties, all experiences passive or active, become thenceforward so many shocks which disintegrate the teguments of the soul and remove the obstacles to the inevitable efflorescence. He who chooses the Infinite has been chosen by the Infinite. He has received the divine touch without which there is no awakening, no opening of the spirit; but once it is received, attainment is sure, whether conquered swiftly in the course of one human life or pursued patiently through many stadia of the cycle of existence in the manifested universe.

* *The Synthesis of Yoga*, pp. 47–62.

Nothing can be taught to the mind which is not already concealed as potential knowledge in the unfolding soul of the creature. So also all perfection of which the outer man is capable, is
only a realising of the eternal perfection of the Spirit within him.
We know the Divine and become the Divine, because we are That
already in our secret nature. All teaching is a revealing, all becoming is an unfolding. Self-attainment is the secret; self-knowledge and an increasing consciousness are the means and the
process.

The usual agency of this revealing is the Word, the thing
heard (*śruta*). The Word may come to us from within; it may
come to us from without. But in either case, it is only an agency
for setting the hidden knowledge to work. The word within may
be the utterance of the inmost soul in us which is always open to
the Divine or it may be the word of the secret and universal Teacher who is seated in the hearts of all. There are rare cases in
which none other is needed, for all the rest of the Yoga is an unfolding under that constant touch and guidance; the lotus of the
knowledge discloses itself from within by the power of irradiat-
ing effulgence which proceeds from the Dweller in the lotus of the
heart. Great indeed, but few are those to whom self-knowledge
from within is thus sufficient and who do not need to pass under
the dominant influence of a written book or a living teacher.

Ordinarily, the Word from without, representative of the
Divine, is needed as an aid in the work of self-unfolding; and it
may be either a word from the past or the more powerful word of
the living Guru. In some cases this representative word is only
taken as a sort of excuse for the inner power to awaken and manifest; it is, as it were, a concession of the omnipotent and omniscient Divine to the generality of a law that governs Nature.
Thus it is said in the Upanishads of Krishna, son of Devaki, that
he received a word of the Rishi Ghora and had the knowledge.
So Ramakrishna, having attained by his own internal effort the
central illumination, accepted several teachers in the different
paths of Yoga, but always showed in the manner and swiftness
of his realisation that this acceptance was a concession to the
general rule by which effective knowledge must be received as by
a disciple from a Guru.

But usually the representative influence occupies a much larger place in the life of the Sadhaka. If the Yoga is guided by a received written Shastra, — some Word from the past which embodies the experience of former Yogins, — it may be practised either by personal effort alone or with the aid of a Guru. The spiritual knowledge is then gained through meditation on the truths that are taught and it is made living and conscious by their realisation in the personal experience; the Yoga proceeds by the results of prescribed methods taught in a Scripture or a tradition and reinforced and illumined by the instructions of the Master. This is a narrower practice, but safe and effective within its limits, because it follows a well-beaten track to a long familiar goal.

For the Sadhaka of the integral Yoga it is necessary to remember that no written Shastra, however great its authority or however large its spirit, can be more than a partial expression of the eternal Knowledge. He will use, but never bind himself even by the greatest Scripture. Where the Scripture is profound, wide, catholic, it may exercise upon him an influence for the highest good and of incalculable importance. It may be associated in his experience with his awakening to crowning verities and his realisation of the highest experiences. His Yoga may be governed for a long time by one Scripture or by several successively, — if it is in the line of the great Hindu tradition, by the Gita, for example, the Upanishads, the Veda. Or it may be a good part of his development to include in its material a richly varied experience of the truths of many Scriptures and make the future opulent with all that is best in the past. But in the end he must take his station, or better still, if he can, always and from the beginning he must live in his own soul beyond the written Truth, — *śabdabrahmātivartate* — beyond all that he has heard and all that he has yet to hear, — *śrotavyasya śrutasya ca.* For he is not the Sadhaka of a book or of many books; he is a Sadhaka of the Infinite.

Another kind of Shastra is not Scripture, but a statement of the science and methods, the effective principles and way of working of the path of Yoga which the Sadhaka elects to follow. Each path has its Shastra, either written or traditional, passing from mouth to mouth through a long line of Teachers. In India a great authority, a high reverence even is ordinarily attached to the written or traditional teaching. All the lines of the Yoga are supposed to be fixed and the Teacher who has received the Shastra by tradition and realised it in practice guides the disciple along the immemorial tracks. One often even hears the objection urged against a new practice, a new Yogic teaching, the adoption of a new formula, "It is not according to the Shastra." But neither in fact nor in the actual practice of the Yogins is there really any such entire rigidity of an iron door shut against new truth, fresh revelation, widened experience. The written or traditional teaching expresses the knowledge and experiences of many centuries systematised, organised, made attainable to the beginner. Its importance and utility are therefore immense. But a great freedom of variation and development is always practicable. Even so highly scientific a system as Rajayoga can be practised on other lines than the organised method of Patanjali. Each of the three paths, *trimārga*,[1] breaks into many bypaths which meet again at the goal. The general knowledge on which the Yoga depends is fixed, but the order, the succession, the devices, the forms must be allowed to vary; for the needs and particular impulsions of the individual nature have to be satisfied even while the general truths remain firm and constant.

An integral and synthetic Yoga needs especially not to be bound by any written or traditional Shastra; for while it embraces the knowledge received from the past, it seeks to organise it anew for the present and the future. An absolute liberty of experience and of the restatement of knowledge in new terms and new combinations is the condition of its self-formation. Seeking to embrace all life in itself, it is in the position not of a pilgrim following the highroad to his destination, but, to that extent at least, of a path-finder hewing his way through a virgin forest. For Yoga has long diverged from life and the ancient systems which sought to embrace it, such as those of our Vedic forefathers, are far away from us, expressed in terms which are no longer accessible, thrown into forms which are no longer applicable. Since then mankind has moved forward on the current of eternal Time and the same problem has to be approached from a new starting-point.

[1] The triple path of Knowledge, Devotion and Works.

By this Yoga we not only seek the Infinite, but we call upon the Infinite to unfold himself in human life. Therefore the Shastra of our Yoga must provide for an infinite liberty in the receptive human soul. A free adaptability in the manner and type of the individual's acceptance of the Universal and Transcendent into himself is the right condition for the full spiritual life in man. Vivekananda, pointing out that the unity of all religions must necessarily express itself by an increasing richness of variety in its forms, said once that the perfect state of that essential unity would come when each man had his own religion, when not bound by sect or traditional form he followed the free self-adaptation of his nature in its relations with the Supreme. So also one may say that the perfection of the integral Yoga will come when each man is able to follow his own path of Yoga, pursuing the development of his own nature in its upsurging towards that which transcends the nature. For freedom is the final law and the last consummation.

Meanwhile certain general lines have to be formed which may help to guide the thought and practice of the Sadhaka. But these must take, as much as possible, forms of general truths, general statements of principle, the most powerful broad directions of effort and development rather than a fixed system which has to be followed as a routine. All Shastra is the outcome of past experience and a help to future experience. It is an aid and a partial guide. It puts up signposts, gives the names of the main roads and the already explored directions, so that the traveller may know whither and by what paths he is proceeding.

The rest depends on personal effort and experience and upon the power of the Guide.

The development of the experience in its rapidity, its amplitude, the intensity and power of its results, depends primarily, in the beginning of the path and long after, on the aspiration and personal effort of the Sadhaka. The process of Yoga is a turning of the human soul from the egoistic state of consciousness absorbed in the outward appearances and attractions of things to a higher state in which the Transcendent and Universal can pour itself into the individual mould and transform it. The first determining element of the Siddhi is, therefore, the intensity of the turning, the force which directs the soul inward. The power of aspiration of the heart, the force of the will, the concentration of the mind, the perseverance and determination of the applied energy are the measure of that intensity. The ideal Sadhaka should be able to say in the Biblical phrase, "My zeal for the Lord has eaten me up." It is this zeal for the Lord, *utsāha*, the zeal of the whole nature for its divine results, *vyākulatā*, the heart's eagerness for the attainment of the Divine, — that devours the ego and breaks up the limitations of its petty and narrow mould for the full and wide reception of that which it seeks, that which, being universal, exceeds and, being transcendent, surpasses even the largest and highest individual self and nature.

But this is only one side of the force that works for perfection. The process of the integral Yoga has three stages, not indeed sharply distinguished or separate, but in a certain measure successive. There must be, first, the effort towards at least an initial and enabling self-transcendence and contact with the Divine; next, the reception of that which transcends, that with which we have gained communion, into ourselves for the transformation of our whole conscious being; last, the utilisation of our transformed humanity as a divine centre in the world. So long as the contact with the Divine is not in some considerable degree established, so long as there is not some measure of sustained identity, *sāyujya*, the element of personal effort must normally predominate. But in proportion as this contact establishes itself, the Sadhaka must become conscious that a force other than his own, a force transcending his egoistic endeavour and capacity, is at work in him and to this Power he learns progressively to submit himself and delivers up to it the charge of his Yoga. In the end his own will and force become one with the higher Power; he merges them in the divine Will and its transcendent and universal Force. He finds it thenceforward presiding over the necessary transformation of his mental, vital and physical being with an impartial wisdom and provident effectivity of which the eager and interested ego is not capable.

It is when this identification and this self-merging are complete that the divine centre in the world is ready. Purified, liberated, plastic, illumined, it can begin to serve as a means for the direct action of a supreme Power in the larger Yoga of humanity or superhumanity, of the earth's spiritual progression or its transformation.

Always indeed it is the higher Power that acts. Our sense of personal effort and aspiration comes from the attempt of the egoistic mind to identify itself in a wrong and imperfect way with the workings of the divine Force. It persists in applying to experience on a supernormal plane the ordinary terms of mentality which it applies to its normal experiences in the world. In the world we act with the sense of egoism; we claim the universal forces that work in us as our own; we claim as the effect of our personal will, wisdom, force, virtue the selective, formative, progressive action of the Transcendent in this frame of mind, life and body. Enlightenment brings to us the knowledge that the ego is only an instrument; we begin to perceive and feel that these things are our own in the sense that they belong to our supreme and integral Self, one with the Transcendent, not to the instrumental ego. Our limitations and distortions are our contribution to the working; the true power in it is the Divine's. When the human ego realises that its will is a tool, its wisdom ignorance and childishness, its power an infant's groping, its virtue a pretentious impurity, and learns to trust itself to that which transcends it, that is its salvation. The apparent freedom and self-assertion of our personal being to which we are so profoundly attached, conceal a most pitiable subjection to a thousand suggestions, impulsions, forces which we have made extraneous to our little person. Our ego, boasting of freedom, is at every moment the slave, toy and puppet of countless beings, powers, forces, influences in universal Nature. The self-abnegation of the ego in the Divine is its self-fulfilment; its surrender to that which transcends it is its liberation from bonds and limits and its perfect freedom.

But still, in the practical development, each of the three stages has its necessity and utility and must be given its time or its place. It will not do, it cannot be safe or effective to begin with the last and highest alone. It would not be the right course, either, to leap prematurely from one to another. For even if from the beginning we recognise in mind and heart the Supreme, there are elements of the nature which long prevent the recognition from becoming realisation. But without realisation our mental belief cannot become a dynamic reality; it is still only a figure of knowledge, not a living truth, an idea, not yet a power. And even if realisation has begun, it may be dangerous to imagine or to assume too soon that we are altogether in the hands of the Supreme or are acting as his instrument. That assumption may introduce a calamitous falsity; it may produce a helpless inertia or, magnifying the movements of the ego with the Divine Name, it may disastrously distort and ruin the whole course of the Yoga. There is a period, more or less prolonged, of internal effort and struggle in which the individual will has to reject the darkness and distortions of the lower nature and to put itself resolutely or vehemently on the side of the divine Light. The mental energies, the heart's emotions, the vital desires, the very physical being have to be compelled into the right attitude or trained to admit and answer to the right influences. It is only then, only when this has been truly done, that the surrender of the lower to the higher can be effected, because the sacrifice has become acceptable.

The personal will of the Sadhaka has first to seize on the egoistic energies and turn them towards the light and the right; once turned, he has still to train them to recognise that always, always to accept, always to follow that. Progressing, he learns, still using the personal will, personal effort, personal energies, to employ them as representatives of the higher Power and in conscious obedience to the higher Influence. Progressing yet farther, his will, effort, energy become no longer personal and separate, but activities of that higher Power and Influence at work in the individual. But there is still a sort of gulf of distance which necessitates an obscure process of transit, not always accurate, sometimes even very distorting, between the divine Origin and the emerging human current. At the end of the progress, with the progressive disappearance of egoism and impurity and ignorance, this last separation is removed; all in the individual becomes the divine working.

As the supreme Shastra of the integral Yoga is the eternal Veda secret in the heart of every man, so its supreme Guide and Teacher is the inner Guide, the World-Teacher, *jagad-guru*, secret within us. It is he who destroys our darkness by the resplendent light of his knowledge; that light becomes within us the increasing glory of his own self-revelation. He discloses progressively in us his own nature of freedom, bliss, love, power, immortal being. He sets above us his divine example as our ideal and transforms the lower existence into a reflection of that which it contemplates. By the inpouring of his own influence and presence into us he enables the individual being to attain to identity with the universal and transcendent.

What is his method and his system? He has no method and every method. His system is a natural organisation of the highest processes and movements of which the nature is capable. Applying themselves even to the pettiest details and to the actions the most insignificant in their appearance with as much care and thoroughness as to the greatest, they in the end lift all into the Light and transform all. For in his Yoga there is nothing too small to be used and nothing too great to be attempted. As the servant and disciple of the Master has no business with pride or egoism because all is done for him from above, so also he has no right to despond because of his personal deficiencies or the stumblings of his nature. For the Force that works in him is impersonal — or superpersonal — and infinite.

The full recognition of this inner Guide, Master of the Yoga, lord, light, enjoyer and goal of all sacrifice and effort, is of the utmost importance in the path of integral perfection. It is immaterial whether he is first seen as an impersonal Wisdom, Love and Power behind all things, as an Absolute manifesting in the relative and attracting it, as one's highest Self and the highest Self of all, as a Divine Person within us and in the world, in one of his — or her — numerous forms and names or as the ideal which the mind conceives. In the end we perceive that he is all and more than all these things together. The mind's door of entry to the conception of him must necessarily vary according to the past evolution and the present nature.

This inner Guide is often veiled at first by the very intensity of our personal effort and by the ego's preoccupation with itself and its aims. As we gain in clarity and the turmoil of egoistic effort gives place to a calmer self-knowledge, we recognise the source of the growing light within us. We recognise it retrospectively as we realise how all our obscure and conflicting movements have been determined towards an end that we only now begin to perceive, how even before our entrance into the path of the Yoga the evolution of our life has been designedly led towards its turning point. For now we begin to understand the sense of our struggles and efforts, successes and failures. At last we are able to seize the meaning of our ordeals and sufferings and can appreciate the help that was given us by all that hurt and resisted and the utility of our very falls and stumblings. We recognise this divine leading afterwards, not retrospectively but immediately, in the moulding of our thoughts by a transcendent Seer, of our will and actions by an all-embracing Power, of our emotional life by an all-attracting and all-assimilating Bliss and Love. We recognise it too in a more personal relation that from the first touched us or at the last seizes us; we feel the eternal presence of a supreme Master, Friend, Lover, Teacher. We recognise it in the essence of our being as that develops into likeness and oneness with a greater and wider existence; for we perceive that this miraculous development is not the result of our own efforts; an eternal Perfection is moulding us into its own image. One who is the Lord or Ishwara of the Yogic philosophies, the Guide in the conscious being (*caitya guru* or *antaryamin*), the Absolute of the thinker, the Unknowable of the Agnostic, the universal Force of the materialist, the supreme Soul and the supreme Shakti, the One who is differently named and imaged by the religions, is the Master of our Yoga.

To see, know, become and fulfil this One in our inner selves and in all our outer nature, was always the secret goal and becomes now the conscious purpose of our embodied existence.

To be conscious of him in all parts of our being and equally in all that the dividing mind sees as outside our being, is the consummation of the individual consciousness. To be possessed by him and possess him in ourselves and in all things is the term of all empire and mastery. To enjoy him in all experience of passivity and activity, of peace and of power, of unity and of difference is the happiness which the *jīva*, the individual soul manifested in the world, is obscurely seeking. This is the entire definition of the aim of integral Yoga; it is the rendering in personal experience of the truth which universal Nature has hidden in herself and which she travails to discover. It is the conversion of the human soul into the divine soul and of natural life into divine living.

The surest way towards this integral fulfilment is to find the Master of the secret who dwells within us, open ourselves constantly to the divine Power which is also the divine Wisdom and Love and trust to it to effect the conversion. But it is difficult for the egoistic consciousness to do this at all at the beginning. And, if done at all, it is still difficult to do it perfectly and in every strand of our nature. It is difficult at first because our egoistic habits of thought, of sensation, of feeling block up the avenues by which we can arrive at the perception that is needed. It is difficult afterwards because the faith, the surrender, the courage requisite in this path are not easy to the ego-clouded soul. The divine working is not the working which the egoistic mind desires or approves; for it uses error in order to arrive at truth, suffering in order to arrive at bliss, imperfection in order to arrive at perfection. The ego cannot see where it is being led; it revolts against the leading, loses confidence, loses courage. These failings would not matter; for the divine Guide within is not offended by our revolt, not discouraged by our want of faith or repelled by our weakness; he has the entire love of the mother and the entire patience of the teacher. But by withdrawing our assent from the guidance we lose the consciousness, though not all the actuality — not, in any case, the eventuality — of its benefit. And we withdraw our assent because we fail to distinguish our higher Self from the lower through which he is preparing his self-revelation. As in the world, so in ourselves, we cannot see God because of his workings and, especially, because he works in us through our nature and not by a succession of arbitrary miracles. Man demands miracles that he may have faith; he wishes to be dazzled in order that he may see. And this impatience, this ignorance may turn into a great danger and disaster if, in our revolt against the divine leading, we call in another distorting Force more satisfying to our impulses and desires and ask it to guide us and give it the Divine Name.

But while it is difficult for man to believe in something unseen within himself, it is easy for him to believe in something which he can image as extraneous to himself. The spiritual progress of most human beings demands an extraneous support, an object of faith outside us. It needs an external image of God; or it needs a human representative, — Incarnation, Prophet or Guru; or it demands both and receives them. For according to the need of the human soul the Divine manifests himself as deity, as human divine or in simple humanity, — using that thick disguise, which so successfully conceals the Godhead, for a means of transmission of his guidance.

The Hindu discipline of spirituality provides for this need of the soul by the conceptions of the Ishta Devata, the Avatar and the Guru. By the Ishta Devata, the chosen deity, is meant, — not some inferior Power, but a name and form of the transcendent and universal Godhead. Almost all religions either have as their base or make use of some such name and form of the Divine. Its necessity for the human soul is evident. God is the All and more than the All. But that which is more than the All, how shall man conceive? And even the All is at first too hard for him; for he himself in his active consciousness is a limited and selective formation and can open himself only to that which is in harmony with his limited nature. There are things in the All which are too hard for his comprehension or seem too terrible to his sensitive emotions and cowering sensations. Or, simply, he cannot conceive as the Divine, cannot approach or cannot recognise something that is too much out of the circle of his ignorant or partial conceptions. It is necessary for him to conceive God in his own image or in some form that is beyond himself but consonant with his highest tendencies and seizable by his feelings or his intelligence. Otherwise it would be difficult for him to come into contact and communion with the Divine.

Even then his nature calls for a human intermediary so that he may feel the Divine in something entirely close to his own humanity and sensible in a human influence and example. This call is satisfied by the Divine manifest in a human appearance, the Incarnation, the Avatar — Krishna, Christ, Buddha. Or if this is too hard for him to conceive, the Divine represents himself through a less marvellous intermediary, — Prophet or Teacher. For many who cannot conceive or are unwilling to accept the Divine Man, are ready to open themselves to the supreme man, terming him not incarnation but world-teacher or divine representative.

This also is not enough; a living influence, a living example, a present instruction is needed. For it is only the few who can make the past Teacher and his teaching, the past Incarnation and his example and influence a living force in their lives. For this need also the Hindu discipline provides in the relation of the Guru and the disciple. The Guru may sometimes be the Incarnation or World-Teacher; but it is sufficient that he should represent to the disciple the divine wisdom, convey to him something of the divine ideal or make him feel the realised relation of the human soul with the Eternal.

The Sadhaka of the integral Yoga will make use of all these aids according to his nature; but it is necessary that he should shun their limitations and cast from himself that exclusive tendency of egoistic mind which cries, "My God, my Incarnation, my Prophet, my Guru," and opposes it to all other realisation in a sectarian or a fanatical spirit. All sectarianism, all fanaticism must be shunned; for it is inconsistent with the integrity of the divine realisation.

On the contrary, the Sadhaka of the integral Yoga will not be satisfied until he has included all other names and forms of Deity in his own conception, seen his own Ishta Devata in all others, unified all Avatars in the unity of Him who descends in the Avatar, welded the truth in all teachings into the harmony of the Eternal Wisdom.

Nor should he forget the aim of these external aids which is to awaken his soul to the Divine within him. Nothing has been finally accomplished if that has not been accomplished. It is not sufficient to worship Krishna, Christ or Buddha without, if there is not the revealing and the formation of the Buddha, the Christ or Krishna in ourselves. And all other aids equally have no other purpose; each is a bridge between man's unconverted state and the revelation of the Divine within him.

The Teacher of the integral Yoga will follow as far as he may the method of the Teacher within us. He will lead the disciple through the nature of the disciple. Teaching, example, influence, — these are the three instruments of the Guru. But the wise Teacher will not seek to impose himself or his opinions on the passive acceptance of the receptive mind; he will throw in only what is productive and sure as a seed which will grow under the divine fostering within. He will seek to awaken much more than to instruct; he will aim at the growth of the faculties and the experiences by a natural process and free expansion. He will give a method as an aid, as a utilisable device, not as an imperative formula or a fixed routine. And he will be on his guard against any turning of the means into a limitation, against the mechanising of process. His whole business is to awaken the divine light and set working the divine force of which he himself is only a means and an aid, a body or a channel.

The example is more powerful than the instruction; but it is not the example of the outward acts nor that of the personal character, which is of most importance. These have their place and their utility; but what will most stimulate aspiration in others is the central fact of the divine realisation within him governing his whole life and inner state and all his activities. This is the universal and essential element; the rest belongs to individual person and circumstance. It is this dynamic realisation that the Sadhaka must feel and reproduce in himself according to his own nature; he need not strive after an imitation from outside which may well be sterilising rather than productive of right and natural fruits.

Influence is more important than example. Influence is not

the outward authority of the Teacher over his disciple, but the power of his contact, of his presence, of the nearness of his soul to the soul of another, infusing into it, even though in silence, that which he himself is and possesses. This is the supreme sign of the Master. For the greatest Master is much less a Teacher than a Presence pouring the divine consciousness and its constituting light and power and purity and bliss into all who are receptive around him.

And it shall also be a sign of the teacher of the integral Yoga that he does not arrogate to himself Guruhood in a humanly vain and self-exalting spirit. His work, if he has one, is a trust from above, he himself a channel, a vessel or a representative. He is a man helping his brothers, a child leading children, a Light kindling other lights, an awakened Soul awakening souls, at highest a Power or Presence of the Divine calling to him other powers of the Divine.

The Sadhaka who has all these aids is sure of his goal. Even a fall will be for him only a means of rising and death a passage towards fulfilment. For once on his path, birth and death become only processes in the development of his being and the stages of his journey.

Time is the remaining aid needed for the effectivity of the process. Time presents itself to human effort as an enemy or a friend, as a resistance, a medium or an instrument. But always it is really the instrument of the soul.

Time is a field of circumstances and forces meeting and working out a resultant progression whose course it measures. To the ego it is a tyrant or a resistance, to the Divine an instrument. Therefore, while our effort is personal, Time appears as a resistance, for it presents to us all the obstruction of the forces that conflict with our own. When the divine working and the personal are combined in our consciousness, it appears as a medium and condition. When the two become one, it appears as a servant and instrument.

The ideal attitude of the Sadhaka towards Time is to have an endless patience as if he had all eternity for his fulfilment and yet to develop the energy that shall realise now and with an ever-increasing mastery and pressure of rapidity till it reaches the miraculous instantaneousness of the supreme divine Transformation.

*

There are many ways of opening to this Divine Consciousness or entering into it. My way which I show to others by a constant practice is to go inward into oneself, to open by aspiration to the Divine and once one is conscious of it and its action, to give oneself to it entirely. This self-giving means not to ask for anything but the constant contact or union with the Divine Consciousness, to aspire for its peace, power, light and felicity, but to ask nothing else and in life and action to be its instrument only for whatever work it gives one to do in the world. If one can once open and feel the Divine Force, the Power of the Spirit working in the mind and heart and body, the rest is a matter of remaining faithful to it, calling for it always, allowing it to do its work when it comes and rejecting every other and inferior force that belongs to the lower consciousness and the lower nature.

(XXVII, p. 416)

The Principle of the Integral Yoga*

THE principle of Yoga is the turning of one or of all powers of our human existence into a means of reaching the divine Being. In an ordinary Yoga one main power of being or one group of its powers is made the means, vehicle, path. In a synthetic Yoga all powers will be combined and included in the transmuting instrumentation.

In Hathayoga the instrument is the body and life. All the power of the body is stilled, collected, purified, heightened, concentrated to its utmost limits or beyond any limits by Asana and other physical processes; the power of the life too is similarly purified, heightened, concentrated by Asana and Pranayama. This concentration of powers is then directed towards that physical centre in which the divine consciousness sits concealed in the human body. The power of Life, Nature-power, coiled up with all its secret forces asleep in the lowest nervous plexus of the earth-being, — for only so much escapes into waking action in our normal operations as is sufficient for the limited uses of human life, — rises awakened through centre after centre and awakens, too, in its ascent and passage the forces of each successive nodus of our being, the nervous life, the heart of emotion and ordinary mentality, the speech, sight, will, the higher knowledge, till through and above the brain it meets with and it becomes one with the divine consciousness.

In Rajayoga the chosen instrument is the mind. Our ordinary mentality is first disciplined, purified and directed towards the divine Being, then by a summary process of Asana and Pranayama the physical force of our being is stilled and concentrated, the life-force released into a rhythmic movement capable of cessation and concentrated into a higher power of its upward action, the mind, supported and strengthened by this greater action and concentration of the body and life upon which

* The Synthesis of Yoga, pp. 583–89.

157

it rests, is itself purified of all its unrest and emotion and its habitual thought-waves, liberated from distraction and dispersion, given its highest force of concentration, gathered up into a trance of absorption. Two objects, the one temporal, the other eternal, are gained by this discipline. Mind-power develops in another concentrated action abnormal capacities of knowledge, effective will, deep light of reception, powerful light of thought-radiation which are altogether beyond the narrow range of our normal mentality; it arrives at the Yogic or occult powers around which there has been woven so much quite dispensable and yet perhaps salutary mystery. But the one final end and the one all-important gain is that the mind, stilled and cast into a concentrated trance, can lose itself in the divine consciousness and the soul be made free to unite with the divine Being.

The triple way takes for its chosen instruments the three main powers of the mental soul-life of the human being. Knowledge selects the reason and the mental vision and it makes them by purification, concentration and a certain discipline of a God-directed seeking its means for the greatest knowledge and the greatest vision of all, God-knowledge and God-vision. Its aim is to see, know and be the Divine. Works, action selects for its instrument the will of the doer of works; it makes life an offering of sacrifice to the Godhead and by purification, concentration and a certain discipline of subjection to the divine Will a means for contact and increasing unity of the soul of man with the divine Master of the universe. Devotion selects the emotional and aesthetic powers of the soul and by turning them all Godward in a perfect purity, intensity, infinite passion of seeking makes them a means of God-possession in one or many relations of unity with the Divine Being. All aim in their own way at a union or unity of the human soul with the supreme Spirit.

Each Yoga in its process has the character of the instrument it uses; thus the Hathayogic process is psycho-physical, the Rajayogic mental and psychic, the way of knowledge is spiritual and cognitive, the way of devotion spiritual, emotional and aesthetic, the way of works spiritual and dynamic by action. Each is guided in the ways of its own characteristic power. But all power is in the end one, all power is really soul-power. In the ordinary process of life, body and mind this truth is quite obscured by the dispersed, dividing and distributive action of Nature which is the normal condition of all our functionings, although even there it is in the end evident; for all material energy contains hidden the vital, mental, psychic, spiritual energy and in the end it must release these forms of the one Shakti, the vital energy conceals and liberates into action all the other forms, the mental supporting itself on the life and body and their powers and functionings contains undeveloped or only partially developed the psychic and the spiritual power of the being. But when by Yoga any of these powers is taken up from the dispersed and distributive action, raised to its highest degree, concentrated, it becomes manifest soul-power and reveals the essential unity. Therefore the Hathayogic process has too its pure psychic and spiritual result, the Rajayogic arrives by psychic means at a spiritual consummation. The triple way may appear to be altogether mental and spiritual in its way of seeking and its objectives, but it can be attended by results more characteristic of the other paths, which offer themselves in a spontaneous and involuntary flowering, and for the same reason, because soul-power is all-power and where it reaches its height in one direction its other possibilities also begin to show themselves in fact or in incipient potentiality. This unity at once suggests the possibility of a synthetic Yoga.

Tantric discipline is in its nature a synthesis. It has seized on the large universal truth that there are two poles of being whose essential unity is the secret of existence, Brahman and Shakti, Spirit and Nature, and that Nature is power of the spirit or rather is spirit as power. To raise nature in man into manifest power of spirit is its method and it is the whole nature that it gathers up for the spiritual conversion. It includes in its system of instrumentation the forceful Hathayogic process and especially the opening up of the nervous centres and the passage through them of the awakened Shakti on her way to her union with the Brahman, the subtler stress of the Rajayogic purification, meditation and concentration, the leverage of will-force, the motive power of devotion, the key of knowledge. But it does not stop short with an effective assembling of the different powers of these specific Yogas. In two directions it enlarges by its synthetic turn

the province of the Yogic method. First, it lays its hand firmly
on many of the main springs of human quality, desire, action and
it subjects them to an intensive discipline with the soul's mastery
of its motives as a first aim and their elevation to a diviner spiritual level as its final utility. Again, it includes in its objects of
Yoga not only liberation,[1] which is the one all-mastering preoccupation of the specific systems, but a cosmic enjoyment[2] of the
power of the Spirit, which the others may take incidentally on the
way, in part, casually, but avoid making a motive or object. It is
a bolder and larger system.

In the method of synthesis which we have been following,
another clue of principle has been pursued which is derived from
another view of the possibilities of Yoga. This starts from the
method of Vedanta to arrive at the aim of the Tantra. In the
tantric method Shakti is all-important, becomes the key to the
finding of spirit; in this synthesis spirit, soul is all-important,
becomes the secret of the taking up of Shakti. The tantric method starts from the bottom and grades the ladder of ascent upwards to the summit; therefore its initial stress is upon the action
of the awakened Shakti in the nervous system of the body and its
centres; the opening of the six lotuses is the opening up of the
ranges of the power of Spirit. Our synthesis takes man as a spirit
in mind much more than a spirit in body and assumes in him the
capacity to begin on that level, to spiritualise his being by the
power of the soul in mind opening itself directly to a higher spiritual force and being and to perfect by that higher force so possessed and brought into action the whole of his nature. For that
reason our initial stress has fallen upon the utilisation of the
powers of soul in mind and the turning of the triple key of knowledge, works and love in the locks of the spirit; the Hathayogic
methods can be dispensed with, — though there is no objection
to their partial use, — the Rajayogic will only enter in as an
informal element. To arrive by the shortest way at the largest
development of spiritual power and being and divinise by it a
liberated nature in the whole range of human living is our ins-
piring motive.

The principle in view is a self-surrender, a giving up of the

[1] *mukti*   [2] *bhukti*

human being into the being, consciousness, power, delight of the Divine, a union or communion at all the points of meeting in the soul of man, the mental being, by which the Divine himself, directly and without veil master and possessor of the instrument, shall by the light of his presence and guidance perfect the human being in all the forces of the Nature for a divine living. Here we arrive at a farther enlargement of the objects of the Yoga. The common initial purpose of all Yoga is the liberation of the soul of man from its present natural ignorance and limitation, its release into spiritual being, its union with the highest self and Divinity. But ordinarily this is made not only the initial but the whole and final object: enjoyment of spiritual being there is, but either in a dissolution of the human and individual into the silence of self-being or on a higher plane in another existence. The Tantric system makes liberation the final, but not the only aim; it takes on its way a full perfection and enjoyment of the spiritual power, light and joy in the human existence, and even it has a glimpse of a supreme experience in which liberation and cosmic action and enjoyment are unified in a final over-coming of all oppositions and dissonances. It is this wider view of our spiritual potentialities from which we begin, but we add another stress which brings in a completer significance. We regard the spirit in man not as solely an individual being travel-ling to a transcendent unity with the Divine, but as a universal being capable of oneness with the Divine in all souls and all Nature and we give this extended view its entire practical con-sequence. The human soul's individual liberation and enjoyment of union with the Divine in spiritual being, consciousness and delight must always be the first object of the Yoga; its free enjoy-ment of the cosmic unity of the Divine becomes a second object; but out of that a third appears, the effectuation of the meaning of the divine unity with all beings by a sympathy and participa-tion in the spiritual purpose of the Divine in humanity. The indi-vidual Yoga then turns from its separateness and becomes a part of the collective Yoga of the divine Nature in the human race. The liberated individual being, united with the Divine in self and spirit, becomes in his natural being a self-perfecting instrument for the perfect outflowering of the Divine in humanity.

This outflowering has its two terms; first, comes the growth
out of the separative human ego into the unity of the spirit, then
the possession of the divine nature in its proper and its higher
forms and no longer in the inferior forms of the mental being
which are a mutilated translation and not the authentic text of
the original script of divine Nature in the cosmic individual.
In other words, a perfection has to be aimed at which amounts to
the elevation of the mental into the full spiritual and supramental
nature. Therefore this integral Yoga of knowledge, love and
works has to be extended into a Yoga of spiritual and gnostic
self-perfection. As gnostic knowledge, will and Ananda are a
direct instrumentation of spirit and can only be won by growing into the spirit, into divine being, this growth has to be the first
aim of our Yoga. The mental being has to enlarge itself into the
oneness of the Divine before the Divine will perfect in the soul
of the individual its gnostic outflowering. That is the reason why
the triple way of knowledge, works and love becomes the key-
note of the whole Yoga, for that is the direct means for the soul
in mind to rise to its highest intensities where it passes upward
into the divine oneness. That too is the reason why the Yoga
must be integral. For if immergence in the Infinite or some close
union with the Divine were all our aim, an integral Yoga would
be superfluous, except for such greater satisfaction of the being
of man as we may get by a self-lifting of the whole of it towards
its Source. But it would not be needed for the essential aim, since
by any single power of the soul-nature we can meet with the
Divine; each at its height rises up into the infinite and absolute,
each therefore offers a sufficient way of arrival, for all the hundred separate paths meet in the Eternal. But the gnostic being is
a complete enjoyment and possession of the whole divine and
spiritual nature; and it is a complete lifting of the whole nature
of man into its power of a divine and spiritual existence. Inte-
grality becomes then an essential condition of this Yoga.

At the same time we have seen that each of the three ways
at its height, if it is pursued with a certain largeness, can take into
itself the powers of the others and lead to their fulfilment. It is
therefore sufficient to start by one of them and find the point at
which it meets the other at first parallel lines of advance and melts

into them by its own widenings. At the same time a more difficult, complex, wholly powerful process would be to start, as it
were, on three lines together, on a triple wheel of soul-power.
But the consideration of this possibility must be postponed till
we have seen what are the conditions and means of the Yoga of
self-perfection. For we shall see that this also need not be postponed entirely, but a certain preparation of it is part of and a
certain initiation into it proceeds by the growth of the divine
works, love and knowledge.

*

All life is the play of universal forces. The individual gives a
personal form to these universal forces. But he can choose whether he shall respond or not to the action of a particular force.
Only most people do not really choose — they indulge the play of
the forces. Your illnesses, depressions etc. are the repeated play
of such forces. It is only when one can make oneself free of them
that one can be the true person and have a true life — but one
can be free only by living in the Divine.

(XXII, p. 318)

The Integral Perfection*

A DIVINE perfection of the human being is our aim. We must know then, first, what are the essential elements that constitute man's total perfection; secondly, what we mean by a divine as distinguished from a human perfection of our being. That man as a being is capable of self-development and of some approach at least to an ideal standard of perfection which his mind is able to conceive, fix before it and pursue, is common ground to all thinking humanity, though it may be only the minority who concern themselves with this possibility as providing the one most important aim of life. But by some the ideal is conceived as a mundane change, by others as a religious conversion.

The mundane perfection is sometimes conceived of as something outward, social, a thing of action, a more rational dealing with our fellow-men and our environment, a better and more efficient citizenship and discharge of duties, a better, richer, kindlier and happier way of living, with a more just and more harmonious associated enjoyment of the opportunities of existence. By others again a more inner and subjective ideal is cherished, a clarifying and raising of the intelligence, will and reason, a heightening and ordering of power and capacity in the nature, a nobler ethical, a richer aesthetic, a finer emotional, a much healthier and better-governed vital and physical being. Sometimes one element is stressed, almost to the exclusion of the rest; sometimes, in wider and more well-balanced minds, the whole harmony is envisaged as a total perfection. A change of education and social institutions is the outward means adopted or an inner self-training and development is preferred as the true instrumentation. Or the two aims may be clearly united, the perfection of the inner individual, the perfection of the outer living.

But the mundane aim takes for its field the present life and its

* *The Synthesis of Yoga*, pp. 590–96.

164

opportunities; the religious aim, on the contrary, fixes before it the self-preparation for another existence after death, its commonest ideal is some kind of pure sainthood, its means a conversion of the imperfect or sinful human being by divine grace or through obedience to a law laid down by a scripture or else given by a religious founder. The aim of religion may include a social change, but it is then a change brought about by the acceptance of a common religious ideal and way of consecrated living, a brotherhood of the saints, a theocracy or kingdom of God reflecting on earth the kingdom of heaven.

The object of our synthetic Yoga must, in this respect too as in its other parts, be more integral and comprehensive, embrace all these elements or these tendencies of a larger impulse of self-perfection and harmonise them or rather unify, and in order to do that successfully it must seize on a truth which is wider than the ordinary religious and higher than the mundane principle. All life is a secret Yoga, an obscure growth of Nature towards the discovery and fulfilment of the divine principle hidden in her which becomes progressively less obscure, more self-conscient and luminous, more self-possessed in the human being by the opening of all his instruments of knowledge, will, action, life to the Spirit within him and in the world. Mind, life, body, all the forms of our nature are the means of this growth, but they find their last perfection only by opening out to something beyond them, first, because they are not the whole of what man is, secondly, because that other something which he is, is the key of his completeness and brings a light which discovers to him the whole high and large reality of his being.

Mind is fulfilled by a greater knowledge of which it is only a half-light, life discovers its meaning in a greater power and will of which it is the outward and as yet obscure functioning, body finds its last use as an instrument of a power of being of which it is a physical support and material starting-point. They have all themselves first to be developed and find out their ordinary possibilities; all our normal life is a trying of these possibilities and an opportunity for this preparatory and tentative self-training. But life cannot find its perfect self-fulfilment till it opens to that greater reality of being of which by this development of a richer power and a more sensitive use and capacity it becomes a well-prepared field of working.

Intellectual, volitional, ethical, emotional, aesthetic and physical training and improvement are all so much to the good, but they are only in the end a constant movement in a circle without any last delivering and illumining aim, unless they arrive at a point when they can open themselves to the power and presence of the Spirit and admit its direct workings. This direct working effects a conversion of the whole being which is the indispensable condition of our real perfection. To grow into the truth and power of the Spirit and by the direct action of that power to be made a fit channel of its self-expression, — a living of man in the Divine and a divine living of the Spirit in humanity, — will therefore be the principle and the whole object of an integral Yoga of self-perfection.

In the process of this change there must be by the very necessity of the effort two stages of its working. First, there will be the personal endeavour of the human being, as soon as he becomes aware by his soul, mind, heart of this divine possibility and turns towards it as the true object of life, to prepare himself for it and to get rid of all in him that belongs to a lower working, of all that stands in the way of his opening to the spiritual truth and its power, so as to possess by this liberation his spiritual being and turn all his natural movements into free means of its self-expression. It is by this turn that the self-conscious Yoga aware of its aim begins: there is a new awakening and an upward change of the life motive. So long as there is only an intellectual, ethical and other self-training for the now normal purposes of life which does not travel beyond the ordinary circle of working of mind, life and body, we are still only in the obscure and yet unillumined preparatory Yoga of Nature; we are still in pursuit of only an ordinary human perfection. A spiritual desire of the Divine and of the divine perfection, of a unity with him in all our being and a spiritual perfection in all our nature, is the effective sign of this change, the precursory power of a great integral conversion of our being and living.

By personal effort a precursory change, a preliminary conversion can be effected; it amounts to a greater or less spiritualising of our mental motives, our character and temperament, and a mastery, stilling or changed action of the vital and physical life. This converted subjectivity can be made the base of some communion or unity of the soul in mind with the Divine and some partial reflection of the divine nature in the mentality of the human being. That is as far as man can go by his unaided or indirectly aided effort, because that is an effort of mind and mind cannot climb beyond itself permanently: at most it arises to a spiritualised and idealised mentality. If it shoots up beyond that border, it loses hold of itself, loses hold of life, and arrives either at a trance of absorption or a passivity. A greater perfection can only be arrived at by a higher power entering in and taking up the whole action of the being. The second stage of this Yoga will therefore be a persistent giving up of all the action of the nature into the hands of this greater Power, a substitution of its influence, possession and working for the personal effort, until the Divine to whom we aspire becomes the direct master of the Yoga and effects the entire spiritual and ideal conversion of the being.

This double character of our Yoga raises it beyond the mundane ideal of perfection, while at the same time it goes too beyond the loftier, intenser, but much narrower religious formula. The mundane ideal regards man always as a mental, vital and physical being and it aims at a human perfection well within these limits, a perfection of mind, life and body, an expansion and refinement of the intellect and knowledge, of the will and power, of ethical character, aim and conduct, of aesthetic sensibility and creativeness, of emotional balanced poise and enjoyment, of vital and physical soundness, regulated action and just efficiency. It is a wide and full aim, but yet not sufficiently full and wide, because it ignores that other greater element of our being which the mind vaguely conceives as the spiritual element and leaves it either undeveloped or insufficiently satisfied as merely some high occasional or added derivatory experience, the result of the action of mind in its exceptional aspects or dependent upon mind for its presence and persistence. It can become a high aim when it seeks to develop the loftier and the larger reaches of our mentality, but yet not sufficiently high, because it does not aspire beyond mind to that of which our purest reason, our brightest mental intuition, our deepest mental sense and feeling, strongest mental will and power or ideal aim and purpose are only pale radiations. Its aim besides is limited to a terrestrial perfection of the normal human life.

A Yoga of integral perfection regards man as a divine spiritual being involved in mind, life and body; it aims therefore at a liberation and a perfection of his divine nature. It seeks to make an inner living in the perfectly developed spiritual being his constant intrinsic living and the spiritualised action of mind, life and body only its outward human expression. In order that this spiritual being may not be something vague and indefinable or else but imperfectly realised and dependent on the mental support and the mental limitations, it seeks to go beyond mind to the supramental knowledge, will, sense, feeling, intuition, dynamic initiation of vital and physical action, all that makes the native working of the spiritual being. It accepts human life, but takes account of the large supraterrestrial action behind the earthly material living, and it joins itself to the divine Being from whom the supreme origination of all these partial and lower states proceeds so that the whole of life may become aware of its divine source and feel in each action of knowledge, of will, of feeling, sense and body the divine originating impulse. It rejects nothing that is essential in the mundane aim, but enlarges it, finds and lives in its greater and its truer meaning now hidden from it, transfigures it from a limited, earthly and mortal thing to a figure of intimate, divine and immortal values.

The integral Yoga meets the religious ideal at several points, but goes beyond it in the sense of a greater wideness. The religious ideal looks, not only beyond this earth, but away from it to a heaven or even beyond all heavens to some kind of Nirvana. Its ideal of perfection is limited to whatever kind of inner or outer mutation will eventually serve the turning away of the soul from the human life to the beyond. Its ordinary idea of perfection is a religio-ethical change, a drastic purification of the active and the emotional being, often with an ascetic abrogation and rejection of the vital impulses as its completest reaching of excellence, and in any case a supraterrestrial motive and reward or result of a life of piety and right conduct. In so far as it admits a change of knowledge, will, aesthesis, it is in the sense of the turning of them to another object than the aims of human life and eventually brings a rejection of all earthly objects of aesthesis, will and knowledge. The method, whether it lays stress on personal effort or upon divine influence, on works and knowledge or upon grace, is not like the mundane a development, but rather a conversion; but in the end the aim is not a conversion of our mental and physical nature, but the putting on of a pure spiritual nature and being, and since that is not possible here on earth, it looks for its consummation by a transference to another world or a shuffling off of all cosmic existence.

But the integral Yoga founds itself on a conception of the spiritual being as an omnipresent existence, the fullness of which comes not essentially by a transference to other worlds or a cosmic self-extinction, but by a growth out of what we now are phenomenally into the consciousness of the onnipresent reality which we always are in the essence of our being. It substitutes for the form of religious piety its completer spiritual seeking of a divine union. It proceeds by a personal effort to a conversion through a divine influence and possession; but this divine grace, if we may so call it, is not simply a mysterious flow or touch coming from above, but the all-pervading act of a divine presence which we come to know within as the power of the highest Self and Master of our being entering into the soul and so possessing it that we not only feel it close to us and pressing upon our mortal nature, but live in its law, know that law, possess it as the whole power of our spiritualised nature. The conversion its action will effect is an integral conversion of our ethical being into the Truth and Right of the divine nature, of our intellectual into the illumination of divine knowledge, our emotional into the divine love and unity, our dynamic and volitional into a working of the divine power, our aesthetic into a plenary reception and a creative enjoyment of divine beauty, not excluding even in the end a divine conversion of the vital and physical being. It regards all the previous life as an involuntary and unconscious or half-conscious preparatory growing towards this change and Yoga as the voluntary and conscious effort and realisation of the change, by

which all the aim of human existence in all its parts is fulfilled,
even while it is transfigured. Admitting the supracosmic truth
and life in worlds beyond, it admits too the terrestrial as a continued term of the one existence and a change of individual and
communal life on earth as a strain of its divine meaning.

To open oneself to the supracosmic Divine is an essential
condition of this integral perfection; to unite oneself with the
universal Divine is another essential condition. Here the Yoga
of self-perfection coincides with the Yogas of knowledge, works
and devotion; for it is impossible to change the human nature
into the divine or to make it an instrument of the divine knowledge, will and joy of existence, unless there is a union with the
supreme Being, Consciousness and Bliss and a unity with its
universal Self in all things and beings. A wholly separative possession of the divine nature by the human individual, as distinct
from a self-withdrawn absorption in it, is not possible. But this
unity will not be an inmost spiritual oneness qualified, so long as
the human life lasts, by a separative existence in mind, life and
body; the full perfection is a possession, through this spiritual
unity, of unity too with the universal Mind, the universal Life,
the universal Form which are the other constant terms of cosmic
being. Moreover, since human life is still accepted as a self-
expression of the realised Divine in man, there must be an action
of the entire divine nature in our life; and this brings in the need
of the supramental conversion which substitutes the native action
of spiritual being for the imperfect action of the superficial
nature and spiritualises and transfigures its mental, vital and
physical parts by the spiritual ideality. These three elements, a
union with the supreme Divine, unity with the universal Self, and
a supramental life action from this transcendent origin and
through this universality, but still with the individual as the soul-
channel and natural instrument, constitute the essence of the
integral divine perfection of the human being.

PART THREE

TOWARD A SPIRITUAL AGE

INTRODUCTION

Ideals and Progress

Like Tagore, Radhakrishnan, Gandhi, and Nehru, Sri Aurobindo combines the dominant strains of India and the West, and envisions a fuller integration of Indian and Western cultures. Unfortunately, Sri Aurobindo also repeats the characteristic Indian failure to recognize the significance of East Asia. (Tagore stands out as the lone exception to the Indian habit of looking to the West and referring to India as "the East.") The charges of lethargy and conservatism that Sri Aurobindo levels against India could be supported by comparison to China or Japan as well as to the modern West. But Sri Aurobindo believes that the two great components of the future evolution of man are Indian spirituality and Western intellectuality. Although the evolution of historical man will almost certainly include other major components—e.g., China and Japan—the model of such interactions may well be the one developed in the following essays on ideals and progress.

The Spiritual Age and Supermind

Sri Aurobindo leaves little doubt that he envisioned our own time as a period of radical transition such as he describes in "The Hour of God." Indian independence in 1947, his death in 1950, descent of the Supermind in 1956, and the creation of Auroville in 1968 are among the events he would count as having a momentous impact on the eventual transition from a mental to a supramental existence. The descent of the Supermind in 1956, believed to be the joint effort of Sri Aurobindo and the Mother, and its concretization in Auroville, introduces an era when "the Spirit moves among men." Accordingly, this is a new age and a new stage of evolution.

173

Using a psychological model, *The Human Cycle* outlines the history of human culture in five stages: first, the Symbolic Stage, typified by the Vedic period in India, in which man expresses his perception of the world in myth, poetry, and art; second, the Typal Stage, exemplified by the Indian *varna* or caste system of types, which is predominantly psychological and ethical; third, the Conventional Stage, typified by the European Middle Ages, in which conventional functions of caste and class become fixed according to external standards rather than individual merit; fourth, the Individualist Stage, typified by the modern West, in which reason, revolt, progress, and freedom are dominant; and fifth, the Subjective Stage, which has emerged in the present century. The sixth stage, the supramental, was not included in *The Human Cycle* (which has remained as it was first written in 1918) but is described in *The Life Divine*, *The Synthesis of Yoga*, and *Savitri*, as well as in *The Mind of Light*, the brief summary of his evolutionary vision which he wrote in 1949, a year before he died.

In "Supermind in the Evolution," from *The Mind of Light*, Sri Aurobindo explains that the descent of the Supermind, which he believed to be imminent, will reveal the universe, in both its absolute and processive phases and on each of its levels, to be a divine "ascent from Matter to supreme Spirit."

Savitri

Sri Aurobindo began writing *Savitri—A Legend and a Symbol* in 1898 at Baroda and continued to revise it until a few days before his death on December 5, 1950. More than any other writing, *Savitri* reveals the experiential basis of Sri Aurobindo's spiritual evolution and yoga.

In the sequence included here, Aswapathy describes the dilemma of having achieved overmental consciousness—namely, the task of bridging the spiritual and physical levels of existence. Aswapathy enjoys a vision of the Divine functioning in the historical process, but he remains on the mental plane. Sri Aurobindo and the Mother, represented by Satyam and Savitri respectively, express the supramental level of the Divine. In response to Aswapathy's plea, the Divine agrees to embody itself in a supramental avatar:

> O strong forerunner, I have heard thy cry.
> One shall descend and break the iron law,
> Change Nature's doom by the love Spirit's power.

Throughout his epic poem, as throughout his *sādhanā,* Sri Aurobindo struggled to "change Nature's doom"; and in *Savitri,* as in his life and legacy, the Mother, or Savitri, represents the receptacle of the Infinite and the conqueror of death. Sri Aurobindo and the Mother, then, are seen as the biune avatars of the supramental—Sri Aurobindo as the forerunner and the Mother as the manifestation of the Divine in the physical world.

IDEALS AND PROGRESS

Our Ideal*

W E BELIEVE in the constant progression
of humanity and we hold that that progression is the working out
of a Thought in Life which sometimes manifests itself on the
surface and sometimes sinks below and works behind the mask
of external forces and interests. When there is this lapse below
the surface, humanity has its periods of apparent retrogression
or tardy evolution, its long hours of darkness or twilight during
which the secret Thought behind works out one of its phases by
the pressure mainly of economic, political and personal interests
ignorant of any deeper aim within. When the thought returns to
the surface, humanity has its periods of light and of rapid efflorescence, its dawns and splendid springtides; and according to
the depth, vitality, truth and self-effective energy of the form of
Thought that emerges is the importance of the stride forward
that it makes during these Hours of the Gods in our terrestrial
manifestation.

There is no greater error than to suppose, as the "practical"
man is wont to do, that thought is only a fine flower and orna-
ment of life and that political, economic and personal interests
are the important and effective motors of human action. We
recognise that this is a world of life and action and developing
organism; but the life that seeks to guide itself only by vital
and material forces is a slow, dark and blundering growth. It
is an attempt to approximate man to the method of vegetable and
animal existence. The earth is a world of Life and Matter, but
man is not a vegetable nor an animal; he is a spiritual and a thinking being who is set here to shape and use the animal mould for
higher purposes, by higher motives, with a more divine instrumentation.

Therefore by his very nature he serves the working of a
Thought within him even when he is ignorant of it in his surface
self. The practical man who ignores or despises the deeper life
of the Idea, is yet serving that which he ignores or despises. Char-

* The Supramental Manifestation, pp. 308–15.

176

lemagne hewing a chaotic Europe into shape with his sword was preparing the reign of the feudal and Catholic interpretation of human life with all that that great though obscure period of humanity has meant for the thought and spiritual development of mankind. But it is when the Thought emerges and guides life that man grows towards his full humanity, strides forward on his path and begins to control the development of Nature in his destiny or at least to collaborate as a conscious mind and spirit with That which controls and directs it.

The progress of humanity has therefore been a constant revolution with its rhythm of alternate darkness and light, but both the day and the night have helped to foster that which is evolving. The periods have not been the same for all parts of the globe. In the historic ages of the present cycle of civilisation the movement has been almost entirely centred in the twin continents of Asia and Europe. And there it has been often seen that when Asia was moving through the light, Europe was passing through one of her epochs of obscurity and on the other hand the nights of Asia's repose or stagnation have corresponded with the days of Europe's mental vigour and vital activity.

But the fundamental difference has been that Asia has served predominantly (not exclusively) as a field for man's spiritual experience and progression; Europe has been rather a workshop for his mental and vital activities. As the cycle progressed, the Eastern continent has more and more converted itself into a storehouse of spiritual energy sometimes active and reaching forward to new development, sometimes conservative and quiescent. Three or four times in history a stream of this energy has poured out upon Europe, but each time Europe has rejected wholly or partially the spiritual substance of the afflatus and used it rather as an impulse to fresh intellectual and material activity and progress.

The first attempt was the filtering of Egyptian, Chaldean and Indian wisdom through the thought of the Greek philosophers from Pythagoras to Plato and the Neo-Platonists; the result was the brilliantly intellectual and unspiritual civilisation of Greece and Rome. But it prepared the way for the second attempt when Buddhism and Vaishnavism, filtered through the Semitic temperament, entered Europe in the form of Christianity. Christianity came within an ace of spiritualising and even of asceticising the mind of Europe; it was baffled by its own theological deformation in the minds of the Greek fathers of the Church and by the sudden flooding of Europe with a German barbarism whose temperament in its merits no less than in its defects was the very anti-type both of the Christian spirit and the Graeco-Roman intellect.

The Islamic invasion of Spain and the southern coast of the Mediterranean—curious as the sole noteworthy example of Asiatic culture using the European method of material and political irruption as opposed to a peaceful invasion by ideas—may be regarded as a third attempt. The result of its meeting with Graecised Christianity was the reawakening of the European mind in feudal and Catholic Europe and the obscure beginnings of modern thought and science.

The fourth and last attempt which is as yet only in its slow initial stage is the quiet entry of Eastern and chiefly of Indian thought into Europe first through the veil of German metaphysics, more latterly by its subtle influence in reawakening the Celtic, Scandinavian and Slavonic idealism, mysticism, religionism, and the direct and open penetration of Buddhism, Theosophy, Vedantism, Bahaism and other Oriental influences in both Europe and America.

On the other hand, there have been two reactions of Europe upon Asia; first the invasion of Alexander with his aggressive Hellenism which for a time held Western Asia, created echoes and reactions in India and returned through Islamic culture upon mediaeval Europe; secondly, the modern onslaught of commercial, political, scientific Europe upon the moral, artistic and spiritual cultures of the East.

The new features of this mutual interpenetration are, first, that the two attacks have synchronised and, secondly, that they have encountered in each case the extreme exaggeration of their opposites. Intellectual and materialistic Europe found India, the Asia of Asia, the heart of the world's spiritual life, in the last throes of an enormous experiment, the thought of a whole nation concentrated for centuries upon the pure spiritual existence to the exclusion of all real progress in the practical and mental life of the race. The entering stream of Eastern thought found in Europe the beginning of an era which rejected religion, philosophy and psychology, — religion as an emotional delusion, philosophy, the pure essence of the mind, as a barren thought-weaving, — and resolved to devote the whole intellectual faculty of man to a study of the laws of material Nature and of man's bodily, social, economic and political existence and to build thereon a superior civilisation.

That stupendous effort is over; it has not yet frankly declared its bankruptcy, but it is bankrupt. It is sinking in a cataclysm as gigantic and as unnatural as the attempt which gave it birth. On the other hand, the exaggerated spirituality of the Indian effort has also registered a bankruptcy; we have seen how high individuals can rise by it, but we have seen also how low a race can fall which in its eagerness to seek after God ignores His intention in humanity. Both the European and the Indian attempt were admirable, the Indian by its absolute spiritual sincerity, the European by its severe intellectual honesty and ardour for the truth; both have accomplished miracles; but in the end God and Nature have been too strong for the Titanism of the human spirit and for the Titanism of the human intellect.

The salvation of the human race lies in a more sane and integral development of the possibilities of mankind in the individual and in the community. The safety of Europe has to be sought in the recognition of the spiritual aim of human existence, otherwise she will be crushed by the weight of her own unillumined knowledge and soulless organisation. The safety of Asia lies in the recognition of the material mould and mental conditions in which that aim has to be worked out, otherwise she will sink deeper into the slough of despond, of a mental and physical incompetence to deal with the facts of life and the shocks of a rapidly changing movement. It is not any exchange of forms that is required, but an interchange of regenerating impulses and a happy fusion and harmonising.

The synchronism and mutual interpenetration of the two great currents of human effort at such a crisis in the history of the race is full of hope for the future of humanity, but full also of possible dangers. The hope is the emergence of a new and better human life founded on a greater knowledge, a pursuit of the new faculties and possibilities opening out before us and a just view of the problem which the individual, the society, the race have to solve. Mankind has been drawn together by the developments of material science and for good or evil its external future is henceforth one; its different parts no longer develop separately and in independence of each other. There opens out at the same time the possibility that by the development and practice of the science and the life of the soul it may be made one in reality and by an internal unity.

The idea by which the enlightenment of Europe has been governed is the passion for the discovery of the Truth and Law that constitutes existence and governs the process of the world, the attempt to develop the life and potentialities of man, his ideals, institutions, organisation by the knowledge of that Law and Truth and the confidence that along this line lies the road of human progress and perfection.

The idea is absolutely just and we accept it entirely; but its application has been erroneous. For the Law and Truth that has to be discovered is not that of the material world — though this is required, nor even of the mental and physical — though this is indispensable, but the Law and Truth of the Spirit on which all the rest depends. For it is the power of the Self of things that expresses itself in their forms and processes.

The message of the East to the West is a true message, "Only by finding himself can man be saved," and "what shall it profit a man though he gain the whole world, if he lose his own soul." The West has heard the message and is seeking out the law and truth of the soul and the evidences of an inner reality greater than the material. The danger is that with her passion for mechanism and her exaggerated intellectuality she may fog herself in an external and false psychism, such as we see arising in England and America, the homes of the mechanical genius, or in intellectual, unspiritual and therefore erroneous theories of the Absolute, such as have run their course in critical and metaphysical Germany.

The idea by which the illumination of Asia has been governed is the firm knowledge that truth of the Spirit is the sole real truth, the belief that the psychological life of man is an instrument for attaining to the truth of the Spirit and that its laws must be known and practised with that aim paramount, and the attempt to form the external life of man and the institutions of society into a suitable mould for the great endeavour.

This idea, too, is absolutely just and we accept it entirely. But in its application, and in India most, it has deviated into a divorce between the Spirit and its instruments and a disparagement and narrowing of the mental and external life of the race. For it is only on the widest and richest efflorescence of this instrumental life that the fullest and most absolute attainment of the spiritual can be securely based. This knowledge the ancients of the East possessed and practised; it has been dimmed in knowledge and lost in practice by their descendants.

The message the West brings to the East is a true message. Man also is God and it is through his developing manhood that he approaches the godhead; Life also is the Divine, its progressive expansion is the self-expression of the Brahman, and to deny Life is to diminish the Godhead within us. This is the truth that returns to the East from the West translated into the language of the higher truth the East already possesses; and it is an ancient knowledge. The East also is awaking to the message. The danger is that Asia may accept it in the European form, forget for a time her own law and nature and either copy blindly the West or make a disastrous amalgam of that which she has in its most inferior forms and the crudenesses which are invading her.

The problem of thought therefore is to find out the right idea and the right way of harmony; to restate the ancient and eternal spiritual truth of the Self so that it shall re-embrace, permeate, dominate, transfigure the mental and physical life; to develop the most profound and vital methods of psychological self-discipline and self-development so that the mental and psychical life of man may express the spiritual life through the utmost possible expansion of its own richness, power and complexity; and to seek for the means and motives by which his external life, his society and his institutions may remould themselves progressively in the truth of the spirit and develop towards the utmost possible harmony of individual freedom and social unity.

This is our ideal and our search. Throughout the world there are plenty of movements inspired by the same drift, but there is room for an effort of thought which shall frankly acknowledge the problem in its integral complexity and not be restrained in the flexibility of its search by attachment to any cult, creed or extant system of philosophy.

The effort involves a quest for the Truth that underlies existence and the fundamental Law of its self-expression in the universe, — the work of metaphysical philosophy and religious thought; the sounding and harmonising of the psychological methods of discipline by which man purifies and perfects himself, — the work of psychology, not as it is understood in Europe, but the deeper practical psychology called in India Yoga and the application of our ideas to the problems of man's social and collective life.

Philosophy and religious thought based on spiritual experience must be the beginning and the foundation of any such attempt; for they alone go behind appearances and processes to the truth of things. The attempt to get rid of their supremacy must always be vain. Man will always think and generalise and try to penetrate behind the apparent fact, for that is the imperative law of his awakened consciousness; man will always turn his generalisations into a religion, even though it be only a religion of positivism or of material Law. Philosophy is the intellectual search for the fundamental truth of things; religion is the attempt to make the truth dynamic in the soul of man. They are essential to each other; a religion that is not the expression of philosophic truth, degenerates into superstition and obscurantism, and a philosophy which does not dynamise itself with the religious spirit is a barren light, for it cannot get itself practised. But again neither of these get their supreme value unless raised into the spirit and cast into life.

What then shall be our ideal? Unity for the human race by an inner oneness and not only by an external association of interests; the resurgence of man out of the merely animal and economic life or the merely intellectual and aesthetic into the glories of the spiritual existence; the pouring of the power of the spirit into the physical mould and mental instrument so that man may develop his manhood into that true supermanhood which shall exceed our present state as much as this exceeds the animal state from which Science tells us that we have issued. These three are one; for man's unity and man's self-transcendence can come only by living in the Spirit.

★

A spiritual ideal has always been the characteristic idea and aspiration of India. But the progress of Time and the need of humanity demand a new orientation and another form of that ideal. The old forms and methods are no longer sufficient for the purpose of the Time-Spirit. India can no longer fulfil herself on lines that are too narrow for the great steps she has to take in the future. Nor is ours the spirituality of a life that is aged and world-weary and burdened with the sense of the illusion and miserable inutility of all God's mighty creation. Our ideal is not the spirituality that withdraws from life but the conquest of life by the power of the spirit. It is to accept the world as an effort of manifestation of the Divine, but also to transform humanity by a greater effort of manifestation than has yet been accomplished, one in which the veil between man and God shall be removed, the divine manhood of which we are capable shall come to birth and our life shall be remoulded in the truth and light and power of the spirit. It is to make of all our action a sacrifice to the master of our action and an expression of the greater self in man and of all life a Yoga.

(XVI, p. 329)

The Conservative Mind and
Eastern Progress*

THE arrival of a new radical idea in the
minds of men is the sign of a great coming change in human life
and society; it may be combated, the reaction of the old
idea may triumph for a time, but the struggle never leaves either
the thoughts and sentiments or the habits and institutions of the
society as they were when it commenced. Whether it knows it
or not, it has gone forward and the change is irretrievable.
Either new forms replace the old institutions or the old while
preserving the aspect of continuity have profoundly changed
within, or else these have secured for themselves a period of
greater rigidity, increasing corruption, progressive deterioration
of spirit and waning of real force which only assures them in the
future a more complete catastrophe and absolute disappearance. The past can arrive at the most at a partial survival or an
euthanasia, provided it knows how to compromise liberally
with the future.

The conservative mind is unwilling to recognise this law
though it is observable throughout human history and we can
easily cull examples with full hands from all ages and all climes;
and it is protected in its refusal to see by the comparative rarity
of rapid revolutions and great cataclysmal changes; it is blinded
by the disguise which Nature so often throws over her processes
of mutation. If we look casually at European history in this
light the attention is only seized by a few conspicuous landmarks,
the evolution and end of Athenian democracy, the transition
from the Roman republic to the empire, the emergence of feudal
Europe out of the ruins of Rome, the Christianisation of Europe,
the Reformation and Renascence together preparing a new
society, the French Revolution, the present rapid movement towards a socialistic State and the replacing of competition by organised co-operation. Because our view of European history is
chiefly political, we do not see the constant mutation of society

* *The Supramental Manifestation*, pp. 322–28.

and of thought in the same relief; but we can recognise two great cycles of change, one of the ancient races leading from the primitive ages to the cultured society of the Graeco-Roman world, the other from the semi-barbarism of feudal Christendom to the intellectual, materialistic and civilised society of modern times.

In the East, on the contrary, the great revolutions have been spiritual and cultural; the political and social changes, although they have been real and striking, if less profound than in Europe, fall into the shade and are apt to be overlooked; besides, this unobtrusiveness is increased by their want of relief, the slow subtlety of their process and instinctive persistence and reverence with which old names and formulas have been preserved while the thing itself was profoundly modified until its original sense remained only as a pious fiction. Thus Japan kept its sacrosanct Mikado as a cover for the change to an aristocratic and feudal government and has again brought him forward in modern times to cover and facilitate without too serious a shock the transition from a mediaeval form of society into the full flood of modernism. In India the continued fiction of the ancient fourfold order of society based on spiritual idealism, social type, ethical discipline and economic function is still used to cover and justify the quite different, complex and chaotic order of caste which, while it still preserves some confused fragments of the old motives, is really founded upon birth, privilege, local custom and religious formalism. The evolution from one type of society to another so opposed to it in its psychological motives and real institutions without any apparent change of formula is one of the most curious phenomena in the social history of mankind and still awaits intelligent study.

Our minds are apt to seize things in the rough and to appreciate only what stands out in bold external relief; we miss the law of Nature's subtleties and disguises. We can see and fathom to some extent the motives, necessities, process of great revolutions and marked changes and we can consider and put in their right place the brief reactions which only modified without actually preventing the overt realisation of new ideas. We can see, for instance, that the Sullan restoration of Roman oligarchy, the Stuart restoration in England or the brief return of monarchy in

France with the Bourbons were no real restorations, but a mo-
mentary damming of the tide attended with insufficient concessions and forced developments which determined, not a return to
the past, but the form and pace of the inevitable revolution. It is
more difficult but still possible to appreciate the working of an
idea against all obstacles through many centuries; we can com-
prehend now, for instance, that we must seek the beginnings of
the French Revolution, not in Rousseau or Mirabeau or the
blundering of Louis XVI, but in movements which date back to
the Capet and the Valois, while the precise fact which prepared
its tremendous outbreak and victory and determined its form was
the defeat of the Calvinistic reformation in France and the absolute triumph of the monarchical system over the nobility and the
bourgeoisie in the reigns of Louis XIII and Louis XIV. That
double victory determined the destruction of the monarchy in
France, the downfall of the Church and, by the failure of the
nobles to lead faithfully the liberal cause whether in religion or
politics, the disappearance of aristocracy.

But Nature has still more subtle and disguised movements in
her dealings with men by which she leads them to change without their knowing that they have changed. It is because she has
employed chiefly this method in the vast masses of the East that
the conservative habit of mind is so much stronger there than in
the West. It is able to nourish the illusion that it has not changed,
that it is immovably faithful to the ideas of remote forefathers,
to their religion, their traditions, their institutions, their social
ideals, that it has preserved either a divine or an animal immobility both in thought and in the routine of life and has been free
from the human law of mutation by which man and his social
organisations must either progress or degenerate but can in no
case maintain themselves unchanged against the attack of Time.
Buddhism has come and gone and the Hindu still professes to belong to the Vedic religion held and practised by his Aryan forefathers; he calls his creed the Aryan Dharma, the eternal religion.
It is only when we look close that we see the magnitude of the
illusion. Buddha has gone out of India indeed, but Buddhism
remains; it has stamped its giant impress on the spirit of the national religion, leaving the forms to be determined by the Tantri-

cism with which itself had made alliance and some sort of fusion in its middle growth; what it destroyed no man has been able to restore, what it left no man has been able to destroy. As a matter of fact, the double cycle which India has described from the early Vedic times to India of Buddha and the philosophers and again from Buddha to the time of the European irruption was in its own way as vast in change religious, social, cultural, even political and administrative as the double cycle of Europe; but because it preserved old names for new things, old formulas for new methods and old coverings for new institutions and because the change was always marked in the internal but quiet and unobtrusive in the external, we have been able to create and preserve the fiction of the unchanging East. There has also been this result that while the European conservative has learned the law of change in human society, knows that he must move and quarrels with the progressist only over the right pace and the exact direction, the eastern or rather the Indian conservative still imagines that stability may be the true law of mortal being, practises a sort of Yogic *āsana* on the flood of Time and because he does not move himself, thinks, — for he keeps his eyes shut and is not in the habit of watching the banks, — that he can prevent the stream also from moving on.

This conservative principle has its advantages even as rapid progress has its vices and its perils. It helps towards the preservation of a fundamental continuity which makes for the longevity of civilisations and the persistence of what was valuable in humanity's past. So, in India, if religion has changed immensely its form and temperament, the religious spirit has been really eternal, the principle of spiritual discipline is the same as in the earliest times, the fundamental spiritual truths have been preserved and even enriched in their contents and the very forms can all be traced back through their mutations to the seed of the Veda. On the other hand, this habit of mind leads to the accumulation of a great mass of accretions which were once valuable but have lost their virtue and to the heaping up of dead forms and shibboleths which no longer correspond to any vital truth nor have any understood and helpful significance. All this putrid waste of the past is held to be too sacred to be touched by any profane hand and yet it chokes up the streams of the national life or corrupts its waters. And if no successful process of purification takes place, a state of general ill-health in the social body supervenes in which the principle of conservation becomes the cause of dissolution.

The present era of the world is a stage of immense transformations. Not one but many radical ideas are at work in the mind of humanity and agitate its life with a vehement seeking and effort at change; and although the centre of the agitation is in progressive Europe, yet the East is being rapidly drawn into this churning of the sea of thought and this breaking up of old ideas and old institutions. No nation or community can any longer remain psychologically cloistered and apart in the unity of the modern world. It may even be said that the future of humanity depends most upon the answer that will be given to the modern riddle of the Sphinx by the East and especially by India, the hoary guardian of the Asiatic idea and its profound spiritual secrets. For the most vital issue of the age is whether the future progress of humanity is to be governed by the modern economic and materialistic mind of the West or by a nobler pragmatism guided, uplifted and enlightened by spiritual culture and knowledge. The West never really succeeded in spiritualising itself and latterly it has been habituated almost exclusively to an action in the external governed by political and economic ideals and necessities; in spite of the reawakening of the religious mind and the growth of a widespread but not yet profound or luminous spiritual and psychical curiosity and seeking, it has to act solely in the things of this world and to solve its problems by mechanical methods and as the thinking political and economic animal, simply because it knows no other standpoint and is accustomed to no other method. On the other hand the East, though it has allowed its spirituality to slumber too much in dead forms, has always been open to profound awakenings and preserves its spiritual capacity intact, even when it is actually inert and uncreative. Therefore the hope of the world lies in the re-arousing in the East of the old spiritual practicality and large and profound vision and power of organisation under the insistent contact of the West and in the flooding out of the light of Asia on the Occident, no longer in forms that are now static, effete, unadaptive, but in new forms stirred, dynamic and effective.

India, the heart of the Orient, has to change as the whole West and the whole East are changing, and it cannot avoid changing in the sense of the problems forced upon it by Europe. The new Orient must necessarily be the result either of some balance and fusion or of some ardent struggle between progressive and conservative ideals and tendencies. If, therefore, the conservative mind in this country opens itself sufficiently to the necessity of transformation, the resulting culture born of a resurgent India may well bring about a profound modification in the future civilisation of the world. But if it remains shut up in dead fictions, or tries to meet the new needs with the mind of the school-man and the sophist dealing with words and ideas in the air rather than actual fact and truth and potentiality, or struggles merely to avoid all but a scanty minimum of change, then, since the new ideas cannot fail to realise themselves, the future India will be formed in the crude mould of the westernised social and political reformer whose mind, barren of original thought and unenlightened by vital experience, can do nothing but reproduce the forms and ideas of Europe and will turn us all into halting apes of the West. Or else, and that perhaps is the best thing that can happen, a new spiritual awakening must arise from the depths of this vast life that shall this time more successfully include in its scope the great problems of earthly life as well as those of the soul and its transmundane destinies, an awakening that shall ally itself closely with the renascent spiritual seeking of the West and with its yearning for the perfection of the human race. This third and as yet unknown quantity is indeed the force needed throughout the East. For at present we have only two extremes of a conservative immobility and incompetence imprisoned in the shell of past conventions and a progressive force hardly less blind and ineffectual because second-hand and merely imitative of nineteenth-century Europe, with a vague floating mass of uncertainty between. The result is a continual fiasco and inability to evolve anything large, powerful, sure and vital, — a drifting in the stream of circumstance, a constant grasping at details and unessentials and failure to reach the heart of the great problems of life which the age is bringing to our doors. Something is needed which tries to be born; but as yet, in the phrase of the Veda, the Mother holds herself compressed in smallness, keeps the Birth concealed within her being and will not give it forth to the Father. When she becomes great in impulse and conception, then we shall see it born.

★

If we consider carefully we shall see that the past is indeed a huge force of conservation, but of conservation that is not immobile, that on the contrary offers itself as material for change and new realisation; that the present is the constant change and new actual realisation which the past desires and compels; and that the future is that force of new realisation not yet actual towards which the past was moving and for the sake of which it lived. Then we perceive that there is no real opposition between these three; we see that they are part of a single movement, a sort of Trinity of Vishnu-Brahma-Maheshwara fulfilling by an inseparable action the one Deity. Yet the human mind in its mania of division and opposition seeks to set them at strife and ranges humanity into various camps, the partisans of the past, the partisans of the present, the partisans of the future, the partisans of all sorts of compromises between the three Forces. Nature makes good use of the struggle between these partisans and her method is necessary in our present state of passionate ignorance and egoistic obstinacy; but nonetheless is it from the point of view of a higher knowledge a pitiably ignorant struggle.

(XVI, p. 319)

THE SPIRITUAL AGE
AND SUPERMIND

The Hour of God*

THERE are moments when the Spirit moves among men and the breath of the Lord is abroad upon the waters of our being; there are others when it retires and men are left to act in the strength or the weakness of their own egoism. The first are periods when even a little effort produces great results and changes destiny; the second are spaces of time when much labour goes to the making of a little result. It is true that the latter may prepare the former, may be the little smoke of sacrifice going up to heaven which calls down the rain of God's bounty.

Unhappy is the man or the nation which, when the divine moment arrives, is found sleeping or unprepared to use it, because the lamp has not been kept trimmed for the welcome and the ears are sealed to the call. But thrice woe to them who are strong and ready, yet waste the force or misuse the moment; for them is irreparable loss or a great destruction.

In the hour of God cleanse thy soul of all self-deceit and hypocrisy and vain self-flattering that thou mayst look straight into thy spirit and hear that which summons it. All insincerity of nature, once thy defence against the eye of the Master and the light of the ideal, becomes now a gap in thy armour and invites the blow. Even if thou conquer for the moment, it is the worse for thee, for the blow shall come afterwards and cast thee down in the midst of thy triumph. But being pure cast aside all fear; for the hour is often terrible, a fire and a whirlwind and a tempest, a treading of the winepress of the wrath of God; but he who can stand up in it on the truth of his purpose is he who shall stand; even though he fall, he shall rise again; even though he seem to pass on the wings of the wind, he shall return. Nor let worldly prudence whisper too closely in thy ear; for it is the hour of the unexpected.

* *The Hour of God.* p. 1.

Conditions for the Coming
of a Spiritual Age*

A CHANGE of this kind, the change from the mental and vital to the spiritual order of life, must necessarily be accomplished in the individual and in a great number of individuals before it can lay any effective hold upon the community. The Spirit in humanity discovers, develops, builds into form in the individual man: it is through the progressive and formative individual that it offers the discovery and the chance of a new self-creation to the mind of the race. For the communal mind holds things subconsciently at first or, if consciously, then in a confused chaotic manner: it is only through the individual mind that the mass can arrive at a clear knowledge and creation of the thing it held in its subconscient self. Thinkers, historians, sociologists who belittle the individual and would like to lose him in the mass or think of him chiefly as a cell, an atom, have got hold only of the obscurer side of the truth of Nature's workings in humanity. It is because man is not like the material formations of Nature or like the animal, because she intends in him a more and more conscious evolution, that individuality is so much developed in him and so absolutely important and indispensable. No doubt what comes out in the individual and afterwards moves the mass, must have been there already in the universal Mind and the individual is only an instrument for its manifestation, discovery, development; but he is an indispensable instrument and an instrument not merely of subconscient Nature, not merely of an instinctive urge that moves the mass, but more directly of the Spirit of whom that Nature is itself the instrument and the matrix of his creations. All great changes therefore find their first clear and effective power and their direct shaping force in the mind and spirit of an individual or of a limited number of individuals.

* *Social and Political Thought*, pp. 231–45; *The Human Cycle* (1962), pp. 330–49.

The mass follows, but unfortunately in a very imperfect and confused fashion which often or even usually ends in the failure or distortion of the thing created. If it were not so, mankind could have advanced on its way with a victorious rapidity instead of with the lumbering hesitations and soon exhausted rushes that seem to be all of which it has yet been capable.

Therefore if the spiritual change of which we have been speaking is to be effected, it must unite two conditions which have to be simultaneously satisfied but are most difficult to bring together. There must be the individual and the individuals who are able to see, to develop, to re-create themselves in the image of the Spirit and to communicate both their idea and its power to the mass. And there must be at the same time a mass, a society, a communal mind or at the least the constituents of a group-body, the possibility of a group-soul which is capable of receiving and effectively assimilating, ready to follow and effectively arrive, not compelled by its own inherent deficiencies, its defect of preparation to stop on the way or fall back before the decisive change is made. Such a simultaneity has never yet happened, although the appearance of it has sometimes been created by the ardour of a moment. That the combination must happen some day is a certainty, but none can tell how many attempts will have to be made and how many sediments of spiritual experience will have to be accumulated in the subconscious mentality of the communal human being before the soil is ready. For the chances of success are always less powerful in a difficult upward effort affecting the very roots of our nature than the numerous possibilities of failure. The initiator himself may be imperfect, may not have waited to become entirely the thing that he has seen. Even the few who have the apostolate in their charge may not have perfectly assimilated and shaped it in themselves and may hand on the power of the Spirit still farther diminished to the many who will come after them. The society may be intellectually, vitally, ethically, temperamentally unready, with the result that the final acceptance of the spiritual idea by the society may be also the beginning of its debasement and distortion and of the consequent departure or diminution of the Spirit. Any or all of these things may happen, and the result will be, as has so often happened in the past, that even though some progress is made and an important change effected, it will not be the decisive change which can alone re-create humanity in a diviner image.

What then will be that state of society, what that readiness of the common mind of man which will be most favourable to this change, so that even if it cannot at once effectuate itself, it may at least make for its ways a more decisive preparation than has been hitherto possible? For that seems the most important element, since it is that, it is the unpreparedness, the unfitness of the society or of the common mind of man which is always the chief stumbling-block. It is the readiness of this common mind which is of the first importance; for even if the condition of society and the principle and rule that govern society are opposed to the spiritual change, even if these belong almost wholly to the vital, to the external, the economic, the mechanical order, as is certainly the way at present with human masses, yet if the common human mind has begun to admit the ideas proper to the higher order that is in the end to be, and the heart of man has begun to be stirred by aspirations born of these ideas, then there is a hope of some advance in the not distant future. And here the first essential sign must be the growth of the subjective idea of life, — the idea of the soul, the inner being, its powers, its possibilities, its growth, its expression and the creation of a true, beautiful and helpful environment for it as the one thing of first and last importance. The signals must be there that are precursors of a subjective age in humanity's thought and social endeavour.

These ideas are likely first to declare their trend in philosophy, in psychological thinking, in the arts, poetry, painting, sculpture, music, in the main idea of ethics, in the application of subjective principles by thinkers to social questions, even perhaps, though this is a perilous effort, to politics and economics, that hard refractory earth matter which most resists all but a gross utilitarian treatment. There will be new unexpected departures of science or at least of research, — since to such a turn in its most fruitful seekings the orthodox still deny the name of science. Discoveries will be made that thin the walls between soul and matter; attempts there will be to extend exact knowledge into the psychological and psychic realms with a realisation of the truth that these have laws of their own which are other than physical, but not the less laws because they escape the external senses and are infinitely plastic and subtle. There will be a labour of religion to reject its past heavy weight of dead matter and revivify its strength in the fountains of the Spirit. These are sure signs, if not of the thing to be, at least of a great possibility of it, of an effort that will surely be made, another endeavour perhaps with a larger sweep and a better equipped intelligence capable not only of feeling but of understanding the Truth that is demanding to be heard. Some such signs we can see at the present time although they are only incipient and sporadic and have not yet gone far enough to warrant a confident certitude. It is only when these groping beginnings have found that for which they are seeking, that it can be successfully applied to the remoulding of the life of man. Till then nothing better is likely to be achieved than an inner preparation and, for the rest, radical or revolutionary experiments of a doubtful kind with the details of the vast and cumbrous machinery under which life now groans and labours.

A subjective age may stop very far short of spirituality; for the subjective turn is only a first condition, not the thing itself, not the end of the matter. The search for the Reality, the true self of man, may very easily follow out the natural order described by the Upanishad in the profound apologue of the seekings of Bhrigu, son of Varuna. For first the seeker found the ultimate reality to be Matter and the physical, the material being, the external man our only self and spirit. Next he fixed on Life as the Reality and the vital being as the self and spirit; in the third essay on Mind and the mental being; only afterwards could he get beyond the superficial subjective through the supramental Truth-Consciousness to the eternal, the blissful, the ever creative Reality of which these are the sheaths. But humanity may not be as persistent or as plastic as the son of Varuna, the search may stop short anywhere. Only if it is intended that he shall now at last arrive and discover, will the Spirit break each insufficient formula as soon as it has shaped itself and compel the thought of man to press forward to a larger discovery and in the end to the largest and most luminous of all. Something of the kind has been happening but only in a very external way and on the surface. After the material formula which governed the greater part of the nineteenth century had burdened man with the heaviest servitude to the machinery of the outer material life that he has ever yet been called upon to bear, the first attempt to break through, to get to the living reality in things and away from the mechanical idea of life and living and society, landed us in that surface vitalism which had already begun to govern thought before the two formulas inextricably locked together lit up and flung themselves on the lurid pyre of the World War. The vital élan brought us no deliverance, but only used the machinery already created with a more feverish insistence, a vehement attempt to live more rapidly, more intensely, an inordinate will to act and to succeed, to enlarge the mere force of living, to pile up a gigantic efficiency of life. It could not have been otherwise even if this vitalism had been less superficial and external, more truly subjective. To live, to act, to grow, to increase the vital force, to understand, utilise and fulfil the intuitive impulse of life are not things evil in themselves: rather they are excellent things, if rightly followed and rightly used, that is to say, if they are directed to something beyond the mere vitalistic impulse and are governed by that within which is higher than Life. The Life-power is an instrument, not an aim; it is in the upward scale the first great subjective supra-physical instrument of the Spirit and the base of all action and endeavour. But a Life-power that sees nothing beyond itself, nothing to be served except its own organised demands and impulses, will be very soon like the force of steam driving an engine without the driver or an engine in which the locomotive force has made the driver its servant and not its controller. It can only add the uncontrollable impetus of a high-crested or broad-based Titanism, or it may be even a nether flaming demonism, to the Nature forces of the material world with the intellect as its servant, an impetus of measureless unresting creation, appropriation, expansion which will end in something violent, huge and "colossal", foredoomed in its very nature to excess and ruin, because light is not in it nor the soul's truth nor the sanction of the gods and their calm eternal will and knowledge.

But beyond the subjectivism of the vital self there is the possibility of a mental and even a psychic subjectivism which would at first perhaps, leaning upon the already realised idea of the soul as Life in action but correcting it, appear as a highly mentalised pragmatism, but might afterwards rise to the higher idea of man as a soul that develops itself individually and collectively in the life and body through the play of an ever-expanding mental existence. This greater idea would realise that the elevation of the human existence will come not through material efficiency alone or the complex play of his vital and dynamic powers mastering through the aid of the intellect the energies of physical Nature for the satisfaction of the life-instincts, which can only be an intensification of his present mode of existence, but through the greatness of his mental and psychic being and a discovery bringing forward an organisation of his vast subliminal nature and its forces. It would see in life an opportunity for the joy and power of knowledge, for the joy and power of beauty, for the joy and power of the human will mastering not only physical Nature, but vital and mental Nature. It might discover her secret yet undreamed-of mind-powers and life-powers and use them for a freer liberation of man from the limitations of his shackled bodily life. It might arrive at new psychic relations, a more sovereign power of the idea to realise itself in the act, inner means of overcoming obstacles of distance and division which would cast into insignificance even the last miraculous achievements of material Science. A development of this kind is far enough away from the dreams of the mass of men, but there are certain pale hints and presages of such a possibility and ideas which lead to it are already held by a great number who are perhaps in this respect the yet unrecognised vanguard of humanity. It is not impossible that behind the confused morning voices of the hour a light of this kind, still below the horizon, may be waiting to ascend with its splendours.

Such a turn of human thought, effort, ideas of life, if it took hold of the communal mind, would evidently lead to a profound revolution throughout the whole range of human existence. It would give it from the first a new tone and atmosphere, a loftier spirit, wider horizons, a greater aim. It might easily develop a Science which would bring the powers of the physical world into a real and not only a contingent and mechanical subjection and open perhaps the doors of other worlds. It might develop an achievement of Art and Beauty which would make the greatness of the past a comparatively little thing and would save the world from the astonishingly callous reign of utilitarian ugliness that even now afflicts it. It would open up a closer and freer interchange between human minds and, it may well be hoped, a kindlier interchange between human hearts and lives. Nor need its achievements stop here, but might proceed to greater things of which these would be only the beginnings. This mental and psychic subjectivism would have its dangers, greater dangers even than those that attend a vitalistic subjectivism, because its powers of action also would be greater, but it would have what vitalistic subjectivism has not and cannot easily have, the chance of a detecting discernment, strong safeguards and a powerful liberating light.

Moving with difficulty upward from Matter to Spirit, this is perhaps a necessary stage of man's development. This was one principal reason of the failure of past attempts to spiritualise mankind, that they endeavoured to spiritualise at once the material man by a sort of rapid miracle, and though that can be done, the miracle is not likely to be of an enduring character if it overleaps the stages of his ascent and leaves the intervening levels untrodden and therefore unmastered. The endeavour may succeed with individuals, — Indian thought would say with those who have made themselves ready in a past existence, — but it must fail with the mass. When it passes beyond the few, the forceful miracle of the Spirit flags; unable to transform by inner force, the new religion tries to save by machinery, is entangled in the mechanical turning of its own instruments, loses the spirit and perishes quickly or decays slowly. That is the fate which overtakes all attempts of the vitalistic, the intellectual and mental, the spiritual endeavour to deal with material man through his physical mind chiefly or alone; the endeavour is overpowered by the machinery it creates and becomes the slave and victim of the machine. That is the revenge which our material Nature, herself mechanical, takes upon all such violent endeavours; she waits to master them by their concessions to her own law. If mankind is to be spiritualised, it must first in the mass cease to be the material or the vital man and become the psychic and the true mental being. It may be questioned whether such a mass progress or conversion is possible; but if it is not, then the spiritualisation of mankind as a whole is a chimera.

From this point of view it is an excellent thing, a sign of great promise, that the wheel of civilisation has been following its past and present curve upward from a solid physical knowledge through a successive sounding of higher and higher powers that mediate between Matter and Spirit. The human intellect in modern times has been first drawn to exhaust the possibilities of materialism by an immense dealing with life and the world upon the basis of Matter as the sole reality, Matter as the Eternal, Matter as the Brahman, *annam brahma*. Afterwards it had begun to turn towards the conception of existence as the large pulsation of a great evolving Life, the creator of Matter, which would have enabled it to deal with our existence on the basis of Life as the original reality, Life as the great Eternal, *prāṇo brahma*. And already it has in germ, in preparation a third conception, the discovery of a great self-expressing and self-finding inner Mind other than our surface mentality as a master-power of existence, that should lead towards a rich attempt to deal with our possibilities and our ways of living on the basis of Mind as the original reality, the great Eternal, *mano brahma*. It will also be a sign of promise if these conceptions succeeded each other with rapidity, with a large but swift evocation of the possibilities of each level; for that would show that there is a readiness in our subconscient Nature and that we need not linger in each stage for centuries.

But still a subjective age of mankind must be an adventure full of perils and uncertainties as are all great adventures of the race. It may wander long before it finds itself or may not find itself at all and swing back to a new repetition of the cycle.

The true secret can only be discovered if in the third stage, in an age of mental subjectivism, the idea becomes strong of the Mind itself as no more than a secondary power of the Spirit's working and of the Spirit as the great Eternal, the original and, in spite of the many terms in which it is both expressed and hidden, the sole reality, *ayam ātmā brahma*. Then only will the real, the decisive endeavour begin and life and the world be studied, known, dealt with in all directions as the self-finding and self-expression of the Spirit. Then only will a spiritual age of mankind be possible. To attempt any adequate discussion of what that would mean, and in an inadequate discussion there is no fruit, would need another volume or two of essays; for we should have to examine a knowledge which is rare and nowhere more than initial. It is enough to say that a spiritual human society would start from and try to realise three essential truths of existence which all Nature seems to be an attempt to hide by their opposites and which therefore are as yet for the mass of mankind only words and dreams, God, freedom, unity. Three things which are one, for you cannot realise freedom and unity unless you realise God, you cannot possess freedom and unity unless you possess God, possess at once your highest self and the self of all creatures. The freedom and unity which otherwise go by that name, are simply attempts of our subjection and our division to get away from themselves by shutting their eyes while they turn somersaults around their own centre. When man is able to see God and to possess him, then he will know real freedom and arrive at real unity, never otherwise. And God is only waiting to be known, while man seeks for him everywhere and creates images of the Divine, but all the while truly finds, effectively erects and worships images only of his own mind-ego and life-ego. When this ego pivot is abandoned and this ego-hunt ceases, then man gets his first real chance of achieving spirituality in his inner and outer life. It will not be enough, but it will be a commencement, a true gate and not a blind entrance.

A spiritualised society would live like its spiritual individuals, not in the ego, but in the spirit, not as the collective ego, but as the collective soul. This freedom from the egoistic standpoint would be its first and most prominent characteristic. But the elimination of egoism would not be brought about, as it is now proposed to bring it about, by persuading or forcing the individual to immolate his personal will and aspirations and his precious and hard-won individuality to the collective will, aims and egoism of the society, driving him like a victim of ancient sacrifice to slay his soul on the altar of that huge and shapeless idol. For that would be only the sacrifice of the smaller to the larger egoism, larger only in bulk, not necessarily greater in quality or wider or nobler, since a collective egoism, result of the united egoisms of all, is as little a god to be worshipped, as flawed and often an uglier and more barbarous fetish than the egoism of the individual. What the spiritual man seeks is to find by the loss of the ego the Self which is one in all and perfect and complete in each and by living in that to grow into the image of its perfection, — individually, be it noted, though with an all-embracing universality of his nature and its conscious circumference. It is said in the old Indian writings that while in the second age, the age of Power, Vishnu descends in the King, and in the third, the age of balance, as the legislator or codifier; in the age of the Truth he descends as Yajna, that is to say, as the Master of works manifest in the heart of his creatures. It is this kingdom of God within, the result of the finding of God not in a distant heaven but within ourselves, of which the state of society in an age of the Truth, spiritual age, would be the result and the external figure.

Therefore a society which was even initially spiritualised, would make the revealing and finding of the divine Self in man the whole first aim of all its activities, its education, its knowledge, its science, its ethics, its art, its economical and political structure. As it was to some extent in the ancient Vedic times with the cultural education of the higher classes, so it would be then with all education. It would embrace all knowledge in its scope, but would make the whole trend and aim and the permeating spirit not mere worldly efficiency, but this self-developing and self-finding. It would pursue physical and psychical science not in order merely to know the world and Nature in her processes and to use them for material human ends, but to know through and in and under and over all things the Divine in the world and the ways of the Spirit in its masks and behind them. It would make it the aim of ethics not to establish a rule of action whether supplementary to the social law or partially corrective of it, the social law that is after all only the rule, often clumsy and ignorant, of the biped pack, the human herd, but to develop the divine nature in the human being. It would make it the aim of Art not merely to present images of the subjective and objective world, but to see them with the significant and creative vision that goes behind their appearances and to reveal the Truth and Beauty of which things visible to us and invisible are the forms, the masks or the symbols and significant figures.

A spiritualised society would treat in its sociology the individual, from the saint to the criminal, not as units of a social problem to be passed through some skilfully devised machinery and either flattened into the social mould or crushed out of it, but as souls suffering and entangled in a net and to be rescued, souls growing and to be encouraged to grow, souls grown and from whom help and power can be drawn by the lesser spirits who are not yet adult. The aim of its economics would be not to create a huge engine of production, whether of the competitive or the co-operative kind, but to give to men — not only to some but to all men each in his highest possible measure — the joy of work according to their own nature and free leisure to grow inwardly, as well as a simply rich and beautiful life for all. In its politics it would not regard the nations within the scope of their own internal life as enormous State machines regulated and armoured with man living for the sake of the machine and worshipping it as his God and his larger self, content at the first call to kill others upon its altar and to bleed there himself so that the machine may remain intact and powerful and be made ever larger, more complex, more cumbrous, more mechanically efficient and entire. Neither would it be content to maintain these nations or States in their mutual relations as noxious engines meant to discharge poisonous gas upon each other in peace and to rush in times of clash upon each other's armed hosts and unarmed millions, full of belching shot and men missioned to murder like hostile tanks in a modern battlefield. It would re-

gard the peoples as group-souls, the Divinity concealed and to
be self-discovered in its human collectivities, group-souls meant
like the individual to grow according to their own nature and by
that growth to help each other, to help the whole race in the one
common work of humanity. And that work would be to find the
divine Self in the individual and the collectivity and to realise
spiritually, mentally, vitally, materially its greatest, largest,
richest and deepest possibilities in the inner life of all and their
outer action and nature.

For it is into the Divine within each man and each people
that the man and the nation have to grow; it is not an external
idea or rule that has to be imposed on them from without.
Therefore the law of a growing inner freedom is that which will
be most honoured in the spiritual age of mankind. True it is that
so long as man has not come within measurable distance of self-
knowledge and has not set his face towards it, he cannot escape
from the law of external compulsion and all his efforts to do so
must be vain. He is and always must be, so long as that lasts,
the slave of others, the slave of his family, his caste, his clan,
his Church, his society, his nation; and he cannot but be that
and they too cannot help throwing their crude and mechanical
compulsion on him, because he and they are the slaves of their
own ego, of their own lower nature. We must feel and obey the
compulsion of the Spirit if we would establish our inner right to
escape other compulsion; we must make our lower nature the
willing slave, the conscious and illumined instrument or the
ennobled but still self-subjected portion, consort or partner of the
divine Being within us, for it is that subjection which is the condition of our freedom, since spiritual freedom is not the egoistic
assertion of our separate mind and life but obedience to the
Divine Truth in ourself and our members and in all around us.
But we have, even so, to remark that God respects the freedom
of the natural members of our being and that he gives them
room to grow in their own nature so that by natural growth and
not by self-extinction they may find the Divine in themselves.
The subjection which they finally accept, complete and absolute,
must be a willing subjection of recognition and aspiration to
their own source of light and power and their highest being.

Therefore even in the unregenerated state we find that the healthiest, the truest, the most living growth and action is that which arises in the largest possible freedom and that all excess of compulsion is either the law of a gradual atrophy or a tyranny varied or cured by outbreaks of rabid disorder. And as soon as man comes to know his spiritual self, he does by that discovery, often even by the very seeking for it, as ancient thought and religion saw, escape from the outer law and enter into the law of freedom.

A spiritual age of mankind will perceive this truth. It will not try to make man perfect by machinery or keep him straight by tying up all his limbs. It will not present to the member of the society his higher self in the person of the policeman, the official and the corporal, nor, let us say, in the form of a socialistic bureaucracy or a Labour Soviet. Its aim will be to diminish as soon and as far as possible the element of external compulsion in human life by awakening the inner divine compulsion of the Spirit within and all the preliminary means it will use will have that for its aim. In the end it will employ chiefly if not solely the spiritual compulsion which even the spiritual individual can exercise on those around him, — and how much more should a spiritual society be able to do it, — that which awakens within us in spite of all inner resistance and outer denial the compulsions of the Light, the desire and the power to grow through one's own nature into the Divine. For the perfectly spiritualised society will be one in which, as is dreamed by the spiritual anarchist, all men will be deeply free, and it will be so because the preliminary condition will have been satisfied. In that state each man will be not a law to himself, but *the* law, the divine Law, because he will be a soul living in the Divine and not an ego living mainly if not entirely for its own interest and purpose. His life will be led by the law of his own divine nature liberated from the ego.

Nor will that mean a breaking up of all human society into the isolated action of individuals; for the third word of the Spirit is unity. The spiritual life is the flower not of a featureless but a conscious and diversified oneness. Each man has to grow into the Divine within himself through his own individual being, therefore is a certain growing measure of freedom a necessity of the being as it develops and perfect freedom the sign and the condition of the perfect life. But also, the Divine whom he thus sees in himself, he sees equally in all others and as the same Spirit in all. Therefore too is a growing inner unity with others a necessity of his being and perfect unity the sign and condition of the perfect life. Not only to see and find the Divine in oneself, but to see and find the Divine in all, not only to seek one's own individual liberation or perfection, but to seek the liberation and perfection of others is the complete law of the spiritual being. If the divinity sought were a separate godhead within oneself and not the one Divine, or if one sought God for oneself alone, then indeed the result might be a grandiose egoism, the Olympian egoism of a Goethe or the Titanic egoism imagined by Nietzsche, or it might be the isolated self-knowledge or asceticism of the ivory tower or the Stylites pillar. But he who sees God in all, will serve freely God in all with the service of love. He will, that is to say, seek not only his own freedom, but the freedom of all, not only his own perfection, but the perfection of all. He will not feel his individuality perfect except in the largest universality, nor his own life to be full life except as it is one with the universal life. He will not live either for himself or for the State and society, for the individual ego or the collective ego, but for something much greater, for God in himself and for the Divine in the universe.

The spiritual age will be ready to set in when the common mind of man begins to be alive to these truths and to be moved or desire to be moved by this triple or triune Spirit. That will mean the turning of the cycle of social development which we have been considering out of its incomplete repetitions on a new upward line towards its goal. For having set out, according to our supposition, with a symbolic age, an age in which man felt a great Reality behind all life which he sought through symbols, it will reach an age in which it will begin to live in that Reality, not through the symbol, not by the power of the type or of the convention or of the individual reason and intellectual will, but in our own highest nature which will be the nature of that Reality fulfilled in the conditions — not necessarily the same as now — of terrestrial existence. This is what the religions have seen with a more or less adequate intuition, but most often as in a glass darkly, that which they called the kingdom of God on earth, — his kingdom within in men's spirit and therefore, for the one is the material result of the effectivity of the other, his kingdom without in the life of the peoples.

*

A spiritual religion of humanity is the hope of the future. By this is not meant what is ordinarily called a universal religion, a system, a thing of creed and intellectual belief and dogma and outward rite. Mankind has tried unity by that means; it has failed and deserved to fail, because there can be no universal religious system, one in mental creed and vital form. The inner spirit is indeed one, but more than any other the spiritual life insists on freedom and variation in its self-expression and means of development. A religion of humanity means the growing realisation that there is a secret Spirit, a divine Reality, in which we are all one, that humanity is its highest present vehicle on earth, that the human race and the human being are the means by which it will progressively reveal itself here. It implies a growing attempt to live out this knowledge and bring about a kingdom of this divine Spirit upon earth. By its growth within us oneness with our fellow-men will become the leading principle of all our life, not merely a principle of co-operation but a deeper brotherhood, a real and an inner sense of unity and equality and a common life. There must be the realisation by the individual that only in the life of his fellow-men is his own life complete. There must be the realisation by the race that only on the free and full life of the individual can its own perfection and permanent happiness be founded. There must be too a discipline and a way of salvation in accordance with this religion, that is to say, a means by which it can be developed by each man within himself, so that it may be developed in the life of the race.

(XV, p. 554)

Supermind in the Evolution*

A NEW humanity would then be a race of mental beings on the earth and in the earthly body but delivered from its present conditions in the reign of the cosmic Ignorance so far as to be possessed of a perfected mind, a mind of light which could even be a subordinate action of the supermind or Truth-Consciousness and in any case capable of the full possibilities of mind acting as a recipient of that truth and at least a secondary action of it in thought and life. It could even be a part of what could be described as a divine life upon earth and at least the beginnings of an evolution in the Knowledge and no longer entirely or predominantly in the Ignorance. How far this would go, whether it would eventually embrace the whole of humanity or only an advanced portion of it, would depend upon the intention in the evolution itself, on the intention in whatever cosmic or transcendent Will is guiding the movements of the universe. We have supposed not only the descent of the supermind upon the earth but its embodiment in a supramental race with all its natural consequences and a new total action in which the new humanity would find its complete development and its assured place in the new order.

But it is clear that all this could only come as a result of the evolution which is already taking place upon earth extending far beyond its present bounds and passing into a radically new movement governed by a new principle in which mind and man would be subordinate elements and no longer mind the utmost achievement or man the head or leader. The evolution we see around us at present is not of that kind and, it might be said, shows few signs of such a possibility, so few that the reason, at present our only sure guide, has no right to hazard belief in it. Earth, the earth we see, with its life deeply immersed and founded in inconscience and ignorance, is not built for such a development or capable of holding such an advent; its materiality and limitations condemn it to be permanently the field of a far inferior order. It

* *The Supramental Manifestation*, pp. 60–66; *The Mind of Light*, pp. 102–9 (copyright 1954 by The Sri Aurobindo Library, Inc. Published by E. P. Dutton & Co., Inc., and used with their permission).

may be said too that for such an order there must be a place somewhere and even if supermind is not a mere unwarranted speculation and is a concrete reality, there is no need and no place for its embodying itself here. Mind as marking the full play of the knowledge possible to the ignorance must have its field somewhere and to keep the earth as its natural field would best serve the economy of cosmic Nature. A materialistic philosophy would admit of no possibility of a divine life in Matter; but even a philosophy admitting a soul or spirit or a spiritual terminus of the evolutionary movement here could very well deny the capacity of earth for a divine life: a divine existence could only be achieved by a departure from earth and the body. Even if cosmic existence is not an illusion or Maya, a divine or a completely spiritual being is likely to be possible only in another less material world or only in the pure spirit. At any rate, to the normal human reason the odds seem to be heavily against any early materialisation on earth of anything divine.

Again, if too strong a stress is laid on the present or apparent character of the evolution here as it is presented to us by physical science, it might be urged that there is no warrant for expecting any emergence of a principle higher than human mind or of any such thing as super-human beings in a world of Matter. Consciousness is itself dependent upon Matter and material agencies for its birth and its operations and an infallible Truth-Consciousness, such as we suppose supermind to be, would be a contradiction of these conditions and must be dismissed as a chimera. Fundamentally, physical science regards evolution as a development of forms and vital activities; the development of a larger and more capable consciousness is a subordinate result of the development of life and form and not a major or essential characteristic or circumstance and it cannot go beyond limits determined by the material origin of mind and life. Mind has shown itself capable of many extraordinary achievements, but independence of the material organ or of physical conditions or a capability for any such thing as a power of direct and absolute knowledge not acquired by material means would be beyond the conditions imposed by Nature. At a certain point therefore the evolution of consciousness can go no further. Even if a something definite and independent which we call a soul exists, it is limited by its natural conditions here where Matter is the basis, physical life the condition, mind the highest possible instrument; there is no possibility of an action of consciousness apart from the body or surpassing this physical, vital or mental Nature. This fixes the limits of our evolution here.

It might be suggested also that until something clearly recognisable like supermind manifests itself with some definiteness and fullness or until it descends and takes possession of our earth-consciousness, we cannot be certain that it exists; till then mind holds the place as a general arbiter or field of reference for all knowledge and mind is incapable of any certain or absolute knowledge; it has to doubt all, to test all and yet to achieve all, but cannot be secure in its knowledge or its achievement. That, incidentally, establishes the necessity of such a principle as the supermind or Truth-Consciousness in any intelligible universe, for without it there is no issue, no goal for either life or knowledge. Consciousness cannot achieve its own entire meaning, its own supreme result without it; it will end in an inconsequence or a fiasco. To become aware of its own truth and all truth is the very aim of its existence and it cannot do so, so long as it has to tend towards truth, towards knowledge in ignorance and through the ignorance: it must develop or it must reach a power of itself whose very nature is to know, to see, to possess in its own power. This is what we call supermind and, once it is admitted, all the rest becomes intelligible. But till then we are in doubt and it may be contended that even if supermind is admitted as a reality, there can be no certainty of its advent and reign: till then all effort towards it may end in failure. It is not enough that the supermind should be actually there above us, its descent a possibility or a future intention in Nature. We have no certainty of the reality of this descent until it becomes an objectivised fact in our earthly being. Light has often tried to descend upon the earth, but the Light remains unfulfilled and incomplete; man may reject the Light, the world is still full of darkness and the advent seems to be little more than a chance; this doubt is to some extent justified by the actualities of the past and still existing possibilities of the future. Its power to stand would disappear only if supermind is once admitted as a consequent part of the order of the universe. If the evolution tends from Matter to Supermind, it must also tend to bring down Supermind into Matter and the consequences are inevitable.

The whole trouble of this incertitude arises from the fact that we do not look straight at the whole truth of the world as it is and draw from it the right conclusion as to what the world must be and cannot fail to be. This world is, no doubt, based ostensibly upon Matter, but its summit is Spirit and the ascent towards Spirit must be the aim and justification of its existence and the pointer to its meaning and purpose. But the natural conclusion to be drawn from the supremacy and summit existence of Spirit is clouded by a false or imperfect idea of spirituality which has been constructed by intellect in its ignorance and even by its too hasty and one-sided grasp at knowledge. The Spirit has been thought of not as something all-pervading and the secret essence of our being, but as something only looking down on us from the heights and drawing us only towards the heights and away from the rest of existence. So we get the idea of our cosmic and individual being as a great illusion, and departure from it and extinction in our consciousness of both individual and cosmos as the only hope, the sole release. Or we build up the idea of the earth as a world of ignorance, suffering and trial and our only future an escape into heavens beyond; there is no divine prospect for us here, no fulfilment possible even with the utmost evolution on earth in the body, no victorious transformation, no supreme object to be worked out in terrestrial existence. But if supermind exists, if it descends, if it becomes the ruling principle, all that seems impossible to mind becomes not only possible but inevitable. If we look closely, we shall see that there is a straining of mind and life on their heights toward their own perfection, towards some divine fulfilment, towards their own absolute. That and not only something beyond and elsewhere is the true sign, the meaning of this constant evolution and the labour of continual birth and rebirth and the spiral ascent of Nature. But it is only by the descent of supermind and the fulfilment of mind and life by their self-exceeding that this secret intention in things, this hidden meaning of

Spirit and Nature can become utterly overt and in its totality realisable. This is the evolutionary aspect and significance of supermind, but in truth it is an eternal principle existing covertly even in the material universe, the secret supporter of all creation, it is that which makes the emergence of consciousness possible and certain in an apparently inconscient world and compels a climb in Nature towards a supreme spiritual Reality. It is, in fact, an already and always existent plane of being, the nexus of Spirit and Matter, holding in its truth and reality and making certain the whole meaning and aim of the universe.

If we disregard our present ideas of evolution, all changes, — if we can regard consciousness and not life and form as the fundamental and essential evolutionary principle and its emergence and full development of its possibilities as the object of the evolutionary urge. The inconscience of Matter cannot be an insuperable obstacle; for in this inconscience can be detected an involved consciousness which has to evolve; life and mind are steps and instruments of that evolution; the purposeful drive and workings of the inconscient material Energy are precisely such as we can attribute to the presence of an involved consciousness automatic, not using thought like the mind but guided by something like an inherent material instinct practically infallible in all its steps, not yet cognitive but miraculously creative. The entirely and inherently enlightened Truth-Consciousness we attribute to Supermind would be the same reality appearing at an ultimate stage of the evolution, finally evolved and no longer wholly involved as in Matter or partly and imperfectly evolved and therefore capable of imperfection and error as in life and mind, now possessed of its own natural fullness and perfection, luminously automatic, infallible. All the objections to a complete evolutionary possibility then fall away; it would, on the contrary, be the inevitable consequence contained not only in Nature as a whole but even in material Nature.

In this vision of things the universe will reveal itself in its unity and totality as a manifestation of a single Being, Nature as its power of manifestation, evolution as its process of gradual self-revelation here in Matter. We would see the divine series of the worlds as a ladder of ascent from Matter to supreme Spirit;

there would reveal itself the possibility, the prospect of a supreme manifestation by the conscious and no longer a veiled and enigmatic descent of the Spirit and its powers in their fullness even into this lowest world of Matter. The riddle of the universe need be no longer a riddle; the dubious mystery of things would put off its enigma, its constant ambiguity, the tangled writings would become legible and intelligible. In this revelation, supermind would take its natural place and no longer be a matter of doubt or questioning to an intelligence bewildered by the complexity of the world; it would appear as the inevitable consequence of the nature of mind, life and Matter, the fulfilment of their meaning, their inherent principle and tendencies, the necessary perfection of their imperfection, the summit to which all are climbing, the consummation of divine existence, consciousness and bliss to which it is leading, the last result of the birth of things and supreme goal of this progressive manifestation which we see here in life.

The full emergence of supermind may be accomplished by a sovereign manifestation, a descent into earth-consciousness and a rapid assumption of its powers and disclosing of its forms and the creation of a supramental race and a supramental life: this must indeed be the full result of its action in Nature. But this has not been the habit of evolutionary Nature in the past upon earth and it may well be that this supramental evolution also will fix its own periods, though it cannot be at all a similar development to that of which earth has hitherto been the witness. But once it has begun, all must unavoidably and perfectly manifest and all parts of Nature must tend towards a greatest possible luminousness and perfection. It is this certainty that authorises us to believe that mind and humanity also will tend towards the realisation that will be far beyond our present dreams of perfection. A mind of light will replace the present confusion and trouble of this earthly ignorance; it is likely that even those parts of humanity which cannot reach it will yet be aware of its possibility and consciously tend towards it; not only so, but the life of humanity will be enlightened, uplifted, governed, harmonised by this luminous principle and even the body become something much less powerless, obscure and animal in its propensities and capable instead of a new and harmonised perfection. It is this possibility that we have to look at and that would mean a new humanity uplifted into Light, capable of a spiritualised being and action, open to governance by some light of the Truth-Consciousness, capable even on the mental level and in its own order of something that might be called the beginning of a divinised life.

*

The thing to be done is as large as human life, and therefore the individuals who lead the way will take all human life for their province. These pioneers will consider nothing as alien to them, nothing as outside their scope. For every part of human life has to be taken up by the spiritual, — not only the intellectual, the aesthetic, the ethical, but the dynamic, the vital, the physical; therefore for none of these things or the activities that spring from them will they have contempt or aversion, however they may insist on a change of the spirit and a transmutation of the form. In each power of our nature they will seek for its own proper means of conversion; knowing that the Divine is concealed in all, they will hold that all can be made the Spirit's means of self-finding and all can be converted into its instruments of divine living.

(XV, p. 251)

SAVITRI

The Vision and the Boon*

Nothing now moved in the vast brooding space:
A stillness came upon the listening world,
A mute immensity of the Eternal's peace.
But Aswapathy's heart replied to her,
A cry amid the silence of the Vasts:
"How shall I rest content with mortal days
And the dull measure of terrestrial things,
I who have seen behind the cosmic mask
The glory and the beauty of thy face?
Hard is the doom to which thou bindst thy sons!
How long shall our spirits battle with the Night
And bear defeat and the brute yoke of Death,
We who are vessels of a deathless Force
And builders of the godhead of the race?
Or if it is thy work I do below
Amid the error and waste of human life
In the vague light of man's half-conscious mind,
Why breaks not in some distant gleam of thee?
Ever the centuries and millenniums pass.
Where in the greyness is thy coming's ray?
Where is the thunder of thy victory's wings?
Only we hear the feet of passing gods.
A plan in the occult eternal Mind
Mapped out to backward and prophetic sight,
The aeons ever repeat their changeless round,
The cycles all rebuild and ever aspire.
All we have done is ever still to do.
All breaks and all renews and is the same.
Huge revolutions of life's fruitless gyre,
The new-born ages perish like the old,

---

* *Savitri—A Legend and a Symbol*, pp. 341–48.

As if the sad Enigma kept its right
Till all is done for which this scene was made.
Too little the strength that now with us is born,
Too faint the light that steals through Nature's lids,
Too scant the joy with which she buys our pain.
In a brute world that knows not its own sense,
Thought-racked upon the wheel of birth we live,
The instruments of an impulse not our own
Moved to achieve with our heart's blood for price
Half-knowledge, half-creations that soon tire.
A foiled immortal soul in perishing limbs,
Baffled and beaten back we labour still;
Annulled, frustrated, spent, we still survive.
In anguish we labour that from us may rise
A larger-seeing man with nobler heart,
A golden vessel of the incarnate Truth,
The executor of the divine attempt
Equipped to wear the earthly body of God,
Communicant and prophet and lover and king.
I know that thy creation cannot fail.
For even through the mists of mortal thought
Infallible are thy mysterious steps,
And, though Necessity dons the garb of Chance,
Hidden in the blind shifts of Fate she keeps
The slow calm logic of Infinity's pace
And the inviolate sequence of its will.
All life is fixed in an ascending scale
And adamantine is the evolving Law;
In the beginning is prepared the close.
This strange irrational product of the mire,
This compromise between the beast and God,
Is not the crown of thy miraculous world.
I know there shall inform the inconscient cells,
At one with Nature and at height with heaven,
A spirit vast as the containing sky
And swept with ecstasy from invisible founts,
A god come down and greater by the fall.
A power arose out of my slumber's cell.

Abandoning the tardy limp of the hours
And the inconstant blink of mortal sight,
There where the Thinker sleeps in too much light
And intolerant flames the lone all-witnessing Eye
Hearing the word of Fate from Silence' heart
In the endless moment of Eternity,
It saw from timelessness the works of Time.
Overpassed were the leaden formulas of the Mind,
Overpowered the obstacle of mortal Space:
The unfolding Image showed the things to come.
A giant dance of Shiva tore the past,
There was a thunder as of worlds that fall;
Earth was o'errun with fire and the roar of Death
Clamouring to slay a world his hunger had made;
There was a clangour of Destruction's wings:
The Titan's battle-cry was in my ears,
Alarm and rumour shook the armoured Night.
I saw the Omnipotent's flaming pioneers
Over the heavenly verge which turns towards life
Come crowding down the amber stairs of birth;
Forerunners of a divine multitude
Out of the paths of the morning star they came
Into the little room of mortal life.
I saw them cross the twilight of an age,
The sun-eyed children of a marvellous dawn,
The great creators with wide brows of calm,
The massive barrier-breakers of the world
And wrestlers with destiny in her lists of will,
The labourers in the quarries of the gods,
The messengers of the Incommunicable,
The architects of immortality.
Into the fallen human sphere they came,
Faces that wore the Immortal's glory still,
Voices that communed still with the thoughts of God,
Bodies made beautiful by the Spirit's light,
Carrying the magic word, the mystic fire,
Carrying the Dionysian cup of joy,
Approaching eyes of a diviner man,

Lips chanting an unknown anthem of the soul,
Feet echoing in the corridors of Time.
High priests of wisdom, sweetness, might and bliss,
Discoverers of beauty's sunlit ways
And swimmers of Love's laughing fiery floods
And dancers within rapture's golden doors,
Their tread one day shall change the suffering earth
And justify the light on Nature's face.
Although Fate lingers in the high Beyond
And the work seems vain on which our heart's force was spent,
All shall be done for which our pain was borne.
Even as of old man came behind the beast
This high divine successor surely shall come
Behind man's inefficient mortal pace,
Behind his vain labour, sweat and blood and tears:
He shall know what mortal mind barely durst think,
He shall do what the heart of the mortal could not dare.
Inheritor of the toil of human time
He shall take on him the burden of the gods;
All heavenly light shall visit the earth's thoughts,
The might of heaven shall fortify earthly hearts;
Earth's deeds shall touch the superhuman's height,
Earth's seeing widen into the infinite.
Heavy unchanged weighs still the imperfect world;
The splendid youth of Time has passed and failed;
Heavy and long are the years our labour counts
And still the seals are firm upon man's soul
And weary is the ancient Mother's heart.
O Truth defended in thy secret sun,
Voice of her mighty musings in shut heavens
On things withdrawn within her luminous depths,
O Wisdom-Splendour, Mother of the universe,
Creatrix, the Eternal's artist Bride,
Linger not long with thy transmuting hand
Pressed vainly on one golden bar of Time,
As if Time dare not open its heart to God.
O radiant fountain of the world's delight
World-free and unattainable above,

O Bliss who ever dwellst deep hid within
While men seek thee outside and never find,
Mystery and Muse with hieratic tongue,
Incarnate the white passion of thy force,
Mission to earth some living form of thee.
One moment fill with thy eternity,
Let thy infinity in one body live,
All-Knowledge wrap one mind in seas of light,
All-Love throb single in one human heart.
Immortal, treading the earth with mortal feet
All heaven's beauty crowd in earthly limbs!
Omnipotence, girdle with the power of God
Movements and moments of a mortal will,
Pack with the eternal might one human hour
And with one gesture change all future time.
Let a great word be spoken from the heights
And one great act unlock the doors of Fate."

   His prayer sank down in the resisting Night
Oppressed by the thousand forces that deny,
As if too weak to climb to the Supreme.
But there arose a wide consenting Voice;
The spirit of beauty was revealed in sound:
Light floated round the marvellous Vision's brow
And on her lips the Immortal's joy took shape.
"O strong forerunner, I have heard thy cry.
One shall descend and break the iron Law,
Change Nature's doom by the lone Spirit's power.
A limitless Mind that can contain the world,
A sweet and violent heart of ardent calms
Moved by the passions of the gods shall come.
All mights and greatnesses shall join in her;
Beauty shall walk celestial on the earth,
Delight shall sleep in the cloud-net of her hair
And in her body as on his homing tree
Immortal Love shall beat his glorious wings.
A music of griefless things shall weave her charm;
The harps of the Perfect shall attune her voice,

The streams of Heaven shall murmur in her laugh,
Her lips shall be the honeycombs of God,
Her limbs his golden jars of ecstasy,
Her breasts the rapture-flowers of Paradise.
She shall bear Wisdom in her voiceless bosom,
Strength shall be with her like a conqueror's sword
And from her eyes the Eternal's bliss shall gaze.
A seed shall be sown in Death's tremendous hour,
A branch of heaven transplant to human soil;
Nature shall overleap her mortal step;
Fate shall be changed by an unchanging will."

As a flame disappears in endless Light
Immortally extinguished in its source,
Vanished the splendour and was stilled the word.
An echo of delight that once was close,
The harmony journeyed towards some distant hush,
A music failing in the ear of trance,
A cadence called by distant cadences,
A voice that trembled into strains withdrawn.
Her form retreated from the longing earth
Forsaking nearness to the abandoned sense,
Ascending to her unattainable home.
Lone, brilliant, vacant lay the inner fields;
All was unfilled inordinate spirit space,
Indifferent, waste, a desert of bright peace.
Then a line moved on the far edge of calm:
The warm-lipped sentient soft terrestrial wave,
A quick and many-murmured moan and laugh,
Came gliding in upon white feet of sound.
Unlocked was the deep glory of Silence' heart;
The absolute unmoving stillnesses
Surrendered to the breath of mortal air,
Dissolving boundlessly the heavens of trance
Collapsed to waking mind. Eternity
Cast down its incommunicable lids
Over its solitudes remote from ken
Behind the voiceless mystery of sleep.

The grandiose respite failed, the wide release.
Across the light of fast-receding planes
That fled from him as from a falling star,
Compelled to fill his human house in Time
His soul drew back into the speed and noise
Of the vast business of created things.
A chariot of the marvels of the heavens
Broad-based to bear the gods on fiery wheels,
Flaming he swept through the spiritual gates.
The mortal stir received him in its midst.
Once more he moved amid material scenes,
Lifted by intimations from the heights
And twixt the pauses of the building brain
Touched by the thoughts that skim the fathomless surge
Of Nature and wing back to hidden shores.
The eternal seeker in the aeonic field
Besieged by the intolerant press of hours
Again was strong for great swift-footed deeds.
Awake beneath the ignorant vault of Night,
He saw the unnumbered people of the stars
And heard the questioning of the unsatisfied flood
And toiled with the form-maker, measuring Mind.
A wanderer from the occult invisible suns
Accomplishing the fate of transient things,
A god in the figure of the arisen beast,
He raised his brow of conquest to the heavens
Establishing the empire of the soul
On Matter and its bounded universe
As on a solid rock in infinite seas.
The Lord of Life resumed his mighty rounds
In the scant field of the ambiguous globe.

★

THE tale of Satyavan and Savitri is recited
in the Mahabharata as a story of conjugal love conquering
death. But this legend is, as shown by many features of the

human tale, one of the many symbolic myths of the Vedic cycle. Satyavan is the soul carrying the divine truth of being within itself but descended into the grip of death and ignorance; Savitri is the Divine Word, daughter of the Sun, goddess of the supreme Truth who comes down and is born to save; Aswapati, the Lord of the Horse, her human father, is the Lord of Tapasya, the concentrated energy of spiritual endeavour that helps us to rise from the mortal to the immortal planes; Dyumatsena, Lord of the Shining Hosts, father of Satyavan, is the Divine Mind here fallen blind, losing its celestial kingdom of vision, and through that loss its kingdom of glory. Still this is not a mere allegory, the characters are not personified qualities, but incarnations or emanations of living and conscious Forces with whom we can enter into concrete touch and they take human bodies in order to help man and show him the way from his mortal state to a divine consciousness and immortal life.

(XXVII, p. 511)

PART FOUR

EPILOGUE

THE MOTHER, 1969, AGE 91

We Are for a New Creation

I invite you to the great adventure, and in this adventure you are not to repeat spiritually what the others have done before us, because our adventure begins from beyond that stage. We are for a new creation, entirely new, carrying in it all the unforeseen, all risks, all hazards—a true adventure of which the goal is sure victory, but of which the way is unknown and has to be traced out step by step in the unexplored. It is something that has never been in the present universe and will never be in the same manner. If that interests you, well, embark. What will happen tomorrow, I do not know. You must leave behind whatever has been designed, whatever has been built up, and then march into the unknown. Come what may.

—The Mother on Auroville, 1957

EPILOGUE

Education

Sri Aurobindo's and the Mother's claim for a Supramental Age, and the Mother's claim in 1956 that the Supermind was manifest on earth through the instrument of her own mind and body, may be viewed less suspiciously if such claims positively effect individual and historical growth. Two endeavors particularly supportive of Sri Aurobindo's and the Mother's claims are their educational system and creation of the city of Auroville. Although their implications cannot be definitely assessed for decades to come, there is ample evidence that both of these ventures have avoided many of the deeply rooted vices of virtually all extant educational and communal systems.

Significantly, the educational philosophy operative at the Ashram and at Auroville has been an integral part of their discipline from the earliest stage of development. As early as 1910, Sri Aurobindo articulated the three requirements for a true educational system:

> The first principle of true teaching is that nothing can be taught. The teacher is not an instructor or task-master, he is a helper and a guide. His business is to suggest and not to impose. He does not actually train the pupil's mind, he only shows him how to perfect his instruments of knowledge and helps and encourages him in the process. He does not impart knowledge to him, he shows him how to acquire knowledge for himself. . . .
>
> The second principle is that the mind has to be consulted in its own growth. The idea of hammering the child into the shape desired by the parent or teacher is a barbarous and ignorant superstition. It is he himself who must be induced to expand in accordance with his own nature. . . . Everyone has in him something divine, something his own, a chance of perfection and strength in however small a sphere which God offers him to take or refuse. The task is to find it, develop

225

it and use it. The chief aim of education should be to help the growing soul to draw out that in itself which is best and make it perfect for a noble use. . . .

The third principle of education is to work from the near to the far, from that which is to that which shall be. The basis of a man's nature is almost always, in addition to his soul's past, his heredity, his surroundings, his nationality, his country, the soil from which he draws sustenance, the air which he breathes, the sights, sounds, habits to which he is accustomed. . . . The past is our foundation, the present our material, the future our aim and summit. Each must have its due and natural place in a national system of education.[1]

The nucleus of the Ashram school was established during the 1940's for the children of the disciples. But by January 1952, the Mother launched the Sri Aurobindo International Centre of Education (SAICE), and the Ashram opened its educational facilities to other Indian and Western children. From its inception the Mother insisted that SAICE represented a major force for spiritual and intellectual progress. At present, SAICE is a coeducational residence school with approximately six hundred students, about half from India and half Western. All the children learn to speak English and French and at least one Indian language (Indian students from the north learn a southern language, and southern students learn a northern language). Boys and girls—as indeed men and women in all parts of the Ashram and Auroville—receive the same education, including athletic activities such as soccer and boxing. The school begins at kindergarten and progresses to the equivalent of graduate study, but diplomas and certificates, examinations and grades are all considered to be utilitarian devices incompatible with the true aim of education.

As is the case with every such venture, the disciples, who inevitably fall short of the master's exacting example, may mistake uniformity and orthodoxy for the creative and unified synthesis Sri Aurobindo and the Mother have sought to establish. If the Mother's confidence that SAICE will eventually "be the greatest seat of knowledge upon earth"[2] is to be justified, the disciples will have to meet the high requirements established by her. Ultimately, it is the spiritual discipline that holds the key: the entire educational scheme depends upon the requirements set forth in Sri Aurobindo's and the Mother's yoga, of which "The Science of Living" is the most succinct, authoritative summary.

The Science of Living

In this essay, subtitled "To Know Oneself and to Control Oneself," the Mother describes the fourfold discipline by which the sincere aspirant can progress toward an integral perfection of the four planes of human existence: physical, vital, mental, and psychic-spiritual. These four areas correspond to the four goals of beauty, power, knowledge, and love. Just as Sri Aurobindo contends that the yogas of work, knowledge, and love are equally important ingredients in the integral yoga of self-perfection, the Mother insists on the need to perfect all four levels of the self, and simultaneously to realize the four goals of human life. Since social forms ordinarily militate against the egoless unity of the individual and the communal, the Mother organized a community called the Sri Aurobindo Ashram, in which disciples could concentrate on the spiritual discipline articulated by Sri Aurobindo. The Ashram, which numbers more than three thousand disciples, remains the core of Sri Aurobindo's and the Mother's work: it is at the Ashram that the Mother presides over such activities as SAICE, World Union, Sri Aurobindo's Action, and Auroville, the first planetary city presently under construction five miles from the Ashram in Pondicherry.

Auroville

Auroville is unquestionably the most ambitious effort by the Mother and disciples to implement Sri Aurobindo's vision of a spiritually disciplined, selflessly active community. Indeed, Auroville is intended as the bridge between man's present stage of evolution and the Divine Life which is the goal of Sri Aurobindo's and the Mother's discipline and historical vision.

Neither the following description nor any combination of reports and photographs can adequately capture the multileveled creativity by which the Aurovillians are attempting to fashion a spiritualized or supramental community. In comparison to the Ashram, Auroville is a more demanding effort because it seeks to combine individual spirituality with a specific communal task. As the Mother explained in June 1971: "The Ashram will keep its role as pioneer, inspirer and guide. Auroville is an experiment in collective realisation."[3]

That the highly demanding ideal established by the Mother is clearly, if unevenly, perceptible at Auroville should help to attract those who are ready, and to discourage those who are not. It is encouraging that there are some who fit the Mother's description of a true Aurovillian:

> To be an Aurovillian one must at least belong to the enlightened humanity and aspire to the higher consciousness, that which will govern the race of tomorrow. Always higher and always better, beyond the egoistic limitations.[4]

Many familiar with Auroville, both as it exists in Pondicherry and as an ideal for communities in other parts of the world, believe that because of it the evolution of man may proceed at an accelerated pace.

Notes

1. "A System of National Education," in *The Hour of God*, XVII, pp. 204–5; see also *Sri Aurobindo and the Mother on Education* (1966), p. 11.

2. K. R. Srinivas Iyengar, *Sri Aurobindo: A Biography and a History* (1972), II, p. 1382.

3. Quoted in *Gazette Aurovilienne*, No. 4, p. 9.

4. Quoted in *ibid.*, No. 3, p. 17.

THE MOTHER ON EDUCATION

The International Centre of Education*

The conditions under which men live upon the earth are the result of their state of consciousness. To seek to change conditions without changing the consciousness is a vain chimera. All who have had the perception of what could be and should be done to improve the situation, in the different domains of human life, economical, political, social, financial, educational or sanitary, are precisely the individuals who have developed their consciousness more or less to an exceptional degree and put themselves in contact with higher planes of consciousness. But their ideas remained on the whole theoretical; or, if an attempt was ever made to realize them practically, it always failed lamentably in the long or short run: for no human organization can change radically unless human consciousness itself changes. Prophets of a new humanity have followed one another, religions, spiritual or social, have been created, their beginnings were at times full of promise: but, as humanity was not transformed at heart, the old errors arising from human nature itself have reappeared gradually and after a time it was found that one was left almost at the same spot from where one had started with so much hope and enthusiasm. In this effort, however, to improve human conditions there have always been two tendencies, which although apparently contrary to each other should rather be complementary and together work out the progress. One seeks a collective reorganization, something that would lead towards an effective unity of mankind: the other declares that all progress is made first by the individual and insists that it is the individual who should be given conditions in which he can progress freely. Both are equally true and necessary, and our effort should be directed along both lines. Collective progress and individual progress are interdependent. Before

*Sri Aurobindo and the Mother on Education (1966), pp. 102–4; Bulletin of the International Centre of Education (Special Issue, 1968), pp. 25–27.

the individual can take a leap forward, it is necessary that something of an antecedent progress be achieved in the collective life. A way has therefore to be found whereby the twofold progress can go on simultaneously.

It is in answer to this pressing need that Sri Aurobindo conceived the scheme of his International Centre of Education, so that the élite of humanity may be made ready who would be able to work for the progressive unification of the race and who at the same time would be prepared to embody the new force descending upon earth to transform it. Some broad ideas would serve as the basis for organizing this center of education and as a guide for the program of studies. Most of these have already been dealt with in the various writings of Sri Aurobindo and in the series of articles on education that have appeared in this Bulletin.

The most important one is that the unity of the human race can be achieved neither through uniformity nor through domination and subjection. A synthetic organization of all nations, each one occupying its own place in accordance with its own genius and the role it has to play in the whole, can alone effect a comprehensive and progressive unification which may have some chance of enduring. And if the synthesis is to be a living thing, the grouping should be done around a central idea as high and wide as possible, and in which all tendencies, even the most contradictory, would find their respective places. That idea is to give man the conditions of life necessary for preparing him to manifest the new force that will create the race of tomorrow.

All urge of rivalry, all struggle for precedence and domination should disappear, giving place to a will for harmonious organization, for clear-sighted and effective collaboration.

To make this possible, children from their very early age must be accustomed not merely to the idea but to its practice. Therefore the International Centre of Education will be international not because students from all countries will be admitted here, nor because the education will be given in their own mother tongue, but particularly because the cultures of the different regions of the earth will be represented here in such a way as to be accessible to all, not merely intellectually, in ideas, theories, principles and languages, but also vitally in habits and customs, in art under all forms—painting, sculpture, music, architecture, decoration—and physically too through natural scenery, dress, games, sports, industries and food. A kind of world exhibition has to be organized in which all the countries will be represented in a concrete and living manner; the ideal is that every nation with a very definite culture would have a pavilion representing that culture, built on a model that most displays the habits of the country: it will exhibit the nation's most representative products, natural as well as manufactured, products also that best express its intellectual and artistic genius and its spiritual tendencies. Each nation would thus find a practical and concrete interest in cultural synthesis and collaborate in the work by taking over the charge of the pavilion that represents it. A lodging house also could be attached, large or small according to the need, where students of the same nationality would be accommodated; they will thus enjoy the very culture of their own motherland, and at the same time receive at the center the education which will introduce them as well to other cultures existing upon earth. Thus the international education will not be simply theoretical, on the school bench, but practical in all details of existence. . . .

The first aim then will be to help individuals to become conscious of the fundamental genius of the nation to which they belong and at the same time to put them in contact with the modes of living of other nations so that they may know and respect equally the true spirit of all the countries upon earth. For all world organization, to be real and to be able to live, must be based upon mutual respect and understanding between nation and nation as well as between individual and individual. It is only in the collective order and organization, in a collaboration based upon mutual good will that lies the possibility of man being lifted out of the painful chaos where he is now. It is with this aim and in this spirit that all human problems will be studied at the Centre of Education: and their solution will be given in the light of the supramental knowledge which Sri Aurobindo has revealed in his writings.

The Science of Living*

An aimless life is always a miserable life.

Everyone of you should have an aim. But do not forget that on the quality of your aim will depend the quality of your life.

Your aim should be high and wide, generous and disinterested; this will make your life precious to yourself and to all.

But whatever your ideal, it cannot be perfectly realized unless you have realized perfection in yourself.

To work for your perfection, the first step is to become conscious of yourself, of the different parts of your being and their respective activities. You must learn to distinguish these different parts one from the other, so that you may find out clearly the origin of the movements that occur in you, the many impulses, reactions and conflicting wills that drive you to action. It is an assiduous study which demands much perseverance and sincerity. For man's nature, especially his mental nature, has a spontaneous tendency to give an explanation favorable to whatever he thinks, feels, says and does. It is only by observing these movements with great care, by bringing them, as it were, before the tribunal of our highest ideal, with a sincere will to submit to its judgment, that we can hope to educate in us a discernment which does not err. For if we truly want to progress and acquire the capacity of knowing the truth of our being, that is to say, the one thing for which we have been really created, that which we can call our mission upon earth, then we must, in a very regular and constant manner, reject from us or eliminate in us whatever contradicts the truth of our existence, whatever

*"The Science of Living: To Know Oneself and to Control Oneself," in *Sri Aurobindo and the Mother on Education* (1966), pp. 49–53.

is in opposition to it. It is thus that little by little all the parts, all the elements of our being, could be organized into a homogeneous whole around our psychic center. This work of unification demands a long time to be brought to some degree of perfection. Hence, to accomplish it, we must arm ourselves with patience and endurance, determined to prolong our life as far as it is necessary for the success of our endeavor.

As we pursue this labor of purification and unification, we must at the same time take great care to perfect the external and instrumental part of our being. When the higher truth will manifest, it must find in you a mental being subtle and rich enough to be able to give to the idea seeking to express itself a form of thought which preserves its force and clarity. This thought, again, when it seeks to clothe itself in words must find in you a sufficient power of expression so that the words reveal and not deform the thought. And this formula in which you embody the truth should be made articulate in all your sentiments, all your willings and acts, all the movements of your being. Finally, these movements themselves should, by constant effort, attain their highest perfection.

All this can be realized by means of a fourfold discipline the general outline of which is given here. These four aspects of the discipline do not exclude each other, one can follow them all at the same time, indeed it is better to do so. The starting point is what can be called the psychic discipline. We give the name "psychic" to the psychological center of our being, the seat within of the highest truth of our existence, that which can know and manifest this truth. It is therefore of capital importance for us to become conscious of its presence within us, to concentrate on this presence and make it a living fact for us and identify ourselves with it.

Through space and time many methods have been framed to attain this perception and finally to achieve this identification. Some methods are psychological, some religious, some even mechanical. In reality, everyone has to find out that which suits him best, and if one has a sincere and steady aspiration, a persistent and dynamic will, one is sure to meet in one way or another, externally by study and instruction, internally by concentration, meditation, revelation and experience, the help one needs to reach the goal. Only one thing is absolutely indispensable: the will to discover and realize. This discovery and this realization should be the primary occupation of the being, the pearl of great price which one should acquire at any cost. Whatever you do, whatever your occupation and activity, the will to find the truth of your being and to unite with it must always be living, always present behind all that you do, all that you experience, all that you think.

To complete this movement of inner discovery, it is good not to neglect the mental development. For the mental instrument can be equally a great help or a great hindrance. In its natural state the human mind is always limited in its vision, narrow in its understanding, rigid in its conceptions, and a certain effort is needed to enlarge it, make it supple and deep. Hence, it is very necessary that one should consider everything from as many points of view as possible. There is an exercise in this connection which gives great suppleness and elevation to thought. It is as follows. A clearly formulated thesis is set; against it is opposed the antithesis, formulated with the same precision. Then by careful reflection the problem must be widened or transcended so that a synthesis is found which unites the two contraries in a larger, higher and more comprehensive idea.

Many exercises of the same kind can be undertaken; some have a beneficial effect on the character and so possess a double advantage, that of educating the mind and that of establishing control over one's feelings and their results. For example, you must not allow your mind to judge things and people; for the mind is not an instrument of knowledge—it is incapable of finding knowledge—but it must be moved by knowledge. Knowledge belongs to a region much higher than that of the human mind, even beyond the region of pure ideas. The mind has to be made silent and attentive in order to receive knowledge from above and manifest it. For it is an instrument of formation, organization and action. And it is in these functions that it attains its full value and real utility.

Another practice may be very helpful for the progress of the consciousness. Whenever there is a disagreement on any matter, as a decision to take, or an act to accomplish, one must not stick to one's own conception or point of view. On the contrary, one must try to understand the other's point of view, put oneself in his place and, instead of quarreling or even fighting, find out a solution which can reasonably satisfy both parties; there is always one for men of good will.

Here must be mentioned the training of the vital. The vital being in us is the seat of impulses and desires, of enthusiasm and violence, of dynamic energy and desperate depression, of passions and revolt. It can set in motion everything, build up and realize; it can also destroy and mar everything. It seems to be, in the human being, the most difficult part to train. It is a long labor requiring great patience, and it demands a perfect sincerity, for without sincerity one will deceive oneself from the very first step, and all endeavor for progress will go in vain. With the collaboration of the vital no realization seems impossible, no transformation impracticable. But the difficulty lies in securing this constant collaboration. The vital is a good worker, but most often it seeks its own satisfaction. If that is refused, totally or even partially, it gets vexed, sulky, and goes on strike. As a result the energy disappears more or less completely and leaves in its place disgust for people and things, discouragement or revolt, depression and dissatisfaction. At these moments one must remain quiet and refuse to act; for it is at such times that one does stupid things and in a few minutes can destroy or spoil what one has gained in months of regular effort, losing thus all the progress made. These crises are of less duration and are less dangerous in the case of those who have established a contact with their psychic being sufficient to keep alive in them the flame of aspiration and the consciousness of the ideal to be realized. They can, with the help of this consciousness, deal with their vital as one deals with a child in revolt, with patience and perseverance showing it the truth and light, endeavoring to convince it and awaken in it the good will which for a moment was veiled. With the help of such patient intervention each crisis can be changed into a new progress, into a further step forward towards the goal. Progress may be slow, falls may be frequent, but if a courageous will is maintained one is sure to triumph one day and see all difficulties melt and vanish before the consciousness of truth.

Lastly, we must, by means of a rational and clear-seeing physical education, make our body strong and supple so that it may become in the material world a fit instrument for the truth-force which wills to manifest through us.

In fact, the body must not rule, it has to obey. By its very nature it is a docile and faithful servant. Unfortunately it has not often the capacity of discernment with regard to its masters, the mind and the vital. It obeys them blindly, at the cost of its own well-being. The mind with its dogmas, its rigid and arbitrary principles, the vital with its passions, its excesses and dissipations soon do everything to destroy the natural balance of the body and create in it fatigue, exhaustion and disease. It must be freed from this tyranny; that can be done only through a constant union with the psychic center of the being. The body has a wonderful capacity of adaptation and endurance. It is fit to do so many more things than one can usually imagine. If instead of the ignorant and despotic masters that govern it, it is ruled by the central truth of the being, one will be surprised at what it is capable of doing. Calm and quiet, strong and poised, it will at every minute put forth effort that is demanded of it, for it will have learned to find rest in action, to replace through contact with the universal forces the energies it spends consciously and usefully. In this sound and balanced life a new harmony will manifest in the body, reflecting the harmony of the higher regions which will give it the perfect proportions and the ideal beauty of form. And this harmony will be progressive, for the truth of the being is never static, it is a continual unfolding of a growing, a more and more global and comprehensive perfection. As soon as the body learns to follow the movement of a progressive harmony, it will be possible for it, through a continuous process of transformation, to escape the necessity of disintegration and destruction. Thus the irrevocable law of death will have no reason for existing any more.

As we rise to this degree of perfection which is our goal, we shall perceive that the truth we seek is made up of four major aspects: love, knowledge, power, and beauty. These four attributes of the truth will spontaneously express themselves in our being. The psychic will be the vehicle of true and pure love, the mind that of infallible knowledge, the vital will manifest an invincible power and strength, and the body will be the expression of a perfect beauty and a perfect harmony.

AUROVILLE*

A Dream

There should be somewhere upon earth a place that no nation could claim as its sole property, a place where all human beings of good will, sincere in their aspiration, could live freely as citizens of the world, obeying one single authority, that of the supreme Truth, a place of peace, concord, harmony, where all the fighting instincts of man would be used exclusively to conquer the causes of his sufferings and miseries, to surmount his weakness and ignorance, to triumph over his limitations and incapacities; a place where the needs of the spirit and the care for progress would get precedence over the satisfaction of desires and passions, the seeking for material pleasures and enjoyment. In this place, children would be able to grow and develop integrally without losing contact with their soul. Education would be given not with a view to passing examinations and getting certificates and posts but for enriching the existing faculties and bringing forth new ones. In this place titles and positions would be supplanted by opportunities to serve and organize. The needs of the body will be provided for equally in the case of each and everyone. In the general organization intellectual, moral and spiritual superiority will find expression not in the enhancement of the pleasures and powers of life but in the increase of duties and responsibilities. Artistic beauty in all forms, painting, sculpture, music, literature, will be available equally to all, the opportunity to share in the joys they give being limited solely by each one's capacities and not by social or financial position. For in this ideal place money would be no more the sovereign lord. Individual value would have a greater importance than the value due to material wealth and social position. Work would not be there as the means for gaining one's livelihood, it would be the means whereby to express oneself, develop one's capacities and possibilities, while doing

*Auroville: The Cradle of a New World (1972).

238

THE MATRIMANDIR, 1987

at the same time service to the whole group, which on its side would provide for each one's subsistence and for the field of his work. In brief, it would be a place where the relations among human beings, usually based almost exclusively upon competition and strife, would be replaced by relations of emulation for doing better, for collaboration, relations of real brotherhood.

The earth is certainly not ready to realize such an idea, for mankind does not yet possess the necessary knowledge to understand and accept it nor the indispensable conscious force to execute it. That is why I call it a dream.

Yet, this dream is on the way to becoming a reality. That is exactly what we are seeking to do at the Ashram of Sri Aurobindo on a small scale, in proportion to our modest means. The achievement is indeed far from being perfect but it is progressive; little by little we advance towards our goal, which, we hope, one day we shall be able to hold before the world as a practical and effective means of coming out of the present chaos in order to be born into a more true, more harmonious new life.

Auroville, the Cradle of a New World

In April 1956 the Mother declared:

The manifestation of the Supramental upon earth is no longer a promise but a living fact, a reality. It is at work here, and one day will come when the most blind, the most unconscious, even the most unwilling shall be obliged to recognize it.

Replacing the future tense of her 1914 vision by the present, the Mother announced:

A new light breaks upon the earth,
A new world is born,
All that were promised are fulfilled.

The following year, the Mother delivered a talk in the Ashram, about this event:

Last year, when I announced to you the manifestation of the supramental consciousness and light and force, I should have added that it was an event forerunner of the birth of a new world. But at that time the new world was so much engulfed in the ancient that even now there are very few people who are aware of its birth and of the difference it brings into the world. Yet the action of the new forces has continued in a very regular, very persistent, very obstinate and, to a certain extent, very effective way. The result of all that has been noted at every step in almost day-to-day experiences.

First of all, it is not merely a new conception of the spiritual life and the divine reality. The old spirituality was an escape towards the divine reality, leaving the world where it was, as it was. Our new vision, on the contrary, is the divinization of life, the transformation of the material into a divine world. But this work could have been a simple continuation, an amelioration, an enlargement of the old world as it was. What has happened is truly a new thing:

A New World Has Been Born. It is not the old that is being transformed, it is quite a new world that has been really concretely born.

At the present hour we are in the very heart of a period of transition, where the two are intertwined; the old persists, still all-powerful, continues to dominate the ordinary consciousness, while the new glides in, still modest, unnoticed to the extent that for the moment it disturbs nothing much externally, and even in the consciousness of most people it is quite imperceptible. And yet it works, it grows till the moment when it will be strong enough to impose itself visibly.

In any case, to simplify one can say that the old world, the creation which Sri Aurobindo calls the Overmental, was in a characteristic way the age of the gods and therefore the age of religions. The flower of man's effort towards that which was higher than him gave birth to numerous religions, to a religious relation between the souls of the select few and the invisible world, and at the summit of all that, as an effort towards a still higher realization, was born this idea of the unity of religions, of something that is unique, which is behind all manifestation—and this idea was really the ceiling of human aspiration. This conception is on the borderland: it is something which still belongs wholly to the overmental world to look at another thing, something of which it has only a presentiment, which is a new creation it tries to attain but is unable to seize. To seize it, what is needed is a reversal. One must come out of the overmental creation. But for that, the new creation, the supramental creation must have taken place.

And now all those old things seem so old, so antiquated, so arbitrary, such a travesty of the true truth.

In the supramental creation there will no more be religions. All life will be the expression, the flowering in forms of the Divine Unity manifesting in the world. And there will be no more what men now call the gods.

But all that is of the future, a future that has begun but will take some time before realizing itself integrally. In the meanwhile, we are in a very special situation, extremely special which has had no precedent. We are attending on the birth of a new world, altogether young, altogether weak—weak not in its essence, but in its external manifestation—not yet recognized, nor yet felt, denied by most; but it is there, it is there endeavoring to grow and quite sure of the result. Yet, the road to reach there is a new road, that has never before been traced; none went by that way, none did that. It is a beginning, a universal beginning. Therefore it is an adventure absolutely unexpected and unforeseeable.

There are people who love adventure, and to them I give a call and I tell them:

I invite you to the great adventure, and in this adventure you are not to repeat spiritually what the others have done before us, because our adventure begins from beyond that stage. We are for a new creation, entirely new, carrying in it all the unforeseen, all risks, all hazards—a true adventure of which the goal is sure victory, but of which the way is unknown and has to be traced out step by step in the unexplored. It is something that has never been in the present universe and will never be in the same manner. If that interests you, well, embark. What will happen tomorrow, I do not know.

You must leave behind whatever has been designed, whatever has been built up, and then proceed on the march into the unknown. Come what may.

Auroville Charter

1. Auroville belongs to nobody in particular. Auroville belongs to humanity as a whole. But to live in Auroville one must be a willing servitor of the Divine Consciousness.
2. Auroville will be the place of an unending education, of constant progress and a youth that never ages.
3. Auroville wants to be the bridge between the past and the future. Taking advantage of all discoveries from without and from within Auroville will boldly spring towards future realizations.
4. Auroville will be a site of material and spiritual researches for a living embodiment of an actual Human Unity.

To Be a True Aurovillian

1. The first necessity is the inner discovery by which one learns who one really is behind the social, moral, cultural, racial and hereditary appearances.

At our inmost center there is a free being, wide and knowing, who awaits our discovery and who ought to become the acting center of our being and our life in Auroville.

2. One lives in Auroville in order to be free of moral and social conventions; but this liberty must not be a new slavery to the ego, its desires and its ambitions.

The fulfillment of desires bars the route to the inner discovery which can only be attained in peace and the transparency of a perfect disinterestedness.

3. The Aurovillian must lose the proprietary sense of possession.

For our passage in the material world, that which is indispensable to our life and to our action is put at our disposal

9

according to the place we should occupy there. The more conscious our contact is with our inner being, the more exact are the means given.

4. Work, even manual work, is an indispensable thing for the inner discovery. If one does not work, if one does not inject his consciousness into matter, the latter will never develop. To let one's consciousness organize a bit of matter by way of one's body is very good. To establish order, around oneself, helps to bring order within oneself.

One should organize life not according to outer, artificial rules, but according to an organized, inner consciousness because if one allows life to drift without imposing the control of a higher consciousness, life becomes inexpressive and irresolute. It is to waste one's time in the sense that matter persists without a conscious utilization.

5. The whole earth must prepare itself for the advent of the new species, and Auroville wants to consciously work towards hastening that advent.

6. Little by little it will be revealed to us what this new species should be, and meanwhile the best measure to take is to consecrate oneself entirely to the Divine.

Administration and Organization

Auroville belongs to nobody in particular. . . . At Auroville, nothing belongs to anyone in particular. It is the ideal place for those who want to know the joy and liberation of not having personal possessions any more. All is a collective property. . . .

Auroville will be a place no nation can claim as its sole property, a place where all human beings of good will, sincere in their aspiration, can live freely as citizens of the world, obeying one single authority, that of the supreme truth.

To avoid the errors and deficiencies of all previous and actual governmental systems, whether theocratic, plutocratic, democratic, and even socialistic or communistic, one basic thing has to be acknowledged and accepted by all.

There is an invisible and superior Power—a superior consciousness (it can have any name—Divine Consciousness, Supreme Truth) which does not belong to the ordinary mental plane of consciousness but WHICH IS ACCESSIBLE TO MAN. This consciousness, which is a power, a force, is capable of ruling material things in a more salutary and truer way—happier for all—than any ordinary human power whatsoever.

It is not a thing that one can "pretend" to have, because at any rate, if it is a pretense, it will become evident. Either one has it or one does not have it.

Besides, it gives one no material power; those who are at the top have necessarily the minimum needs; their material needs diminish as their capacity of the vision of the material increases. The experience in which these things lose their importance and their value is automatic and spontaneous; it is not the result of effort.

The second thing is that a person, put into contact with this higher consciousness, has spontaneously a POWER OF CONVICTION greater than any possible to a consciousness in contact with intermediary regions. This power of conviction is a power of transformation of matter.

As soon as one comes down from this supreme height (even a slight descent) there come into play various influences. It is only what is at the very top, which has perfect purity, that has the power of spontaneous conviction. Therefore, all that one can do to replace that, is an approximation, and it is not better than democracy, a system that wants to govern by the greatest number and the lowest rung.

If a representative of the supreme consciousness is not there, he can be replaced by the government of a small number, between four and eight, using an "intuitive" intelligence, an intuition expressed intellectually. "Intuition" is more important than "intelligence." It may have inconveniences from the practical point of view but the result has a better chance of being nearer the Truth which this higher consciousness endeavors to manifest, than all that has so far been tried by different governments.

Those who possess that consciousness can belong to any

class of society: it is not a privilege which comes from birth, it is the result of an effort, a personal growth. It is individuals who have reached a higher consciousness that have the right to rule—not others—and it does not matter to which class the individual belongs.

It is necessary that all who participate in the experiment of Auroville should be absolutely convinced that the higher consciousness is the best judge of the most material things. What has undermined India is the idea that the higher consciousness deals with higher things and that things here below do not interest it at all and it understands nothing of these matters! It is the highest consciousness that sees most clearly what must be the needs of the most material things. With this basis, a new type of government may be tried for the collective organization.

The Mother is considered by all Aurovillians as the best judge for all that concerns Auroville. . . .

To live only according to one's inspiration, one's inner feeling, requires all workers of Auroville to be yogis, conscious of the Divine Truth. Until such time comes, there must be a hierarchic organization grouped around the most enlightened center and submitting to a collective discipline.

Discipline is necessary for life. To live, the body itself is subjected in its functions to a vigorous discipline. Any relaxing of this discipline produces illness.

Organization is a discipline of action, but for Auroville we aspire to go beyond arbitrary and artificial organization. We want an organization which is the expression of a higher consciousness working to manifest the truth of the future.

An organization is needed for the work to be done—but the organization itself must remain flexible and plastic in order to progress always and to modify itself according to the need. . . .

The Aurovillians will not receive any wages. There won't be any exchange of money in Auroville. It is only with the outside world that Auroville will have money relations. Money will be no more the sovereign lord; individual value will have a greater importance than the value due to material wealth and social position. It is the lack of push towards the future that impedes the flow of money.

The push towards the future is to be ready to give up all gains, moral and material, in order to acquire what the future can give us. Very few are like that; there are many who would like to have what the future will bring, but they are not ready to give up what they have in order to acquire the new wealth.

It is only when people really feel that it is their good fortune to help Auroville to grow that funds will come abundantly.

Food

First, each country will have its pavilion and, in the pavilion, there will be a kitchen of that country, that is to say, the Japanese will be able to eat as they want to, etc. . . . .

But in the town itself, there will be food for the vegetarians as well as food for nonvegetarians, and also there will be an attempt to find the food of tomorrow.

All this labor for assimilation that makes you so heavy, it takes so much time and energy of the person, it ought to be done "before" and it must be given something which is at once capable of being assimilated, as it is done now: for example, there are vitamins that are directly assimilable and also proteins, nutritious principles that are found in such and such things and that are not bulky. Chemically, one is enough advanced, and one is able to simplify.

People do not like it simple, because they take an intense delight in eating, but when one does not take pleasure in eating, one requires nourishment and does not lose time in that: the time for eating, the time for digesting.

And so, here there must be a trial kitchen, a kind of culinary laboratory for experimenting. People will go here and there or otherwhere according to their taste and their inclination.

Marriage

In Auroville there will be no marriages. If a man and woman love each other and want to live together, they may do so and without ceremony. If they want to separate, they are free to do so. Why should people be compelled to stay together when they have ceased to love each other?

What has value in one epoch has none any longer in another as human consciousness goes on progressing. But one must take great care to replace a law that is no longer obeyed by a higher and truer law that helps the progress towards the future realization. One has no right to renounce a law unless one is capable of knowing and following a higher and better law. . . .

To a couple—on how to unite themselves:

To unite your physical existences and your material interests, to associate yourselves so as to face together the difficulties and successes, the defeats and victories of life—this is the very basis of marriage—but you know already that it does not suffice.

To be united in feelings, to have the same tastes and the same aesthetic pleasures, to vibrate together in a common response to the same things, one by the other and one for the other—it is good, it is necessary—but it is not enough.

To be one in profound sentiments, your affection, your feelings of tenderness for each other not varying in spite of all the shocks of existence; withstanding weariness, nervous irritations and disappointments, to be always and in every case happy, most happy to be together; to find, under all circumstances, one in the presence of the other, rest, peace and joy—it is good, it is very good, it is indispensable—but it is not enough.

To unite your mentalities, your thoughts harmonizing and becoming complementary to each other, your intellectual preoccupations and discoveries shared between you; in a word, to make your spheres of mental activity identical through a broadening and an enrichment acquired by the two at the same time—it is good, it is absolutely necessary—but it is not enough.

Beyond it all, at the bottom, at the center, at the summing of the being, there is a Supreme Truth of the being, an Eternal Light, independent of all circumstances of birth, of country, of environment, of education; the origin, cause and master of our spiritual development—it is That that gives a definite orientation to our existence; it is That that decides our destiny; it is in the consciousness of this that you should unite. To be one in aspiration and ascension, to advance with the same step on the spiritual path—such is the secret of a durable union.

No Religion

Auroville is for those who want to live a life essentially divine but who renounce all religions whether they be ancient, modern or future.

It is only in experience that there can be knowledge of the truth. No one ought to speak of the Divine unless he has had experience of the Divine. Get experience of the Divine, then alone will you have the right to speak of it.

The objective study of religions will be a part of the historical study of the development of human consciousness.

Religions make up part of the history of mankind and it is in this guise that they will be studied at Auroville—not as beliefs to which one ought or ought not to fasten, but as part of a process in the development of human consciousness which should lead man towards his superior realization.

Program:—Research through experience of the
Supreme Truth
A Life Divine
but
NO RELIGIONS.

AFTERWORD
by Robert A. McDermott

Imagining the Spiritual Mission of
Sri Aurobindo and the Mother

The epigraph following the dedication of this book to Sri Aurobindo reads: "Such a great soul is very difficult to find" (Bhagavad Gita, 7:19). But what is it to "find"—or to look for—a great soul? Assuming "great soul" to be an intelligible concept, and further, that great souls do, or perhaps did, exist, how could we judge the relative greatness of Sri Aurobindo, or Sri AurobindoEMother, by reading this anthology of his writings? Of the approximately ten thousand individuals who purchased this book since it was published in 1973, and the many others who presumably read the three thousand copies sold to libraries, how many of these readers were able or inclined to judge whether Sri Aurobindo (and the Mother) is "such a great soul?" Or for how many Western readers did Aurobindo remain an Indian author of Victorian English, a spiritual visionary in a time characterized by materialism and utilitarian practicality? Perhaps the extraordinary claims in this book, and the manner in which Sri Aurobindo describes and defends them, provide all the reason necessary as to why relatively few Westerners have "found" Sri Aurobindo and the Mother. Or perhaps relatively few Westerners know how to look for or know whether they have found a great soul.

Using the pragmatic habit of mind he helped to establish as characteristically American, William James went in search of great souls and tested the worth of each by the fruits of their experience. In his *The Varieties of Religious Experience*, James argued that the only way to study religion is to call in the experts, those individuals whose lives exhibit an uncommon awareness of a presence taken to be divine. He concluded his survey by affirming that the fruits of religious experience are the best things that history has to show.

What are the characteristics of the experiences which Sri

Aurobindo and the Mother disclose in these pages, and what are the fruits of these experiences? If we were to evaluate the quality of their writings or disciples, or the quality and extent of their influence on individuals and the larger culture, we would almost certainly judge the fruits of their influence to be positive. Unfortunately, however, it would be difficult to gain a clear perspective on such a disparate phenomenon, and as a result, those drawn to Sri Aurobindo's yoga and vision would find more evidence for their positive influence than would those unattracted to such teachings. If Sri Aurobindo and the Mother themselves were asked to submit their work to the pragmatic test of the quality of their influence, they might answer by pointing to a particularly subtle line from Sri Auro-bindo's poem *Savitri*. One could imagine, for example, Sri Aurobindo and the Mother appreciating an attempt to fathom their life and work by meditating on a line such as the following:

The whole wide world is only he and she (*Savitri*, 63).

Obviously, no single line of poetry, no matter how suggestive, can stand for thirty volumes by Sri Aurobindo, twenty volumes by the Mother, and two spectacularly rich lives. But as a thimble full of water can reveal the consistency of a huge body of water, a single line, when made the subject of right meditation, and informed by extensive writings and a lifework, can be extremely revealing for anyone in search of a great soul. Ruud Lohman, for example, a Dutch Catholic priest who worked at Auroville for fifteen years before his sudden death in 1986, was a searcher who meditated on the above line—"The whole world is only he and she"—and enabled it to disclose important meanings not merely in the line, or in *Savitri*, but in the entire vision and force which Sri Aurobindo and the Mother represent in his life.

In his little book of essays, written between 1972 and 1986, *A House for the Third Millennium: Essays on Matrimandir*, Lohman provides an excellent example of the way in which Sri Aurobindo's writings can bear fruit in our thinking, in our receptivity to a spiritual insight, to a revelation. Sri Aurobindo and Mother teach a higher, wider harmony. In fusing their consciousness, Sri Aurobindo and Mother, He and She, represent the overcoming of opposites which is the task of all evolution. The spirit is not only in the Matrimandir, the Mother temple, but outside as well—not only in the flame at the center and the stillness of the meditation space, but equally in the material and the muscle used in construction. Lohman finds words for his meditation on the Matrimandir:

> It is only the He in me that is capable of loving Her, of
> pursuing Her through the centuries:
>> All here where each thing seems its lonely self
>> Are figures of the sole transcendent One:
>> Only by him they are, his breath is their life;
>> An unseen Presence moulds the oblivious clay.
>> A playmate in the mighty Mother's game,
>> One came upon the dubious whirling globe
>> To hide from her pursuit in force and form (*Savitri*, 60)

He gives up his eternity to be with Her, He hides in forms and forces for Her to rediscover and love Him. He hides in me, in you, in us, masks of His divinity. The secret is so obvious that it is hard to see it. The secret is that it is not behind, or beyond, or above all this, no, it is all this. It is I and my brain cells, my hands and the steel I touch, and it is you and things you eat and the thoughts you think and the people you communicate with. There are no two different realities. It is the same reality, His and Hers, and yours, and mine. It is not when the evolution is complete and full-grown that He and She will move into their palace; it is much more dramatic and more loving and more beautiful: the evolution with all its ups and downs, its steps back and little steps forward, history with all its wars and cultures and art and heroes and soliders, is their place, their chamber of love in which they embrace. It is not when Matrimandir is ready that She will move in in some subtle or supranatural form and inhabit it as a queen adored by her subjects. It rather is all the perspiration, all the aspiration, all the physical work, all the designs, all the money, all the steel, all the concrete, all the shapes and spirals and curves of the building that is He and She. There is nothing else. All is either He or She or, when fulfilled by love, both.

> They are married secretly in our thought and life.
> The universe is an endless masquerade:
> For nothing here is utterly what it seems,
> It is a dream-fact vision of a truth
> Which but for the dream would not be wholly true,
> A phenomenon stands out significant
> Against dim backgrounds of eternity;
> We accept its face and pass by all it means;
> A part is seen, we take it for the whole.
> Thus have they made their play with us for roles:
> Author and act with himself as scene,
> He moves there as the Soul, as Nature she (*Savitri*, 61)

To unite with their love-play, to be in it, to be of it, to feel it, to know it, must then be the sense of all this phenomenal show, and the sheer joy of it. For every *why?* there is only one ultimate answer: *love*. And not even that fuzzy kind of ethereal love the preachers preach about of "love thy neighbor..." etc., but some robust, straightforward "real" love down to your flesh and bones and glands and organs. Sri Aurobindo as usual doesn't beat around the bush: "To commit adultery with God is the perfect experience for which the world was created" (*The Hour of God*, 129).[1]

Ruud Lohman's essays on the Matrimandir obviously suggest that he considered Sri Aurobindo and the Mother to be "a great soul." His "finding" Sri Aurobindo, and his meditation on the line from *Savitri*—"This whole wide world is only he and she"—is another example of a "he and she": Sri Aurobindo and the Mother provide a library full of words, images, and ideas, and Ruud, priest and worker, theologian and Aurovillian, brings his spiritual hunger and receptivity to Aurobindo's and the Mother's soul force. The *lila*, the play, goes on, for the *ananda*, the delight of it.

For others in search of a great soul, *Savitri* might not be

[1]Ruud Lohman, *A House for the Third Millennium: Essays on Matrimandir* (Pondicherry: Sri Aurobindo Ashram, 1986), 82-84.

the best place to look, but no matter: the fruits of Aurobindo's experience range over his life story, his philosophy of spiritual evolution, his yoga teaching, karma and rebirth, and his vision of a transformed world—the further manifestation of which is the Mother's vision of Auroville, the most perfect expression of which is the Matrimandir. All of these profound and profoundly important topics invite the kind of meditative reflection which Ruud Lohman brought to, and from, *Savitri* and his work on the Matrimandir.

Aurobindo's and the Mother's spiritual biographies—or, we perhaps should say, their two observable biographies (plural) and their spiritual biography (singular)—provide an excellent starting place for thinking about, with, through, the great soul of Aurobindo-Mother. When he was not yet Sri Aurobindo, but Aurobindo Ghose, a prisoner in the Alipur Jail in Calcutta, awaiting trial for seditious activity against the British rule of India, he was blessed by a transformative "He and She" experience: Krishna entered him, so that he realized, not only intellectually but spiritually, a union with Krishna's divine will which enabled him "to have an equal heart for high and low, friend and opponent, success and failure, yet not to do his work negligently" (*Ky*, 3, and above, p. 8). Krishna gave to Aurobindo a power of harmonious vision similar to that which he gave to Arjuna: the other prisoners and the jailers now seemed to Aurobindo to be part of an underlying harmony, part of the spiritual reality of Krishna. Although frustrated and deserted, Aurobindo was able to overcome hatred, alienation, and misunderstanding by the healing power of Krishna consciousness. Not that Aurobindo, prisoners, or jailers lost their identities: they all stayed in character, but Aurobindo could now see the extent to which these characters were (and are) on the surface. The inner, true, essential self in all cases is not the surface character, personality, or role, but the divine core, the Krishna standing behind and within each one.

When Aurobindo met Mira Richard, they immediately knew that the other was the full complement—the He and She needed for the divine drama. She brought to this divinely sponsored coalition Western esotericism supplemented by several years of Zen Buddhist training in Japan and a deep affinity with Indian yoga, especially with Tantra (the discipline of realizing the spiritual transformation of matter, including the increasing spiritualization of the human body). Aurobindo brought English language and education as well as a profoundly Indian spirituality.

The idea of a spiritual collaboration, of the uniting of two souls, requires the kind of meditative reflection which Ruud Lohman brought to *Savitri* and to the Matrimandir. How are we to understand the consciousness of the Indian-male-mystic-poet-yogi becoming identical with the consciousness of the French-female-artist-occultist? One way to start is to establish that they are not united on the level of Aurobindo Ghose and Mira Richard: the souls of these personalities are presumably no more capable of such a union of consciousness than are our souls at our level of spiritual attainment. Rather, their union is at the level of Sri Aurobindo and the Mother, as coavatars. Is this not the signature of the avatar status—that they are capable of taking on the consciousness and the destiny of another? When we join with another, such a union might include the physical, emotional, and mental, but will be imperfect at each of these levels and will not reach to a spiritual level. To the extent that we are not avatars (or initiates, or buddhas), our souls remain imperfectly related to other souls, as well as to our mental, vital, and physical lives. When Sri Aurobindo says that his consciousness and the Mother's are one and the same, he must mean something like the "He and She" of the line in *Savitri*, which in turn echoes Krishna's claim to include within himself legions of higher beings and civilizations. If we are to picture and articulate the union of the Sri Aurobindo consciousness and the Mother consciousness, we will have to follow Sri Aurobindo into supramental poetry—a poetry which issues from spiritual experience, as did his *Savitri*, and as did a host of other creations and revelations which issued from the individual yet unified Sri Aurobindo-Mother consciousness.

As the disciple who was preparing to write a biography of Sri Aurobindo was not dissuaded from doing so by his master's insistence that his life was not on the surface for man to see, so will we fail to understand Sri Aurobindo on the surface of external events, or in terms of his accessible personality, the historical person, Mira Richard. Sri Aurobindo's announcement concerning the identity of his and the Mother's consciousness came as a result of his experience of the Overmind, a realization preparatory to the descent of the Supermind through the Mother thirty years later. Until the overmental descent, Sri Aurobindo presumably did not know—at least not sufficiently to announce or to act upon—that his consciousness and the Mother's expressed the divine will for themselves and for their disciples. Furthermore, the death of Sri Aurobindo on December 5, 1950, did not signify the death of the spiritual reality, psychic entity avatar, which lived through the personality Aurobindo Ghose; the death of the Mother, at age 95, on November 17, 1973, did not terminate the active spiritual force, *shakti* or Mother, behind the double task of spiritualizing matter and creating a new world for which Auroville is intended as a living laboratory. The possibility of Sri Aurobindo cooperating with the Mother for the descent of Supermind in 1956, six years after his death, or the Mother's cooperation with Aurovillians on behalf of the work underway at Auroville (e.g. the creation and subsequent force of the Matrimandir, the Mother-temple), are subjects on which not only disciples but all spiritual seekers are invited to meditate.

For some readers of the New Testament, Jesus is a moral and religious teacher but is not the Christ, a divine being with a unique relation to the Father. A similar dispute has raged concerning Buddha. Sri Aurobindo reminds anyone who would study a spiritual life that "it is the inner life that gives to the outer any power it may have and the inner life of a spiritual man is something vast and full, and at least in the great figures, so crowded and teeming with significant things that no biographer or historian could even hope to seize it all or tell it." He continues:

> The outward facts as related of Christ or Buddha are not much more than what has happened in many other lives—what is it that gives Buddha or Christ their enormous place in the spiritual world? It was because something manifested through

them that was more than any outward event or any teaching
(*Letters on Yoga*, 428).

To understand what manifested through Buddha or
Christ requires a lifetime (or more) of meditative study; to
understand Sri Aurobindo and the Mother in their avatar roles
requires a similar effort—with no guarantee of success, though
the effort itself is its own reward. The essence of yoga, after all,
is to do what is required—in this case, to penetrate to the inner
meaning of the life and mission of Sri Aurobindo-Mother,
without regard to the fruits of such effort.

In addition to struggling with the spiritual significance of
Sri Aurobindo-Mother in one's life, Sri Aurobindo and the
Mother also insist that one attempt to understand and join
forces with their mission in relation to the entire sweep of
evolution from matter to Supermind, and the transformation
of each level of evolution, from the mental down to the vital
and the physical. This enormous vision and challenge is complemented by an equally important—and to Western minds,
altogether un-usual—double concept of karma and rebirth. To
understand fully Sri Aurobindo and the Mother is to confront
their conviction that their incarnation in this lifetime was made
possible or followed spiritually from previous lifetimes, in
which they each attained important spiritual powers necessary
for the task given them in this century—and, further, that they
will continue to be active in the spiritual world until they return
at a future time to aid in the evolution of consciousness, not as
Aurobindo Ghose and Mira Richard, but as the spiritual realities known imperfectly in this incarnation as Sri Aurobindo
and the Mother.

Karma and Rebirth in the
Evolution of Consciousness

If, following William James, we call in the experts in order
to determine the nature and significance of religious experience, we can do the same on behalf of religious thought: what
are we to make of Aurobindo's spiritually based theory of
evolution, and the complex phenomenon of karma and rebirth

by which it proceeds? For Aurobindo, a proper understanding
of evolu-tion—i.e., that space and time, the universe, is possible because of a prior involution (involvement) of Spirit—is
the foundation stone of his entire teaching. He also emphasizes, however, that it is the question of human destiny—and the
solution provided by karma and rebirth—around which all of
our questions revolve. The significance for his teaching of
involution and evolution is succinctly stated in his three-page
summary, "The Teaching of Sri Aurobindo":

> Sri Aurobindo's teaching states that this one being [the
> eternal divine Self] and consciousness is involved here in mat-
> ter. Evolution is the process by which it liberates itself; con-
> sciousness appears in what seems to be inconscient [un-
> conscious], and once having appeared is self-impelled to grow
> higher and higher and at the same time to enlarge and develop
> toward a greater and greater perfection. Life is the first step in
> this release of consciousness; mind is the second. But the
> evolution does not finish with mind; it awaits a release into
> something greater, a consciousness which is spiritual and sup-
> ramental. The next step of the evolution must be toward the
> development of Supermind and spirit as the dominant power in
> the conscious being. For only then will the involved divinity in
> things release itself entirely and it become possible for life to
> manifest perfection (p. 39, above).

This conception of evolution as a manifestation of a previously
involved divinity is the essential theoretical context within
which all other theoretical questions must be answered, beginning with the questions with which humanity is primarily
concerned—questions of its own destiny.

In his highly readable and well-argued little volume on
rebirth and karma, *The Problem of Rebirth*, Aurobindo
asserts that the one basic question around which all philosophy
revolves is the meaning of human life—its source, direction
and destiny. He argues that we will not satisfactorily answer
this question (or cluster of questions) unless we take into
account the clues provided by karma and rebirth:

> The one question which through all its complexities is the
> sum of philosophy and to which all human inquiry comes

round in the end, is the problem of ourselves—why we are here
and what we are, and what is behind and before and around us,
and what we are to do with ourselves, our inner significance,
and our outer environment. In the idea of evolutionary rebirth,
if we can once find it to be a truth and recognize its antecedents
and consequences, we have a very sufficient clue for an answer
to all these connected sides of the one perpetual question. A
spiritual evolution of which our universe is the scene and earth
its ground and stage, though its plan is still kept back above
from our yet limited knowledge—this way of seeing existence is
a luminous key which we can fit into many doors of obscurity.
But we have to look at it in the right focus, to get its true
proportions and, especially, to see it in its spiritual significance
more than in its mechanical process (*The Supramental Manifestation*, 113).

The same approach is needed for an understanding of
karma and rebirth as is needed to grasp other spiritual pheon-
omena such as the mission of Sri Aurobindo and the Mother,
or the triple process of involution, evolution, and transformation: "Finding" Sri Aurobindo-Mother, or "finding" karma
and rebirth means seeing these phenomena in their spiritual
rather than in their external manifestations.

To understand cosmic and human evolution is to see or
know (in spiritual experience, these are identical) that the entire
evolutionary process, in its most particular as well as in its
general terms, issues from and aims to express the fullest
possible meanings inherent in the divine source of all. Again, it
is the inner that is regarded as more real, more valuable, than
the outer: the inner life of Sri Aurobindo ("not on the surface
for man to see"), the inner meaning of the collaboration
between Sri Aurobindo and the Mother, and the inner process
of rebirth and karma which in each case provide the solution to
the mystery of human destiny. Every rebirth represents a unique expression of the divine, and simultaneously, an advance
of evolution toward a divine life on earth:

The spiritual process of which our human birth is a step
and our life is a portion, appears as the bringing out of a
greatness, *asya mahaminan*, which is secret, inherent, and self-
imprisoned, absorbed in the form and working of things. Our

world-action figures an evolution, an outrolling of a manifold
power gathered and coiled up in the crude intricacy of matter.
The upward progress of the successive births of things is a rise
into waking and larger and larger light of a consciousness shut
into the first hermetic cell of sleep of the eternal energy (*The
Supramental Manifestation*, 238).

Successive births and rebirths struggle upward toward a
greater freedom from matter, toward a fuller manifestation of
divinity, in order to experience the inherent *ananda* (joy,
delight) of the creative process itself. In this respect, all creativity joins with the motive of the divine—to experience and
express maximum *ananda*:

> If, then, being free to move or remain eternally still, to
> throw itself into forms or retain the potentiality of forms in
> itself, it indulges its powers of movement and formation, it can
> be only for one reason, for delight (*The Life Divine*, 91).

> As the poet, artist, or musician when he creates does really
> nothing but develop some potentiality in his unmanifested self
> into a form of manifestation, and as the thinker, statesman,
> mechanist only bring out into a shape of things that which lay
> hidden in themselves, was themselves, is still themeslves when it
> is cast into form, so is it with the world and the Eternal. All
> creation or becoming is nothing but this self-manifestation
> (*The Life Divine*, 112).

This definition of creativity, including birth and rebirth, as
self-manifestation of potentiality, all of which is of and from
the divine, can either be passed over as an intellectual theory or
can be made the object of meditative reflection. Aurobindo
presents this theory, as he presents all of his theories, as an aid
to spiritual insight and practice. While it is easier not to bother
with such a metaphysical, if not mysterious and unanswerable,
question as "why the world at all?"—Aurobindo would have us
brood on this question for its spiritual content and challenge. It
is an exercise in *jnana*—or knowledge-yoga to grapple with a
thought such as: "the Absolute can have no purpose in manifestation except of manifestation itself" (*The Life Divine*, 834).

This statement follows from Aurobindo's own spiritual experience and invites the reader of his writings on evolution (Part One, above) to accept as one's own the motive and will of the divine—to "seek for delight...to find and possess and fulfill it" (*The Life Divine*, 219).

Seeking the delight of existence must become the motive not only of life in general, but of every life, through each birth and rebirth. Each individual is expected to join with *shakti*, the divine will and energy, in helping to realize the spiritual potential of matter, life, and mind. The great struggle initiated by Sri Aurobindo and the Mother is for the realization of the divine energy at the levels above mind—levels of consciousness referred to as intuition, illumined mind, overmind, and Supermind. This gradual self-manifestation of the divine might be referred to in Indian terms as the Brahmanization of the world and in Christian terms as the Kingdom of God on earth. Sri Aurobindo refers to it as founding the Life Divine.

Aurobindo's account of this hoped for triumph gives full measure to the significance and ultimate transformation of matter. With an eye to both philosophy (specifically metaphysics—the philosophical study of being or existence in its most general terms) and to the practical requirements of spiritual discipline, Aurobindo argues against both those who deny the significance of matter and those who are caught in its snare. According to the intergralist perspective which char-acterizes both his philosophy and his yoga, Aurobindo criticizes the materialist's denial of spirit and the spiritualist's denial of matter. Philosophy and yoga are joined in his vision and in his practical spiritual advice concerning the delight of creation, just as they were joined in the Upanishads. Three thousand years ago, the *Taithiriya Upanishad* expressed this idea of *ananda*, delight of creation, which Sri Aurobindo has amplified in modern terms: From Delight all these beings are born, by Delight they exist and grow, to Delight they return (II.7).

In opposition to the world-negating spirituality (which Sri Aurobindo identified with much of Indian thought, including Buddhism and the Advaita Vedanta of Shankara), he insists on the value of matter as well as spirit:

> The affirmation of a divine life upon earth and an immortal sense in mortal existence can have no base unless we recognize not only eternal spirit as the inhabitant of this bodily mansion, the wearer of this mutable robe, but accept matter of which it is made, as a fit and noble material out of which he weaves constantly his garbs, builds recurrently the unending series of his mansions (*The Life Divine*, 6).

Sri Aurobindo's most dramatic affirmation of the interplay between spirit and matter, and the resulting spiritualization of matter, is to be found in his experience and concept of the Supermind. Sri Aurobindo and the Mother understood their spiritual mission—their work as coavatars—to consist primarily in cooperating with the Supermind in the eventual spiritualization or supramentalization of matter, including the human body.

The supramental level of consciousness, or mode of transformation, involves divine involution and evolution: it is an involution in that it is a descent from the divine, and of the divine, into mind, life, and matter. It is also a phase of evolution, the fourth and highest phase to date, in that it is the level above mind toward which humanity appears to be doing anything but searching for the Supermind, or any similar spiritual transformative power. Sri Aurobindo acknowledges that throughout the entire course of evolution, the physical, vital, and mental have exercised near-total dominance over the spiritual, and consequently, the difficulty which contemporary humanity will experience in affirming the existence of Supermind or the possibility of a spiritually transformed body. The descent and manifestation of Supermind could dispel such doubt, but only if it were to enter human consciousness and actually begin the process of liberating our mental, vital, and physical lives from their present limitations. Aurobindo's two conditions for the coming spiritual age—a few invididuals who experience the transformative power of spirit, and a mass of humanity able to assimilate such advanced experience—is particularly apt here (above p. 193).

Sri Aurobindo argues that we are blinded to the possibility of a principle such as Supermind because of our inadequate vision and discipline, both of which fail at integration of matter and spirit. Whereas we should experience and understand the whole of the universe as a complex but organic manifestation of the one divine reality, we tend to divide the world, or our world, into separate compartments wherein the spiritual, if it is acknowledged at all, remains removed from the physical, vital, and mental. In response to this view, Aurobindo offers a vision of the world as an evolving and integral expression of the divine which will soon manifest more dramatically and unmistakably than at any previous time.

> The spirit has been thought of not as something all-pervading and the secret essence of our being, but as something only looking down on us from the heights and drawing us only toward the heights and away from the rest of existence. So we get the idea of our cosmic and individual being as a great illusion, and departure from it and extinction in our consciousness of both individual and cosmos as the only hope, the sole release. Or we build up the idea of the earth as a world of ignorance, suffering, and trial and our only future an escape into heavens beyond; there is no divine prospect for us here, no fulfillment possible even with the utmost evolution on earth in the body, no victorious tansformation, no supreme object to be worked out in terrestrial existence. But if Supermind exists, if it descends, if it becomes the ruling principle, all that seems impossible to mind becomes not only possible but inevitable (*The Supramental Manifestation*, 63).

The Supermind would enable a humanity cooperating with its transformative power to gather into a higher harmony the polarities which limit the mind, emotions, and physical body in their respective spheres: the mind would overcome its natural inclination to divide reality into mutually exclusive parts, the vital or emotional would overcome the desire to possess objects and experiences as mine, and at the physical level, all physical impulses and appetites such as eating and sex would be "accepted as part of the divine life and pass under this law" (*The Supramental Manifestation*, 28). The average person is presumably not interested in such a transformation, but slowly, according to Aurobindo, consciousness continues to evolve from an imperfect mental life to a more perfect supramental life. Although imperceptible to most, the powerful effects of "the great soul," the one who is very difficult to find—and to accept, which means the same—continue to be felt by some portions of humanity. Religions exist for this reason: to transmit to the larger community the advances of the great souls to those who spiritually live off the achievements. Through this transmission, the great souls and religious communities cooperate in making possible a fuller, more perfect manifestation of the divine.

The great souls, furthermore, continue contributing to the evolution of consciousness immediately after death, from the spiritual world, and when they subsequently return to earth bearing the capacities attained in their preceding lifetime. The Mother explained that Sri Aurobindo had helped to bring down the descent of the Supermind even though—or rather because—he was on the other side. According to their disciples, the force of Sri Aurobindo and the Mother continues in the communities which grew up around them during their lifetimes. The disciples also carry their spiritual achievements, their work toward the transformation of the mental, vital, and physical, into the spiritual world and put it at the service of the total evolutionary process. Unlike the great souls, however, disciples generally remain ignorant of their previous lives. Early in the text of the Bhagavad Gita, Lord Krishna rather pityingly reveals to his disciple, Arjuna, the truth of rebirth: "Many of My births that are past and gone, thine also, O Arjuna; all of them I know, but thou knowest not..."(4:5). It is not through the dialogue, or intellectual argumentation, but rather by his progress in yoga practice that Krishna enables Arjuna (or humanity) to grasp the fact of karma and rebirth. Sri Aurobindo similarly argues that spiritual experience alone can lead to the acceptance of this subtle spiritual law:

> The soul needs no proof of its rebirth any more than it needs proof of its immortality. For there comes a time when it is consciously immortal, aware of itself in its eternal and immu-

table essence. Once that realization is accomplished, all intellectual questionings for and against the immortality of the soul fall away like a vain clamour of ignorance around the self-evident and ever-present truth (*The Supramental Manifestation*, 88).

The self that is aware of previous earth lives is, of course, the eternal, spiritual self, not the personality which was fashioned by the spirit for this lifetime. Had Aurobindo Ghose not evolved into Sri Aurobindo, or had Mira Richard not attained the realization of herself as the Mother, they would not have gained a knowledge of their previous lives, any more than Arujuna would have had such knowledge had he not replaced his ordinary consciousness by a genuine Kirshna consciousness. Arjuna, Aurobindo, and Mira Richard died to the old self and were born to the new—which self is in fact the old or original spirit self which succeeded in overcoming, or transforming, the ordinary self by which it was previously limited.

Ironically, it is precisely the ordinary self which is typically desperate for knowledge of karma and rebirth. Aurobindo affirms the value of the ordinary self—the physical, vital, and mental parts of the human being, or levels of consciousness—but he sees it as an instrument of the soul, not as an end in itself. Neither the human body, nor the emotions nor the individual mind—the three components which I regard as "me"—are reborn. Their effects are written on the soul, but in themselves their existence is limited to one earthly life. It is the soul, or what Aurobindo refers to in the following passage as the psychic being, which is of lasting value:

> It is not the personality, the character, that is of the first importance in rebirth—it is the psychic being who stands behind the evolution of the nature and evolves with it. The psychic, when it departs from the body, shedding even the mental and vital on its way to its resting place, carries with it the heart of its experiences—not the physical events, not the vital movements, not the mental buildings, not the capacities or characters, but something essential that is gathered from them, what might be called the divine element for the sake of which the rest existed. That is the permanent addition, it is that that

helps in the growth towards the divine. That is why there is usually no memory of the outward events and circumstances of past lives—for this memory there must be a strong development towards unbroken continuance of the mind, the vital, even the subtle physical; for though it all remains in a kind of seed memory, it does not ordinarily emerge. What was the divine element in the magnanimity of the warrior, that which expressed itself in his loyalty, nobility, high courage, what was the divine element behind the harmonious mentality and generous vitality of the poet and expressed itself in them, that remains and in a new harmony of character may find a new expression or, if the life is turned towards the divine, be taken up as powers for the realization or for the work that has to be done for the divine (*Letters on Yoga*, 452).

The self to which most of us are committed most of the time did not exist in the past and will not be reborn in the future. The effects of the past selves have fashioned my present self according to the law, or laws, of karma, and the effects of my present life will karmically influence the self that I will be in the future, but "I" in this statement refers to my soul or psychic being, not the physical, vital, or mental self which I live for and love. I contribute to my own soul evolution and the evolution of humanity by aiding the manifestation of the divine through more advanced soul qualities.

Evolution proceeds by—or is impeded by—the constant influx of the soul capacities built up in previous lives.

As the evolving being develops still more and becomes more rich and complex, it accumulates its personalities, as it were. Sometimes they stand behind the active elements throwing in some color, some trait, some capacity here and there—or they stand in front and there is a multiple personality, a many-sided character or a many-sided, sometimes what looks like a universal capacity [sic]. But if a former personaliy, a former capacity, is brought forward, it will not be to repeat what was already done, but to cast the same capacity into new forms and new shapes and fuse it into a new harmony of the being which will not be a reproduction of what was before (*Letters on Yoga*, 451-52).

In effect, Sri Aurobindo is here positing a double evolution: as the world evolves through successive states of earthly and human history, so does each soul successively accumulate new personalities, each appropriate for its own history and for the historical period in which it must realize its destiny. This combination of soul history and world-historical environment, both karmically guided, presupposes that the world in general and the individual soul in particular are striving, however unconsciously, to attain a divine perfection in and through earthly life. In order for this double realization to take place, the individual must contact the spiritual capacity of matter, life, and mind: "The soul comes into birth for experience, for growth, for evolution till it can bring the divine into matter" (*Letters on Yoga*, 451).

Although the spiritual quality of the self and the universe is ordinarily veiled, it can be penetrated, and when it is, both the self and the universe are thereby spiritually advanced. It is largely on the basis of this conception of the soul working in concert with the evolutionary process that Aurobindo criticizes traditional conceptions of rebirth. According to Aurobindo, the position of Advaita Vedanta (an absolute monist philosophy based on the Upanishads) affirms the reality of the self as one with Brahman, but fails to take seriously the reality of soul or its relationship to the world of change. Whereas he criticizes the Vedantist position for not emphasizing the reality of the self in the world, he criticizes the traditional Buddhist view for its denial of a permanent self:

> It views the recurrence of birth as a prolonged mechanical chain; it sees, with a sense of suffering and distaste, the eternal revolving of an immense cosmic wheel of energy with no divine sense in its revelations, its beginning an affirmation of ignorant desire, its end a nullifying bliss of escape. The whole wheel turns uselessly, forever disturbing the peace of Nonbeing and creating souls whose one difficult chance and whole business is to cease (*The Supramental Manifestation*, 116).

Aurobindo's response to the Buddhist position shows the extent of his commitment to the reality of both the self and the world, and to their creative collaboration as they evolve in cooperation with the divine purpose:

But what if rebirth were in truth no long dragging chain, but rather at first a ladder of the soul's ascension and at last a succession of mighty spiritual opportunities? It will be so if the infinite existence is not what it seems to the logical intellect, an abstract entity, but what it is to intuition and in deeper soul experience, a conscious spiritual reality, and that reality as real here as in any far-off absolute superconscience. For then universal nature would be no longer a mechanism with no secret but its own inconscient mechanics and no intention but the mere recurrent working; it would be the conscient energy of the universal spirit hidden in the greatness of its process, *mahimanam asya*. And the soul ascending from the sleep of matter through plant and animal life to the human degree of the power of life and there battling with ignorance and limited to take possession of its royal and infinite kingdom would be the mediator appointed to unfold in nature the spirit who is hidden in her subtleties and her vastness. That is the significance of life and the world which the idea of evolutionary rebirth opens to us; life becomes at once a progressive ascending series for the unfolding of the spirit. It acquires a supreme significance: the way of the spirit in its power is justified, no longer a foolish and empty dream, an eternal delirium, great mechanical toil, or termless futility, but the sum of works or a large spiritual will and wisdom: the human soul and the cosmic spirit look into each other's eyes with a noble and divine meaning (*The Supramental Manifestation*, 12-21).

Integral Yoga
and the Task of the Present Age

Aurobindo's yoga teaching is based on the yogas of the Bhagavad Gita—knowledge, action, devotion, and meditation—but goes beyond the Gita in requiring the yoga practitioner to be as concerned with the evolution of humanity as with one's own spiritual liberation. Each of the yogas of the Gita is affirmed and extended in Aurobindo's integral approach: in the Gita, Arjuna is invited to know—or see—Brahman through the appearance of the incarnate god Krishna, and in Aurobindo's Integral Yoga, the seeker is expected to know the fullest possible manifestation of the divine from its initial involution in time and space, through the physical, vital, mental, and supramental stages of evolution. To the karma-yoga of the Gita, Aurobindo adds that the karma-yogi must serve without attachments to the fruits of one's action all of the tasks and all of the participants in the *lila* (drama) of the human community in its evolutionary struggle. The Gita teaches a pure devotion to, or love of, Krishna, and Integral Yoga adds that the devotee must also extend this commitment to include a self-sacrificial love of all manifestations of the divine.

To the Gita's affirmation of the traditional meditative discipline summarized in Patanjali's *Yoga Sutras*, Aurobindo adds an emphasis on the experience of the divine energy, so that meditation should focus on and lead to a transformation of the will. Furthermore, in Aurobindo's synthesis of yoga, the yogas of the Gita are shown to be mutually dependent, and truly integrated:

> By way of this integral knowledge we arrive at the unity of the aims set before themselves by the three paths of knowledge, works, and devotion. Knowledge aims at the realization of true self-existence, works at the realization of the divine conscious-will which secretly governs all works, devotion at the realization of the bliss which enjoys as the lover all beings and all existences—Sat, Chit-Tapas, and Ananda. Each therefore aims at possessing Sachchidananda through one or other aspect of his triune divine nature (*The Synthesis of Yoga*, 406).

In addition to the yogas traditionally associated with the Gita—knowledge, action, and devotion, and the fourth, meditation, which is not always listed with the other three—Aurobindo emphasizes tantric yoga, or the discipline of spiritualizing nature. He describes this tantric discipline as follows: "To raise nature in man into manifest power and spirit is its method and it is the whole nature that it gathers up for the spiritual conversion" (*The Synthesis of Yoga*, 585).

In Aurobindo's Integral Yoga, *tantra* refers to the union of the yoga practitioner with *shakti*, the energy of the divine Mother, in order to effect a transformation of material life. Tantric yoga, or simply tantra, serves an important function in Aurobindo's total spiritual teaching because it focuses on the contemporary opportunity and need to serve and to help manifest the divine will, particularly in union with the supramental force now functioning through individuals of high spiritual attainment such as Sri Aurobindo and the Mother. Aurobindo's yoga teaching, however, is not based exclusively on either tantra or on the Gita, but on both, as well as on his, or their, contemporary Indian and Western spiritual experience.

It is noteworthy that Aurobindo's spiritual experience received a Western coloration from two sources, his education in England from elementary school through graduation from King's College, Cambridge University, and the influence of the Mother, but he shows little or no trace of the influence of Christian spirituality, or of a connection to the Christ. In a letter in 1936 to a disciple (concerning the opinion of a third person) Aurobindo confessed his nonattraction to Christ as well as his profound reverence for Krishna:

> I feel it difficult to say anything about [X's] Christ and Krishna. The attraction which she says people feel for Christ has never touched me, partly because I got disgusted with the dryness and deadness of Christianity in England and partly because the Christ of the gospels (apart from a few pregnant episodes) is luminous no doubt, but somewhat shadowy and imperfectly constructed in his luminosity: there is more of the ethical put forward than of the spiritual or divine man. The Christ that has strongly lived in the Western saints and mystics is the Christ of St. Francis of Assisi, St. Theresa, and others. But apart from that, is it a fact that Christ has been strongly and vividly loved by Christians? Only by a very few, it seems to me. As for Krishna, to judge him and his revealing tradition by the Christ figure and Christ tradition is not possible. The two stand in two different worlds. There is nothing in Christ of the great and boundless and sovereign spiritual knowledge and power of realization we find in the Gita, nothing of the emotional force, passion, beauty of the Gopi-symbol and all that lies behind it, nothing of the many-sided manifestation of the Krishna figure. Christ has other qualities: there is no gain in putting them side by side and trying to weigh them against each other (*On Himself*, 137-38).

One wonders, on reading this passage, whether Sri Aurobindo is not partly influenced here by the Aurobindo Ghose who experienced Christianity both in England and through the British governors of India during his days as an Indian nationalist. He wisely criticizes the Western habit of comparing— never completely free of sectarian narrowness—Christ with Krishna, Buddha, and other great souls. Aurobindo has definite relationships and corresponding ideas concerning these figures, but avoids pitting them, or the religious traditions built around them, against each other.

Aurobindo nevertheless acknowledges that for him neither Buddha nor Christ have brought the degree of spiritual transformation brought by Krishna. He did not see it as his task to develop comparisons between his conception of the supramental transformation and Christian incarnational theology. His thought neither affirms nor discourages a third party from studying—or, better, trying to experience spiritually—the inner similarity and spiritual complementarity between his vision of spiritual evolution and Christian evolutionism articulated by contemporary thinkers such as Pierre Teilhard de Chardin and Rudolf Steiner. There is need for a fuller understanding of comparisons and complementarities—without sectarian narrowness—concerning the respective spiritual powers represented by these three dominant spiritual figures, Krishna, Buddha, and Christ, and for their continuing role in contemporary spiritual and cultural life.

In the case of Integral Yoga, Aurobindo combines a profound affirmation of the positive features found in traditional spiritual teachings with a radically new insight concerning recent developments in human evolution. With respect to the Gita, for example, he considers Krishna an avatar, a divine being incarnated on behalf of the human struggle toward a higher and truer consciousness of the divine, but he considers Krishna's message as articulated in the Gita and in traditional Hinduism to be inadequate in relation to his understanding of the next evolutionary state—the supramental transformation of matter. He considers Buddha, Krishna, and Christ as avatars who each brought a distinctive contribution to humanity, and he affirms that these contributions are still significant for the bulk of spiritual seekers. He adds, however, that beginning with the supramental descent in the second half of the present century, it will be increasingly possible and important to adherents of religious traditions—followers of Krishna, Buddha, and Christ—to experience their respective missions and forces in more spiritual ways. Aurobindo regrets that Hindus, Buddhists, and Christians alike have generally reduced the spiritual mission of Krishna, Buddha, and Christ to an ethical and social level (*Essays on the Gita,* 161-62), but far from seeing no value in these traditions, he recognizes that they are the seedbed for the spiritual age and the spiritually evolved incarnations soon to come.

Aurobindo warned against comparisons ripped from their evolutionary context, but he surely would have seen the merit in exploring possible points of corroboration between his spiritual vision and contemporary spiritual insights in other traditions. In view of his emphasis on the manifestation of the divine in matter, life, and mind, and his corresponding attempt to replace the traditional Indian view of the created world as *maya* (illusion) with an emphasis on the reality of earthly evolution, it would be worth developing the implications of Aurobindo's position in relation to the dominant Christian view of creation and earthly evolution. The first obvious difference between Aurobindo's teaching and standard Christianity would focus on the absence in Christianity of the double concept of karma and rebirth—specifically on the possibility of the soul's progress in concert with the entire sweep of earthly evolution. Aurobindo's thought largely ignores claims for and against the transformative effect of the incarnation of Christ, and focuses appropriately instead on the spiritual phenomenon and transformative power which he himself experienced—the descent of the Supermind in the second half of this century as the decisive intervention of the divine in human history.

Aurobindo's emphasis on the spiritual source and goal of evolution, as well as the transformative effect of divine intervention, would provide a broad base of agreement for an Aurobindo-Christian synthesis. Although it has often failed to do so, the Christian tradition (e.g., by building on the

Bonaventurean-Franciscan tradition) can provide a positive spiritual source and goal of evolution, as well as the transformative effect of divine intervention. Although it has often failed to do so, the Christian tradition can prove a positive interpretation of the role of matter. More specifically, the incarnation of the Christ in a human body that suffered and bled into the earth would seem to be at least analogous to the role of *shakti*, divine energy, which Aurobindo puts at the center of his vision and yoga teaching. Further, Aurobindo's account of the characteristics and possible effects of the supramental descent seem to suggest spiritual experiences and transformations which Christians attribute to the continuing influence, called grace, of the Christ in human history and earth evolution.

Nowhere is the battle between matter and spirit, coupled with an unconscious commitment to evolution, more obviously in the balance than in the youthful, materialistic yet religious culture of the United States. Aurobindo was not alone in seeing the great spiritual significance of the American experiment, the American errand into the wilderness.

In his response to a request for a message on the occasion of his birthday celebrated by his disciples in New York in 1949, Sri Aurobindo sent a three-page statement which outlines the complementary strengths of the East (by which he means India and Buddhist Asia) and the West (by which he means Europe and North America). He offers three observations, each of which is useful for an understanding of Sri Aurobindo's significance for the West (and particularly for America) at the present time. First he observes that contrary to the usual perception of East and West, their histories are not entirely opposed or mutually exclusive: the East, which is typically perceived as characteristically spiritual and mystical, nevertheless "has had its materialistic tendencies, its material splendors, its similar or identical dealings with life and matter and the world in which we live," and "the West has had no less than the East its spiritual seekings and, though not in such profusion, its saints and sages and mystics" (*On Himself*, 414). Aurobindo's second point focuses on the contrast which has become increasingly definitive during the last several centuries. With the commitment to science, the modern West has increasingly neglected, and finally denied, the spiritual realm:

> The West has concentrated more and more on the world, on the dealings of mind and life with our material existence, on our mastery over it, on the perfection of mind and life and some fulfillment of the human being here: latterly this has gone so far as the denial of the Spirit and even the enthronement of matter as the sole reality (*On Himself*, 414-15).

Aurobindo's third point, in conclusion, is simply that the deep experience and knowledge of Spirit which is still alive in the East could, and should, be seen as the true goal of the commitment to evolution characteristic of the West. The intelligence and energy with which the West struggles on behalf of evolution must be made to acknowledge and to serve the evolution of consciousness, not merely its expression in the material world. If the West could see behind its commitment to matter and nature, to the spiritual source and goal of the evolutionary process, the combination would be the richest possible. He concludes his message with this hope:

> The ascent of the human soul to the supreme Spirit is that soul's highest aim and necessity, for that is the supreme reality; but there can be too the descent of the Spirit and its powers into the world and that would justify the existence of the material world also, give a meaning, a divine purpose to the creation and solve its riddle. East and West could be reconciled in the pursuit of the highest and largest ideal, Spirit embrace matter and matter find its own true reality and the hidden reality in all things in the Spirit (*On Himself*, 416).

Sri Aurobindo's legacy represents a uniquely promising attempt to provide a spiritual base and goal for America's commitment to the material, as well as a discipline whereby all material life may be made into an instrument of progress for the individual and the human community.

BIBLIOGRAPHIES

AND

GLOSSARY

CONTENTS OF
THE CENTENARY LIBRARY

A GUIDE TO FURTHER
READING AND INFORMATION

Anyone seriously interested in Sri Aurobindo's writings will want to use the thirty-volume Sri Aurobindo's Birth Centenary Library (SABCL), each volume of which is described in the preceding pages. The selections in this anthology have been photo-offset from this edition. While the SABCL is out of print, many libraries have sets and almost all the volumes are available as individual books from Sri Aurobindo Association, 1218 Wittenberg Road, Mt. Tremper, NY 12457.

Unless otherwise stated, all works are published by the Sri Aurobindo Ashram, Pondicherry 605002, India. References to volumes in the SABCL are cited by CL and a volume number. Paperback editions are marked by an asterisk.

1. Introduction: Life and Teaching

Sri Aurobindo on Himself and on the Mother (1953; CLXXVI) is the richest source of biographical information about Sri Aurobindo. Nirodbaran's *Correspondence with Sri Aurobindo* (1969) and Dilip Kumar Roy's "Conversation" with Sri Aurobindo in *Among the Great* (Bombay: Jaico Publishing House, 1950*), pp. 199-306, are also reliable and revealing.

Of the general introductions to Sri Aurobindo's life and thought, the most widely read is Satprem, *Sri Aurobindo or the Adventure of Consciousness* (New York: Institute for Evolutionary Research, 1984), which consists of brief passages by Sri Aurobindo joined by Satprem's running commentary. A special issue of *Cross Currents,* XXII (Winter 1972), "Sri Aurobindo: His Life, Thought and Legacy," ed. Robert A. McDermott, contains writings by Sri Aurobindo and the Mother on yoga, evolution, and Auroville.

Perhaps the best one-volume secondary source is R.R. Diwakar, *Mahayogi Sri Aurobindo* (Bombay: Bharatiya Vidya Bhavan, 1967*); this work is well complemented by Sisirkumar Mitra, *The Liberator: Sri Aurobindo, India and the World* (Bombay: Jaico Publishing House, 1970*). The Western reader will appreciate Peter Heehs' *Sri Aurobindo: A Brief Biography* (New Delhi: Oxford University Press, 1989). The serious student of Sri Aurobindo, however, will wish to consult K.R. Srinivas Iyengar, *Sri Aurobindo: A Biography and a History* (1990*), a 1400-page study that will probably remain the definitive work for many years.

The most recently published include: *Sri Aurobindo: A Brief Biography* by Peter Heens (New Delhi: Oxford University Press, 1989) and *Beyond the Human Species: The Life and Work of Sri Aurobindo and the Mother* by George Van Vreckhem (St. Paul, Minn.: Paragon House, 1998).

2. Philosophy

The Life Divine (CL XVIII, XIX), first serialized in *Arya* and revised during the 1930s, articulates Sri Aurobindo's theories of existence, knowledge, evolution, and the Divine. The last six chapters (CL XIX, pp. 824–1070) offer the most precise and comprehensive account of Sri Aurobindo's philosophical vision.

In addition to *The Mind of Light*, Introduction and Bibliography by Robert A. McDermott (New York: E.P. Dutton, 1971*), which is perhaps the most readable brief summary of Sri Aurobindo's evolutionary philosophy in his own words, there are two excellent anthologies: P.B. Saint-Hilaire [Pavitra], *The Future Evolution of Man* (1990*) and Rishabhchand and Shyamsundar, eds., *The Destiny of Man* (1969*).

Among secondary sources, the clearest brief summary of Sri Aurobindo's philosophical system is S.K. Maitra, *An Introduction to the Philosophy of Sri Aurobindo* (1965*). An excellent study by an American scholar is Beatrice Bruteau, *Worthy Is the World: The Hindu Philosophy of Sri Aurobindo* (Rutherford, NJ.: Fairleigh Dickinson University Press, 1971). Haridas Chaudhuri, *Sri Aurobindo: Prophet of the Life Divine* (1950; reissued by the California Institute of Asian Studies, 1973*) is an ideal introduction to Sri Aurobindo's philosophy as a synthesis of Indian and Western thought. With Frederic Spiegelberg, Professor Chaudhuri has also edited *The Integral Philosophy of Sri Aurobindo* (London: George Allen & Unwin, 1960), which contains thirty essays on Sri Aurobindo's thought by Indian and Western scholars. Professors Chaudhuri and McDermott have compiled the "Special Centenary Symposium on the Thought of Sri Aurobindo (1872–1950)" in *The International Philosophical Quarterly*, XII (June 1972). *Aurobindo's Philosophy of Brahman* by Steven Phillips with an introduction by Robert Nozick (Leiden, E.J. Brill, 1986) is an important recent contribution to understanding Sri Aurobindo's philosophy.

3. Integral Yoga

Sri Aurobindo's yoga system is most thoroughly articulated in *The Synthesis of Yoga* (1965; CL XX-XXI), and is helpfully amplified in three volumes of correspondence entitled *Letters on Yoga* (1971; CL XXII–XXIV). The most useful single-volume anthology of writings on yoga by Sri Aurobindo and the Mother is *A Practical Guide to Integral Yoga* (1985). Probably the most helpful secondary source is Morwenna Donnelly, *Founding the Life Divine: The Integral Yoga of Sri Aurobindo* (London: Rider and Company, 1955*). The serious student will want to consult Kees Bolle, *The Persistence of Religion: An Essay on Tantrism and Sri Aurobindo's Philosophy* (Leiden: E.J. Brill, 1965), especially pp. 79–102. Writings on yoga by Nolini Kanta Gupta and M.P. Pandit are also valuable.

4. Scriptures: Translations and Commentaries

The Secret of the Veda (1971; CL X) and *Hymns to the Mystic Fire* (1952; CL XI) consist of translations from the Rig Veda and of brief essays on the Vedas and on Aryan speech. These works are rendered more intelligible by A.B. Purani, compiler, *Sri Aurobindo's Vedic Glossary* (1962). Sri Aurobindo's commentaries on the Upanishads (1971; CL XII) emphasize their Vedic and Tantric elements. *From Crisis to Liberation: The Gita's Gospel in Sri Aurobindo's Light* (1987) by H. Maheshwari is a chapter by chapter discussion of the moral, psychological, philosophical, and spiritual issues presented in the Gita.

5. Social and Political Thought

The primary source for Sri Aurobindo's early political thought is CL I-IV. *The Ideal of the Karmayogan* (1966*) and *Speeches* (1969*) are the most representative separate editions. Sri Aurobindo's mature social and political thought is contained in *The Human Cycle, The Ideal of Human Unity,* and *War and Self-Determination* (1971; C V).

Among secondary sources, the most useful short treatment is Karan Singh, *Prophet of Indian Nationalism: A Study of Political Thought of Sri Aurobindo Ghose, 1893–1910* (London: George Allen and Unwin, 1963). For a fuller treatment, see V.P. Varma, *The Political Philosophy of Sri Aurobindo* (New York: Asia Publishing House, 1960). Sisirkumar Mitra has written and edited several works on Sri Aurobindo's importance as a social and political force in India.

6. Education

Sri Aurobindo's writings on education are continued in *Sri Aurobindo and the Mother on Education* (1990*) and *The International Centre of Education at the Sri Aurobindo Ashram* (Special Issue of *Mother India,* November-December 1968). The best study of these ideas is in Pavitra [P.R. Saint-Hilaire], *Education and the Aim of Human Life* (1990*). For education at Auroville, see *Equals One,* No. 4, 1968: "Auroville: System of Education."

7. Indian Culture

Sri Aurobindo's *Foundations of Indian Culture* (1959*; CL XIV) articulates the spiritual basis of Indian art, religion, and literature. His lesser works on various aspects of Indian culture include "The Brain of India," "The Chariot of Jagannatha," "The National Value of Art," and "The Renaissance in India." Additional writings on Indian culture are scattered throughout his collected works, especially in *The Harmony of Virtue* (CL III) and *The Hour of God* (CL XVII).

8. Literature

Sri Aurobindo's literary works include poetry (CL V), plays (CL VI), short stories (CL VII), translations (CL VIII), and literary criticism (CLIX). *Savitri* (CLXXVIII-XXIX), probably the longest poem in the English language, is the subject of extensive commentaries by Sri Aurobindo, the Mother, and many of the disciples, including *Sri Aurobindo's Savitri: An Approach and a Study* (5th edition, 1989) by A.B. Purani. *The Poetic Genius of Sri Aurobindo* (1974) by K.D. Sethna discusses Sri Aurobindo's poetry and his theories

9. The Mother

Sri Aurobindo's writings on the Mother are contained in the last part of *Sri Aurobindo on Himself* (1953; CL XXVI) and in *The Mother* (CL XXV). Most of the secondary sources on Sri Aurobindo also discuss the Mother. The Mother's own writings include several booklets of talks and correspondence. Many questions with the Mother's written replies, first published in the *Bulletin,* are now being issued in a series of volumes, the first of which are *Questions and Answers 1950–51* (1972) and *Questions and Answers 1956* (1973). The Mother's work on physical transformation, recorded by Satprem, has been serialized in the *Bulletin* since 1965 under the heading "Notes along the Way." In 1973 these edited transcripts as well as all of her other talks and writings were published in sixteen volumes as *The Collected Works of the Mother* (1978). Complete transcriptions of her conversations with Satprem comprising thirteen volumes are published by the Institute for Evolutionary Research as *Mother's Agenda* (New York Institute for Evolutionary Research, 1979).

10. Bibliographies

For a comprehensive listing, with cross-references, of writings by and about Sri Aurobindo, the Mother, and the Ashram and its activities, see H.K. Kaul, *Sri Aurobindo: A Descriptive Bibliography* (New Delhi: Munshiram Manoharlal, 1972). There is also an annotated bibliography by Robert A. McDermott in *The Mind of Light,* pp. 120-28. Perhaps the most useful and easily accessible description of further reading is the "Mind of Light" book catalog published by the Sri Aurobindo Association in Berkeley, California.

11. Periodicals

The following periodicals are published by the Sri Aurobindo Ashram, Auroville, and International Centers and are available either directly or through centers:

The Advent. A quarterly devoted to Sri Aurobindo's vision of the future.

All India Magazine. A monthly journal compiled from the writings of Sri Aurobindo and the Mother.

Auroville Today. A monthly newsletter with articles and photos on themes and events in Auroville; www.auroville.org.

The Bulletin of the Sri Aurobindo International Center of Education. A quarterly journal in English and French containing essays and talks of the Mother, and reports of the center's activities.

The Call Beyond. A monthly journal from the Sri Aurobindo Ashram (Delhi Branch).

Collaboration. A quarterly published by the Sri Aurobindo Association containing excerpts of Sri Aurobindo and the Mother's writings, articles, and news of individuals and centers. *Mother India.* A monthly review of culture.

Sri Aurobindo's Action. The organization's monthly newspaper. *Sri Aurobindo Archives and Research.* A biannual journal containing unpublished writings of Sri Aurobindo.

World Union. A quarterly reflecting the organization's interest in the spiritual basis of world peace.

12. The Ashram, Auroville, Centers, and Activities

Sri Aurobindo's most extended discussion of the Ashram is in "The Mother and the Working of the Ashram," in *The Mother* (1982, pp. 219–322; CL XXV, pp. 219–322). A succinct summary entitled *Sri Aurobindo and His Ashram* (1987) gives some background and description of the community in Pondicherry. Anyone can visit the Ashram at any time and may receive information on accommodations by writing to: The Secretary, Sri Aurobindo Ashram, Pondicherry 605002, India.

Auroville is represented in America by Auroville International U.S.A., P.O. Box 877, Santa Cruz, CA 95061; www.aviusa.org. AVI-USA is a nonprofit organization which distributes a newsletter and has the most recent information on procedures for visiting Auroville. One may order *Auroville Today*, a highly informative monthly newsletter published in Auroville, through them. Auroville can be communicated with directly by writing to: The Secretariat, Auroville, 605101, India. Both the ashram and Auroville have limited guest facilities and should be contacted well in advance.

The most appropriate source in the U.S. for a list of centers, books, newsletters, information, and activities related to Sri Aurobindo's yoga is Matagiri Sri Aurobindo Association. The founders welcome those wishing to visit or use the extensive library to contact them at Matagiri, 1218 Wittenberg Road, Mt. Tremper, NY 12457. Individuals will be referred to other centers and study groups in their area.

GLOSSARY OF
IMPORTANT NAMES AND TERMS

Advaita Vedanta. Dominant school of Indian philosophy; teaches the nonduality of Brahman*; based on the Vedas.*

Ahiṃsā. Noninjury; part of the moral philosophy of Gandhi.*

Ānanda. Perfect happiness or bliss; one of the three attributes of Brahman* or Sat-Chit-Ānanda.*

Arjuna. Warrior in the Bhagavadgita* to whom the Lord Krishna* revealed himself as avatar.*

Āsana. Physical postures; part of *hathayoga.*

Ashram. Religious community based on the spiritual teaching of a guru.*

Ātman. Universal Self or Spirit.

Avatar. Person in whom the Divine Consciousness manifests itself (e.g., Rama,* Krishna,* Buddha*).

Avidyā. Ignorance; failure to realize the unity of existence.

Bande Mataram. "I Bow to the Mother (Country)", national song of India since 1906.

Bhagavadgita (Gita). "Song of the Lord"; teaching of Krishna* to Arjuna*; develops three yogas: *jñāna,* *karma,* and *bhakti;* most authoritative Hindu scripture; composed *ca.* 100 B.C.–A.D. 100.

Bhagavan. God as love.

Bhakti. Love of, or devotion to, the Divine. *Bhaktiyoga:* discipline of devotion or self-surrender.

Brahman. Absolute reality; the Divine as one.

Buddha. Gautama, the Enlightened One. Sixth-century spiritual teacher whose influence spread throughout Asia. (Sri Aurobindo considered the Buddha to be an avatar,* but viewed Buddhism as world-negating.)

Dharma. Variety of Hindu social, moral, and religious obligations.

Gandhi, Mohandas K. (1869–1948). Called Mahātmā, "great soul," leader of the Indian independence movement and advocate of *ahiṃsā.*

Guna. Quality; the three primary qualities that form the nature of the created world: *sattva* (knowledge, illumination), *rajas* (action, energy), *tamas* (darkness, lethargy).

Guru. Teacher; spiritual guide.

Hathayoga. Physical discipline, consisting essentially of *āsanas* and *prānāyām.*

285

Integral Yoga. Sri Aurobindo's synthesis of several yogas, principally *jñāna,* * *karma,* * *bhakti,* * *tantra,* * and the yoga of self-perfection. (Distinct from the yoga of the same name subsequently developed by Swami Satchidananda.)

Īshvara. Lord, God as master of creation.

Jñāniyoga. The discipline of spiritual knowledge.

Karma. Law of value entailed by every action; *karmayoga:* the discipline of selfless action.

Krishna. Avatar* of Vishnu*; revealed in the Bhagavadgita.*

Kundalini. Coiled and sleeping force residing near the base of the spine; the arousal of *kundalini* is essential in *tantra.* *

Līlā. Game; existence regarded as the play of the Divine.

Mahābhārata. One of the two great epics of India; a vast assemblage of Indian history, folklore, ethics, and spirituality; original source of the Bhagavadgita.

Māyā. The mystery of existence; the illusion that particulars are as real as Brahman.*

Māyāvāda. The Vedantist theory of the world as created by the power of an illusion, and therefore less than real.

Moksha. Spiritual liberation; release from the bondage of the ego.

Mother. Manifestation of *shakti* *; traditional Indian title referring to spiritual eminence in female form, especially as a complement to a male spiritual personality or force (e.g., Sita to Rama, Radha to Krishna, the Mother to Sri Ramakrishna, and the Mother of the Sri Aurobindo Ashram to Sri Aurobindo).

Nehru, Jawaharlal (1889–1964). With Gandhi, leader of the Nationalist Movement; Prime Minister 1947–64.

Nirvana. Extinction of ordinary existence due to the elimination of the ego and egoistic desire.

Overmind. Plane of consciousness between the individual human mind and the Supermind*; believed to have descended into the earth consciousness through Sri Aurobindo on November 24, 1926.

Pondicherry. Ancient port, south of Madras; capital of French India until 1947; location of the Sri Aurobindo Ashram since 1926.

Prakriti. Basic principle of the manifest world; active complement of *purusha.* *

Prānāyām. Discipline of ordered breathing; part of *hathayoga.* *

Purusha. Spirit; inactive, essential being supporting *prakriti.* *

Radha. Consort of Krishna* in the *Mahābhārata.* *

Radhakrishnan, Sarvapalli (1888—). Most prominent interpreter of Indian philosophy; President of India 1962–67.

Rajayoga. Discipline of quieting the mind; according to Patanjali's *Yoga Sūtras,* includes concentration, meditation, and contemplation.

Ramakrishna, Sri. Nineteenth-century mystic; guru* of Swami Vivekananda.*

Rama, Sita. Hero and heroine of the Indian epic *Rāmāyana*.

Richard, Mira (b. February 21, 1878). French mystic; since 1926 Mother of the Sri Aurobindo Ashram.

Richard, Paul. French diplomat and spiritual seeker; friend of Sri Aurobindo and Rabindranath Tagore; married to Mira Richard prior to her spiritual collaboration with Sri Aurobindo.

Ṛsis (rishis). Sages who composed the Vedas*; conveyers of Vedic knowledge.

Sadhak. Spiritual aspirant.

Sādhanā. Spiritual or yogic practice.

Samādhi. In yoga, the union of the individual mind with the supreme or cosmic consciousness.

Sānkhya. One of the six orthodox systems of Indian philosophy; emphasizes the plurality of consciousness (*purusha**) and the universality of nature (*prakriti**).

Sat-Chit-Ānanda. Being-consciousness-bliss; three characteristics of Brahman.*

Savitri. Sri Aurobindo's epic of spiritual ascent and transformation of the physical world; uses the puranic (ancient) story of Satyam and Savitri, representing Sri Aurobindo and the Mother as instruments of supramental transformation.

Shakti. Divine or cosmic energy; conscious force of Spirit. Manifest through the Mother.*

Siddhi. Attainment of occult powers.

Śiva (*Shiva*). Third god in the Hindu trinity (with Brahmā and Vishnu*, noted for destruction and transformation of the cosmos; cosmic harmony and rhythm.

Sri. Title indicating spiritual eminence.

Sri Chinmoy. Yogi prominent in America since the late 1960's, educated at the Sri Aurobindo Ashram; under the Mother's spiritual direction for twenty years; teachings based on Sri Aurobindo's Integral Yoga.*

Supermind. Truth-consciousness; the level of consciousness above mind which links the lower levels (matter, life, psyche, and mind) to the higher levels of being (bliss, consciousness-force, and existence); the conscious instrument of spiritual evolution; unifies particulars of the manifest world without losing its own perfect unity; aided by the Overmind.*

Tagore, Rabindranath (1861–1941). Most prominent exponent and exemplar of the Indian, especially Bengali, cultural ideal during the first half of the twentieth century; Nobel Prize for literature, 1912; founder of Shantiniketan, noted cultural and educational center near Calcutta.

Tantra. Discipline of physical energy (based on *shakti*).

Vedanta. End or acme of the Vedas*; Advaita* is its most prominent school.

Vedas. The scriptural basis of most Hindu religious and philosophical systems (including Vedic hymns and the Upanishads).

Vishnu. Second person of the Hindu triad (with Brahmā and Śiva*); his avatars* include Rama* and Krishna.*

Vivekananda, Swami. Early-twentieth-century follower of Sri Ramakrishna; spiritual leader and organizer of the Ramakrishna order of monks.

Yoga. Literally "to join," especially to the Divine; includes various disciplines: *hatha,* *raja,* *jñāna,* *karma,* *bhakti,* *tantra,* and Integral or *purna* (Sri Aurobindo's synthesis of these yogas).

Yogi. One who practices yoga.

Printed in the United States
217231BV00001B/8/P